A–Z of Countryside Law

Also by the same author
A-Z of Policing Law

A–Z of Countryside Law

Roger Lorton LL B, M.Phil.

London: The Stationery Office

© Roger Lorton 2000

All rights reserved. No part of this publication may be reproduced, stored in a retrieval system, or transmitted in any form or by any means, electronic, mechanical, photocopying, recording or otherwise without the permission of the publisher.

Applications for reproduction should be made in writing to The Stationery Office Limited, St Crispins, Duke Street, Norwich NR3 1PD.

Roger Lorton has asserted his moral rights under the Copyright, Designs and Patents Act 1988, to be identified as the author of this work.

A CIP catalogue record for this book is available from the British Library
A Library of Congress CIP catalogue record has been applied for

First published 2000
ISBN 0 11 702383 3

Published by The Stationery Office and available from:
The Stationery Office
(mail, telephone and fax orders only)
PO Box 29, Norwich, NR3 1GN
0171 873 0011
Telephone orders/ General enquiries 0870 600 5522
Fax orders 0870 600 5533

www.itsofficial.net

The Stationery Office Bookshops
123 Kingsway, London WC2B 6PQ
0207 242 6393 Fax 0207 242 6412
68–69 Bull Street, Birmingham B4 6AD
0121 236 9696 Fax 0121 236 9699
33 Wine Street, Bristol BS1 2BQ
0117 9264306 Fax 0117 9294515
9–21 Princess Street, Manchester M60 8AS
0161 834 7201 Fax 0161 833 0634
16 Arthur Street, Belfast BT1 4GD
02890 238451 Fax 02890 235401
The Stationery Office Oriel Bookshop
18–19, High Street, Cardiff CF1 2BZ
029 2039 5548 Fax 029 2038 4347
71 Lothian Road, Edinburgh EH3 9AZ
0870 606 5566 Fax 0870 606 5588

The Stationery Office's Accredited Agents (see Yellow Pages)
and through good booksellers

Publisher's note: No responsibility for any loss arising from any action as a result of this publication can be accepted by the author or publisher.

Typeset by Kaarin Wall
Printed in the United Kingdom, on material containing 75% post-consumer waste and 25% ECF pulp, for the Stationery Office
TJ000568   C10   02/00

CONTENTS

Access – A Right to Roam	1	Disease	55
Agencies	3	Dogs	56
Air Weapons	7	Driving – Off-road	59
Amphibians	8	Estuaries and Foreshore	60
Badgers	10	Falconry	61
Bats	12	Farming and Conservation	62
Bees	13	Fences, Gates and Stiles	66
Birds and Eggs	14	Firearms and Shooting	67
Bridle-ways	19	Fires and Smoke	70
Bulls and Cattle	21	Fish and Fishing	71
Canals	22	Floods and Flooding	75
Caravans and Camping	24	Fly Tipping	77
Children	26	Footpaths	79
Clay Target Shooting	27	Forestry	81
Cockfighting	29	Fossil Collecting	83
Common Land	30	Foxes and Fox Hunting	83
Conservation	31	Game Birds	85
Coursing	37	Game Dealers	87
Crops and Grain	38	Game Licences	90
Crossbows and Archery	40	Game Rights	91
Cruelty to Animals	41	Gamekeepers	93
Cycles	44	Green Lanes	94
Damage	46	Hares	95
Dangerous and Destructive Animals	47	Hedges and Hedgerows	98
		Highways and Roads	99
Deer	49	Horses	102

Hunting	105	Rabies	162
Insects and Other Invertebrates	107	Rifles	163
Killing Birds and Animals	110	Rivers, Streams and Other Watercourses	166
Knives	113	Salmon and Trout	167
Land	114	Scotland	173
Lead Shot	117	Shotguns	176
Limestone Pavements	119	Straying	179
Litter	120	Theft	180
Livestock	121	Town and Country Planning	183
Metal Detectors	123	Traps and Snares	186
Monuments and Archaeological Sites	124	Treasure Trove	189
Mushrooms and Fungi	125	Trees	190
National Parks	126	Trespass	191
Noise	128	Vagrants	194
Northern Ireland	129	Vermin	195
Nuisances	134	Village Greens	196
Pesticides	137	Wales	198
Pests	138	Water	199
Plants and Flowers	139	Weeds	200
Poaching	143	Wild Mammals	202
Poison	146	Wildfowl	203
Police	148	Zoos and Animal Parks	207
Pollution	150		
Protected Animals	152		
Protests and Protestors	156		
Quarries and Mines	159		
Rabbits	160		

PREFACE

My objective in writing this book was originally to bring together all the laws that impacted in some way on our countryside or which affect the people that live, work or play there. I did not realise just how many there were until my list exceeded 200 Acts and Regulations. As a result this book now encompasses not only the expected hunting, shooting and fishing legislation but also sections on weeds, public and private nuisances, hedges, trees, footpaths, animals, hunting, insects and much, much more.

I would now like to claim this as the definitive reference on all countryside law, but sadly one book is not capable of achieving this. What has been achieved is a work that identifies all the main laws currently concerned with our countryside and outlines their effects. This should be sufficient for the majority of readers; for scholars I have included the references they will need if they wish to research the relevant legislation – and I wish them well in this for much of this law is old and has been changed to a greater or lesser degree by subsequent legislation.

While attempting to make the law easy to understand, I have still felt it necessary to use the language of the various statutes and it has not always been possible to meet the needs of different genders. Therefore I rely upon the Interpretation Act 1978 which states that in any Act, unless the contrary intention appears:

(a) words importing the masculine gender include the feminine;
(b) words importing the feminine gender include the masculine;
(c) words in the singular include the plural;
(d) words in the plural include the singular.

These last few weeks I have waited with anticipation for the outline of a new Countryside Bill aimed at dealing with issues of access. It has not yet arrived and while I have incorporated into this book many of the recommendations of the government's working parties and consultation papers, I can only guess at what it will contain. The law is a living, growing subject and while change may be slow it is certain to come – eventually.

Roger Lorton
January 2000

TABLE OF LEGISLATION

	Page
Abandonment of Animals Act 1960	43
Access to Neighbouring Land Act 1992	116
Administration of Estates Act 1925	116
Agricultural Produce (Grading and Marking) Act 1928	39
Agricultural Statistics Act 1979	123
Agriculture Act 1947	9, 84, 96, 138, 160, 196
Agriculture Act 1970	40
Agriculture Act 1986	65
Agriculture and Horticulture Act 1964	39
Agriculture (Avoidance of Accidents to Children) Regulations 1958	27
Agriculture (Miscellaneous Provisions) Act 1943	40
Agriculture (Miscellaneous Provisions) Act 1968	121
Agriculture (Miscellaneous Provisions) Act 1972	148
Agriculture (Miscellaneous Provisions) Act 1976	39
Agriculture (Poisonous Substances) Act 1952	147
Agriculture (Safety, Health and Welfare Provisions) Act 1956	26
Agriculture (Scotland) Act 1948	9, 85, 97, 139, 174, 188, 196
Amenity Lands Act (Northern Ireland) 1965	36
Ancient Monuments and Archaeological Areas Act 1979	76, 123, 124
Animal Health Act 1981	15, 22, 43, 55, 58, 121, 162, 175, 180, 196
Animal Health and Welfare Act 1984	122
Animals (Cruel Poisons) Act 1962	148
Animals (Scientific Procedures) Act 1986	42, 147
Bee Diseases Control Order 1982	14
Bee Diseases Control Order (Northern Ireland) 1998	14
Beef Special Premiums Regulations 1993	65
Bees Act 1980	13
Caravan Sites Act 1968	25
Caravan Sites and Control of Development Act 1960	24
Cereals Marketing Act 1965	39
City of London Police Act 1839	29
Civic Government (Scotland) Act 1982	70, 174
Clean Air Act 1993	151
Cockfighting Act 1952	29
Commons Act 1876	30
Commons Act 1899	31
Commons Act 1908	31

	Page
Commons Registration Act 1965	2, 30, 116, 196
Conservation (Natural Habitats, etc.) Regulations 1994	9, 13, 36, 76, 110, 112, 119, 140, 142, 152, 154, 191, 196
Control of Dogs Order 1992	58, 176
Control of Pesticides Regulations 1986	137
Control of Pollution Act 1974	129, 175
Control of Pollution (Silage, Slurry and Agricultural Fuel Oil) Regulations 1991	167
Corn Returns Act 1882	40
Corn Returns (Delegation of Functions) Order 1981	40
Countryside Act 1949	94
Countryside Act 1968	19, 20, 33, 45, 80
Criminal Damage Act 1971	39, 46, 58, 158, 187
Criminal Justice Act 1988	114
Criminal Justice and Public Order Act 1994	25, 26, 107, 146, 157, 176, 193
Criminal Law Act 1977	193
Criminal Law (Consolidation) (Scotland) Act 1995	47, 114, 175, 176
Criminal Procedure (Scotland) Act 1995	150
Crop Residues (Burning) Regulations 1993	70
Crossbows Act 1987	40, 175
Cycle Tracks Act 1984	20, 45, 81
Dangerous Dogs Act 1989	58
Dangerous Dogs Act 1991	58
Dangerous Wild Animals Act 1976	47, 175, 207
Dartmoor Commons Act 1985	31
Deer Act 1991	49, 52, 88, 143, 144, 193
Deer (Close Seasons) (Scotland) Order 1984	54, 175
Deer (Firearms, etc.) (Scotland) Order 1985	51, 175
Deer (Scotland) Act 1959	143, 144, 174
Deer (Scotland) Act 1996	49, 51, 54, 88, 89, 144, 175
Destructive Imported Animals Act 1932	48
Dogs Act 1871	58
Dogs Act 1906	57, 58, 180
Dogs (Protection of Livestock) Act 1953	56, 175
Environment Act 1995	99, 127, 151
Environmental Protection Act 1990	6, 58, 70, 77, 78, 120, 128,135, 150, 175
Environmental Protection (Restriction on Use of Lead Shot) (England) Regulations 1999	117, 204
Farm and Garden Chemicals Act 1967	138
Fire Services Act 1947	71

	Page
Firearms Act 1968	7, 27, 67, 68, 134, 149, 163, 175, 177, 193
Firearms Act 1988	67, 175
Firearms Order (Northern Ireland) 1981	68, 179
Firearms Rules 1969	67
Firearms Rules 1989	67, 177
Food and Environmental Protection Act 1985	137
Forestry Act 1967	31, 81
Forestry Act 1979	81
Forestry Act 1986	83
Freshwater Fisheries (Scotland) Act 1902	172, 174
Freshwater and Salmon Fisheries (Scotland) Act 1976	172
Game Act 1831	85, 88, 90, 91, 92, 95, 97, 143, 144, 146, 161, 193
Game Birds Preservation Order (Northern Ireland) 1999	86, 87
Game Laws (Amendment) Act 1960	143, 146
Game Licences Act 1860	87, 90, 93, 96, 175
Game Preservation Act (Northern Ireland) 1928	86, 87, 88
Game (Scotland) Act 1772	87, 174
Game (Scotland) Act 1832	86, 87, 89, 91, 143, 144, 174
Government of Wales Act 1998	198
Grey Squirrels (Warfarin) Order 1973	148
Ground Game Act 1880	91, 92, 96, 160, 175
Ground Game (Amendment) Act 1906	97, 160
Guard Dogs Act 1975	58
Hares Act 1848	90, 96
Hares Preservation Act 1892	96
Hares (Scotland) Act 1848	97, 174
Heather and Grass Burning (England and Wales) Regulations 1986	71
Hedgerows Regulations 1997	98
Highways Act 1835	21, 44, 100, 102, 103
Highways Act 1980	20, 21, 25, 31, 45, 66, 67, 69, 70, 77, 78, 79, 81, 99, 100, 105, 151, 179, 200
Hill Farming Act 1946	71
Horses (Protective Headgear for Young Riders) Act 1990	27, 104
Horticultural Produce Act 1986	39
Importation of Bees Order 1997	14
Integrated Administration and Control System Regulations 1993	65
Land Charges Act 1972	116

	Page
Land Drainage Act 1991	167
Land Registration Acts 1925 to 1988	116
Landlord and Tenants Acts 1927 to 1988	116
Law of Property Act 1925	31, 114, 116
Law of Property Act 1969	117
Licensing Act 1872	21, 44, 69, 105
Limitations Act 1980	117
Litter Act 1983	120
Litter (Fixed Penalty) Order (Northern Ireland) Order 1998	121
Litter (Northern Ireland) Order 1994	121
Local Government Act 1972	128
Manoeuvres Act 1958	81
Metropolitan Commons Act 1866	30, 198
Metropolitan Green Belt Act 1938	186
Metropolitan Police Act 1839	29
Mines and Quarries Act 1954	159
National Parks and Access to the Countryside Act 1949	4, 36, 81, 94, 126
Nature Conservation and Amenity Lands (Northern Ireland) Order 1985	36
Night Poaching Act 1828	93, 95, 143, 144, 161, 175, 193
Night Poaching Act 1844	96, 143, 144, 161
Noise Act 1996	128
Norfolk and Suffolk Broads Act 1988	127
Occupier's Liability Act 1957	27
Occupier's Liability Act 1984	27
Offences Against the Person Act 1861	158
Open Cast Coal Act 1958	102
Pedal Bicycles (Safety) Regulations 1984	45
Pedal Cycles (Construction and Use) Regulations 1983	45
Pesticides (Maximum Residue Levels in Crops, Food and Feeding Stuffs) (Amendment) Regulations 1994	137
Pests Act 1954	97, 160, 161, 187
Planning (Listed Buildings and Conservation Areas) Act 1990	47
Plant Health Act 1967	39
Plant Health (Forestry) (Great Britain) Order 1993	39
Plant Health (Great Britain) Order 1993	39
Plant Protection Products (Basic Conditions) Regulations 1997	137
Plant Varieties and Seeds Act 1964	39
Poaching Prevention Act 1862	96, 143, 161, 175
Police and Criminal Evidence Act 1984	71, 149, 150, 158
Pollution (Angler's Lead Weights) Regulations 1986	73, 118

	Page
Pollution Prevention and Control Act 1999	151
Prevention of Crimes Act 1953	41, 113, 114
Prevention of Damage by Pests Act 1949	138, 195
Protection from Eviction Act 1977	117
Protection from Harassment Act 1997	107, 117
Protection of Animals Act 1911	14, 22, 29, 37, 41, 58, 61, 84, 97, 103, 106, 146, 161, 187, 203, 207
Protection of Animals (Amendment) Act 1954	43
Protection of Animals (Amendment) Act 1988	176
Protection of Animals (Scotland) Act 1912	14, 22, 29, 38, 43, 58, 85, 97, 105, 107, 148, 174, 188, 203, 207
Protection of Badgers Act 1992	10, 175
Protection of Birds Act 1954	204
Public Health Act 1936	166, 200
Public Health Act 1961	78
Public Health (Amendment) Act 1907	21
Public Order Act 1986	157, 175
Quarries Regulations 1999	160
Rabies (Importation of Dogs, Cats etc.) Order 1974	162
Refuse Disposal (Amenity) Act 1978	77, 120, 151, 175
Riding Establishments Act 1964	104
Rights of Way Act 1990	20, 81, 102
Road Traffic Act 1988	20, 44, 58, 59, 102
Road Vehicles (Construction and Use) Regulations 1986	44, 129
Roads (Scotland) Act 1984	102, 175, 180
Salmon Act 1986	89, 171, 175
Salmon Act 1996	172
Salmon and Freshwater Fisheries Act 1975	72, 143, 145, 147, 167
Salmon and Freshwater Fisheries (Protection) (Scotland) Act 1951	74, 143, 145, 173, 174
Salmon Fisheries (Scotland) Act 1868	172, 206
Salmon Fishery Act 1865	172
Sea Fisheries Regulation Act 1966	206
Sheep Annual Premium and Suckler Cow Premium Quotas Regulations 1993	65
Solway Act 1804	74, 172
Spring Traps (Approval) Order 1995	97, 187
Spring Traps (Scotland) (Approval) Order 1996	97, 189
Suckler Cow Premium Regulations 1993	65
Theft Act 1968	39, 72, 87, 94, 145, 169, 180, 193
Town and Country Planning Act 1947	183
Town and Country Planning Act 1990	28, 78, 80, 102, 183

xiii

	Page
Town and Country Planning (General Permitted Development) Order 1995	28
Town and Country Planning (Scotland) Act 1997	78, 185
Town and Country Planning (Trees) Regulations 1999	190
Town Police Clauses Act 1847	21, 29, 70
Transport Act 1968	3, 22
Treasure Act 1996	189
Trespass (Scotland) Act 1865	25, 174, 193, 195
Trout (Scotland) Act 1933	173, 174
Tweed Fisheries Act 1857	74, 172, 174
Vagrancy Act 1824	193, 194
Water Industry Act 1991	199
Water Resources Act 1991	151, 166, 167, 199
Weeds Act 1959	200
Welfare of Animals (Northern Ireland) Act 1972	38, 43, 207
Welfare of Animals (Transport) Order 1997	87, 103, 122
Welfare of Calves at Markets Regulations (Northern Ireland) 1998	123
Welfare of Livestock (Deer) Order 1980	123
Wild Mammals (Protection) Act 1996	42, 84, 106, 161, 202
Wildlife and Countryside Act 1981	8, 10, 12, 14, 36, 38, 41, 42, 48, 49, 58, 61, 69, 74, 76, 84, 85, 87, 89, 95, 96, 106, 107, 110, 118, 119, 126, 130, 138, 140, 147, 152, 161, 175, 186, 191, 201, 202, 203
Wildlife and Countryside (Amendment) Act 1985	36
Wildlife and Countryside (Registration to Sell, etc. Certain Dead Wild Birds) Regulations 1982	155
Wildlife and Countryside 1981 (Variation of Schedules 5 and 8) Order 1998	143
Wildlife (Northern Ireland) Order 1985	9, 10, 12, 14, 19, 38, 40, 41, 43, 48, 49, 61, 62, 75, 77, 84, 85, 87, 97, 107, 110, 126, 130, 139, 155, 161, 186, 191, 201, 202, 203
Zoo Licensing Act 1981	207

ACCESS – A RIGHT TO ROAM

See also Bridle-ways; Conservation; Footpaths; Green Lanes; Highways and Roads

In the 1998/99 session of Parliament a Private Member's Bill was introduced that proposed to grant a public right to roam in open countryside in England and Wales. The Bill was controversial and, inevitably, failed before it could complete its run through the various stages required for it to become law. However, the issue remains high on the Government's agenda and the Department of the Environment has consulted widely in order to push the concept through. At the time of writing no detailed proposals have been submitted to Parliament although the Government's intentions were made clear at the 1999 Labour Party conference. The consultation process, together with the wording of the original Bill, are indicative of these intentions and may provide an insight into future proposals.

The failed Right to Roam Bill included the following provisions:

(a) any person shall have the right to enter on to, roam on and pass over open country on foot for the purposes of open-air recreation;
(b) breaking or damaging any fence, hedge or gate would immediately remove that right from that person;
(c) an 'open country map' would be prepared by a National Surveying Authority, identifying the open country to which the law would apply;
(d) common land would automatically be included;
(e) offences would be committed: (i) where any means of access to open country was wilfully obstructed; and, (ii) where any false or misleading sign was placed in order to deter access.

'Open country' was defined as any area consisting wholly or predominantly of mountain, moor, heath or down, common land and any other land specifically included as such. Exceptions were to include land covered by buildings, land being used for the purposes of a park, garden or pleasure ground, quarries and railways.

Arguments against the Bill were based largely on infringements of the rights of ownership, the potential damage that could occur to the land and the extent of disturbance to wildlife. These arguments were sufficiently lengthy for the Bill to run out of its allotted time.

Current proposals from the Department of the Environment, Transport and the Regions that may be included in the 1999/2000 session of Parliament appear to be a little more constrained and include:

(a) encouraging the creation of new footpaths and bridleways by local authorities;
(b) encouraging local authorities to complete the identification and classification of rights of way initiated by the Commons Registration Act 1965;
(c) the reclassification of Roads Used as Public Paths as bridleways;
(d) an easing of the procedures involved in diverting or closing rights of way on application by land managers or the public;
(e) the extension of powers under the Road Traffic Regulation Act 1984[1] to include nature conservation as a reason for issuing a traffic regulation order;
(f) ensuring that local authorities in exercising their powers under these proposals should have regard to the Habitats Directive;
(g) local authority powers to erect gates, prohibit the use of a highway at certain times, deny access to pedestrians, divert highways, close footpaths or bridleways and prohibit the driving of motor vehicles;
(h) a duty placed on local highway authorities to improve access for disabled people.

The failed Bill and the current proposals seem to be a world apart as far as the concept of a general right of access is concerned, as the proposals focus only on the extension of existing rights or the creation of rights based on the 20-year rule. It remains to be seen how these proposals fare if introduced as a new Bill in the forthcoming session of Parliament.

Legal access to large parts of our countryside already exists however, including access to national parks and urban commons. The Forestry Commission and National Trust offer further opportunities to explore the countryside and a variety of access schemes exist throughout the UK. The Scottish Assembly is also proposing legislation to create their own national park system and to clarify existing access rights. These opportunities are dealt with elsewhere in this book, as are some of the issues involved with land ownership and private property. The law will have to seek a balance between the different interests concerned with the countryside and it is unlikely that total freedom of access across private property will find a place on the statute books.

1 This permits highway authorities to regulate traffic in order to conserve natural beauty or to promote recreation or nature study.

AGENCIES

See also Conservation; Fish and Fishing

Two government departments have major statutory duties in relation to countryside and environmental issues: (i) the Department of the Environment, Transport and the Regions, and (ii) the Ministry of Agriculture, Fisheries and Food.[1] In addition, the National Assemblies for Wales and Scotland are increasingly taking responsibility for environmental matters falling within their countries.[2] Under these bodies are agencies and boards having specific responsibilities for the implementation of environmental policies and the designation and management of conservation areas.

British Waterways

British Waterways is a corporate public body set up under the Transport Act 1968. It has responsibility for the management, maintenance and conservation of more than 3200km of canals and navigable rivers. Local planning authorities are required to consult the British Waterways Board on any planning applications that may concern any navigation under its control.

Countryside Agency

The Countryside Agency is a statutory body created in 1999 from a merger between the Countryside Commission and the Rural Development Commission. The Agency's stated aims are to conserve and enhance the countryside alongside the promotion of economic opportunities for country dwellers. The Countryside Agency has responsibility for the designation in England of areas of outstanding natural beauty (AONBs), heritage coastline, national trails and national parks, as well as the development of community forests in partnership with the Forestry Commission.

Countryside Commission

Originally called the National Parks Commission, this body was formed under the National Parks and Access to the Countryside Act 1949 to oversee the creation of the national parks and act as an advisory body on landscape and countryside issues. The Countryside Agency has now taken on many of the Countryside Commission's functions.

Countryside Council for Wales

As the advisory body for Wales, the Countryside Council has had its position reaffirmed by the newly elected National Assembly for Wales and no immediate changes to its role appear likely. Responsibilities include the designation of AONBs, sites of special scientific interest (SSSIs) and national parks together with the management of the national nature reserves situated within Wales[3]. Statutory responsibilities that lay with the Nature Conservancy Council and the Countryside Commission now fall to this body in Wales.

English Heritage

English Heritage is concerned with conservation and management of historic and listed buildings, ancient monuments and archaeological sites.

English Nature

A government-funded body, the purpose of English Nature is the conservation of England's wildlife and natural features. This is achieved through the designation and control of national nature reserves and the notification of SSSI. English Nature has some of the statutory responsibilities that once fell to the Countryside Commission and the Nature Conservancy Council and acts as an advisory body to local authorities, conservation groups and the Secretary of State for the Environment.

Environment Agency

The Environment Agency is tasked with achieving general improvements in the quality of air, land and water. It has incorporated the National Rivers Authority and taken responsibility for more than 800km of inland waterways in addition to pollution control and river basin management, waste management and recycling and salmon and freshwater fisheries. One of its aims is to encourage the conservation of natural resources, animals and plants. The Agency also issues licences for rod angling and net fishing.

Environment and Heritage Service

This body is responsible within Northern Ireland for the designation of AONBs, country parks, SSSI, national nature reserves, environmentally sensitive areas as well as special areas of conservation and protection areas. The Service also deals with buildings in a similar way to English Heritage.

Farming and Rural Conservation Agency

This Agency offers advice and technical support to the Ministry of Agriculture, Fisheries and Food, and is also concerned with land use planning, environmental protection, environmental schemes and wildlife management. The Agency is the contact for local planning authorities regarding regional strategies affecting agriculture, planning applications leading to the loss of land and the restoration of land to agricultural use.

Forestry Commission

The Forestry Commission is a Government department concerned with the implementation of Government policy in relation to woodland and forests. Divided into two executive agencies, responsibility for the management of nationally owned woodland falls to Forest Enterprise, while scientific research is the task of Forest Research. The Commission's stated objective is to protect and expand Britain's forests and woodlands and increase their value to society and the environment.

Joint Nature Conservation Committee

A group concerned with coordinating the objectives of the Countryside Council for Wales, Scottish Natural Heritage and English Nature. The Committee acts as an advisory body for ministers on nature conservation issues.

National Rivers Authority

Now part of the Environment Agency, the National Rivers Authority is responsible for flood monitoring, flood defences and flood warnings and the improvement of river navigation.

Nature Conservancy Council

Founded in 1946 and given statutory authority in 1973 the functions of this national advisory body have now been divided[4] between English Nature and the Countryside Council for Wales.

Rivers Agency

The Rivers Agency is responsible for flood monitoring, flood defences, flood warnings and the improvement of river navigation in Northern Ireland.

Scottish Environment Protection Agency

Within Scotland this Agency has responsibilities for the protection of the environment, pollution control and waste management.

Scottish Natural Heritage

This body has taken over many of the functions of the Nature Conservancy Council and the Countryside Commission. It is responsible for the designation and management of national scenic areas, SSSIs, national nature reserves and the implementation of European Directives on habitats and wild birds.

---

1   While the duties of these will be passed over to the new National Assemblies, it may be some time before their impact is felt.
2   The Assembly for Northern Ireland is destined to follow.
3   Some reserves are managed by other conservation organisations, overseen by the CCW.
4   Environmental Protection Act 1990.

AIR WEAPONS

See also Damage; Firearms and Shooting; Theft

An air weapon is a low powered[1] firearm that is not especially dangerous. Unlike the majority of guns that use an explosive force to propel their missiles, air weapons use compressed air or carbon dioxide.[2] Although exact figures are not available, air weapons are probably the most prolific firearms in private ownership in the UK. Some estimates suggest that there may be more than two million air weapons in circulation and statistics clearly show that air weapons account for the vast majority of crime involving firearms.[3]

Currently, no licence is required for possession of an air weapon and they remain largely uncontrolled. The Firearms Act 1968 sought to apply some limitations and as a result an air weapon cannot be:

(a) purchased or hired by anyone under the age of 17;
(b) sold or hired to anyone under the age of 17;
(c) with a person under 17 in a public place, unless in a securely fastened gun cover which prevents firing;
(d) with a person under 14 years of age in any place unless supervised by someone aged 21 years or older,[4] or when engaged as a member of a rifle club or at a shooting gallery;[5]
(e) given as a gift to a person under 14 years.[6]

There are no restrictions on the ownership of air weapons by people over the age of 17 years but it should be noted that air weapons remain 'firearms' for the purposes of criminal offences. This means that if an air weapon is used to commit a robbery it will attract the same penalty as a robbery where a shotgun is used.[7] In addition to criminal damage, regularly committed offences involving air weapons include trespassing on land, having a loaded air weapon in a public place and assault.

Where injuries occur as a result of any specific intention or recklessness, then criminal charges are likely and the police have extensive powers to seize and inspect these firearms. Refusal to hand over an air weapon for inspection is a criminal offence.

The civil courts also offer remedies for damage or injury caused by inappropriate use of an air weapon and compensation may be sought from the guilty party or those responsible for him or her.

1. Current approved muzzle velocities are 12ft lbs for air rifles and 6ft lbs for pistols.
2. Carbon dioxide is often used as the propellant for the type of weapons found in paint-ball games.
3. Statistics for 1997 show that of 12 410 criminal offences involving firearms, 7506 were through the use of air weapons and of these three-quarters involved criminal damage.
4. And where used on any premises, the missiles from the air weapon must not travel beyond the boundary of that property.
5. Such as those found at fairgrounds.
6. No offence is committed where the person is engaged as a member of a rifle club or at a miniature rifle range where the weapons are below .23 inch calibre.
7. Robbery is punishable by life imprisonment.

AMPHIBIANS

See also Killing Birds and Animals; Northern Ireland; Protected Animals

The Wildlife and Countryside Act 1981[1] provides specific protection for amphibians. The great crested newt and the natterjack toad are fully protected. Others may be taken from the wild, although it is against the law to sell, offer or expose for sale or possess for sale any amphibian. This has been further amended by a general sales licence[2] that currently prohibits only the sale of adult specimens during the relevant breeding season for that species. However, the general licence does not permit the sale of any of these species at any time of the year if they were taken from the wild during the breeding season. Specimens of the smooth newt taken from the counties of Devon, Cornwall and Somerset, and palmate newts taken from Cambridgeshire, Essex, Leicestershire, Lincolnshire, Norfolk, Northamptonshire, Staffordshire, Suffolk and Warwickshire may not be sold at any time.

Wild great crested newts and natterjack toads are also protected under the Conservation (Natural Habitats, etc.) Regulations 1994. Under these Regulations, it is an offence to deliberately capture or kill either of these species or to deliberately disturb them, take or destroy their eggs or damage or destroy any breeding site or resting place. It is also an offence to keep, transport, sell or exchange or offer for sale or exchange them alive or dead and this includes any part of such an animal and anything derived from one. It will be a defence to show that the animal had been lawfully killed or taken or lawfully sold. There are also general defences under the Regulations regarding acts of mercy, incidental results of otherwise lawful operations and anything done in pursuance of a requirement by the Ministry of Agriculture, Fisheries and Food.[3] Licences may be granted for scientific and educational purposes.

Local planning authorities are required to take the habitats of the following amphibians into account when considering planning applications:

Schedule 5 Animals which are protected[4]

Common name	Scientific name	Breeding Season[5]
Frog, Common	*Rana temporaria*	15 January – 15 April
Newt, Great Crested (or Warty)	*Triturus cristatus*	
Newt, Palmate	*Triturus helveticus*	1 April – 1 August
Newt, Smooth	*Triturus vulgaris*	1 April – 1 August
Toad, Common	*Bufo bufo*	1 February – 1 May
Toad, Natterjack	*Bufo calamita*	

---

1 The Wildlife (Northern Ireland) Order 1985 includes the common or smooth newt (*Triturus vulgaris*) under its equivalent schedule. The common frog and common newt may not be sold either dead or alive at any time.

2 Issued under the Wildlife and Countryside Act 1981, this is valid in England, Wales and Scotland until January 2001.

3 This exception is concerned with requirements under the Agriculture Act 1947 and the Agriculture (Scotland) Act 1948 for the prevention of damage by pests and order made under the Animal Health Act 1981, as amended.

4 Wildlife and Countryside Act 1981.

5 Dates are inclusive.

BADGERS

See also Firearms; Killing Birds and Animals; Northern Ireland; Police

Though the Wildlife and Countryside Act 1981 and the Wildlife (Northern Ireland) Order 1985 restrict the methods by which any wild animal may be killed or taken, the Protection of Badgers Act 1992 provides specific protection for wild badgers and makes it an offence for any person to:

(a) wilfully kill, injure or take, or attempt to kill, injure or take, a badger;[1]
(b) have in his possession, or under his control, any dead badger or any part of, or anything derived from, a dead badger;[2]
(c) cruelly ill-treat a badger;
(d) use any badger tongs in the course of killing or taking, or attempting to kill or take, a badger;
(e) dig for a badger;
(f) use for the purpose of killing or taking a badger any firearm other than a smooth bore weapon of not less than 20 bore or a rifle using ammunition having a muzzle energy not less than 160ft lbs and a bullet weighing not less than 38 grains;
(g) damage a badger sett[3] or any part of it;[4]
(h) destroy a badger sett;[4]
(i) obstruct access to, or any entrance of, a badger sett;[4]
(j) cause a dog to enter a badger sett;[4,5]
(k) disturb a badger when it is occupying a badger sett;[4]
(l) sell[6] a live badger, offer one for sale or have a live badger in his possession or under his control;
(m) mark, attach a ring, tag or other marking device to a badger.

None of the above will be an offence if the act is performed under the terms of a licence.[7] Other defences include acts of mercy, unavoidable killing or injuring as an incidental result of some other lawful action and anything done under the authorisation of the Animals (Scientific Procedures) Act 1986.

The Protection of Badgers Act 1992 includes a specific exception to the offences under (a), (b), (g), (h), (i), (j) or (k) where action is necessary to prevent serious damage to land, crops, poultry or other property. But this will not apply where the need was foreseen and a licence could have been applied for, or had been applied for but refused. Possession of a live badger will not be an offence if it has been disabled otherwise than by the possessor's act and has been taken by him solely for the purpose of tending it and it is necessary for that purpose for it to remain in his possession or under his control.

Fox hunting requires the reduction of potential sanctuaries for the hunted fox and this has traditionally required the stopping-up of badger setts. In recognition of this need, the 1992 Act includes an exception to (g), (i) and (k) for the purpose of hunting foxes with hounds. In such a case no offence will be committed where the entrance to a sett is obstructed only with approved materials,[8] no digging takes place into the tops or sides of the entrance and the materials are in place only for a limited period of time.[9]

In order to investigate any suspected offences under this Act, the police are empowered to stop and search any people or vehicles that they reasonably believe may be involved. If any person is found committing either of (a) or (b) on any land it shall be lawful for the owner or occupier of the land, employee or constable to require that person to leave the land and also to give details of their name and address. Any refusal will be a further offence.

1 Defined as any animal of the species *Meles meles*.
2 A person is not guilty of this offence if he can show that the badger had not been killed, or had been killed otherwise than in contravention of the provisions of this Act or the earlier Badger Act 1973 (repealed). Nor will an offence be committed if the badger or other thing in his possession had been sold and at the time of sale the purchaser had no reason to believe that the badger had been killed in contravention of any Act.
3 Any structure or place which displays signs indicating current use by a badger.
4 Intending to do any of these or being reckless as to whether his actions would have any of these consequences.
5 The use of a dog may result in its destruction or disposal and the disqualification of the offender from keeping another dog.
6 Includes hire, barter and exchange and cognate expressions shall be construed accordingly.

7   These may be issued for scientific or educational purposes, for the purposes of zoological gardens, in order to ring or mark any badger, for the preservation of ancient monuments and for the purpose of development under the Town and Country Planning Acts. Licences may also be issued to prevent the spread of disease or to prevent serious damage to land, crops, poultry or other property.

8   Only untainted straw or hay, leaf litter, bracken, loose soil, bundles of sticks or faggots, paper sacks (empty or filled with untainted straw, hay, bracken or loose soil) are permitted and only if not packed tightly into the entrances.

9   In the case of untainted straw or hay, leaf litter, bracken and loose soil the materials shall not be placed in the entrances except on the day of the hunt or after midday on the preceding day. Bundles of sticks, faggots or paper sacks may be placed at the entrance to the sett only on the day of the hunt and must be removed the same day.

BATS

See also Killing Birds and Animals; Northern Ireland; Protected Animals

Bats are protected by the provisions of the Wildlife and Countryside Act 1981,[1] the Wildlife (Northern Ireland) Order 1985 and the Conservation (Natural Habitats, etc.) Regulations 1994 and it is an offence for any person to kill, injure or capture any bat of the family Rhinolophidae or Vespertilionidae. Prohibitions extend to include:

(a) possession of any live or dead bat, or of any part of, or anything derived from, such an animal;

(b) intentionally damaging or destroying any structure or place which any wild bat uses for shelter or protection;

(c) obstructing access to any such structure or place used for shelter or protection;

(d) disturbing a bat while it is occupying any structure or place which it uses for these purposes;

(e) selling, offering for sale, possessing or transporting for the purposes of sale, any live or dead bat, or any part of or anything derived from a bat;

(f) publishing any advertisement likely to be understood as conveying that bats are bought or sold.

It is not unlawful, however, to disturb a bat or destroy its shelter where such an act takes place in any dwelling-house or where the act is an incidental result of an otherwise lawful action. This will only apply to acts taking place in the living areas of a dwelling-house and only to the extent necessary to remove the bat. No defence would be available therefore in the case of any disturbance to bats living in an unoccupied loft space or where the bat is needlessly killed. The law does not require that householders put up with bats living on their property however, and where a bat is found to be living in an area of a dwelling, other than a living area, the advice of the appropriate Country Conservation Agency[2] must be sought. Advice will be provided on the best time to exclude all roosting bats and on the most appropriate method.

No offence is committed either under the legislative restrictions where a bat is killed, injured or captured provided it can be shown that the action was:

(a) an act of mercy;
(b) necessary for the purpose of preventing serious damage to crops, vegetables, fruit or growing timber;
(c) an incidental result of an otherwise lawful action;
(d) authorised by the Ministry of Agriculture under the Agriculture Act 1947,[3] Agriculture (Scotland) Act 1948 or the Animal Health Act 1981.

In the few instances where bats may be lawfully killed or taken, the method used is restricted by both the Wildlife and Countryside Act 1981 and the Conservation (Natural Habitats, etc.) Regulations 1994.[4]

---

1   Schedule 5 to the Act lists all wild animals subject to protection.
2   Formerly the task of the Nature Conservancy Council this responsibility now falls to English Nature, the Countryside Council for Wales and Scottish Natural Heritage.
3   These exceptions relate to the prevention of damage by pests.
4   See page 110.

BEES

See also Cruelty to Animals; Insects and Other Invertebrates; Killing Birds and Animals; Northern Ireland; Protected Animals

Bees are protected by specific legislation in the Bees Act 1980, which is concerned with the control of those pests and diseases that may affect them. This Act provides the Minister of Agriculture, Fisheries and Food[1] with powers to make orders regulating the importation of bees[2] and to set standards for bee products, hives, containers or other appliances used in connection with the keeping or transportation of bees. Provisions may also be made for the destruction of diseased bees[3] and fines of up to £5000 are available to enforce the various controls.

As animals, bees are also protected by legislation regulating their treatment. Difficulty arises however, in determining whether bees are wild or captive animals. If domesticated or captive, the Protection of Animals Act 1911[4] may protect bees against cruel treatment such as the administration of poisonous or injurious substances. Tamed and captive animals are 'property' for the purposes of the Theft Act 1968 and are capable of being stolen or damaged. In this context the status of bees was subject to a ruling in *Kearry* v. *Pattinson* (1939), where it was held that bees only became 'property' when hived. This ruling suggests that swarming bees are wild. While some provisions of the Wildlife and Countryside Act 1981[5] offer general protection to wild animals,[6] none seem appropriate to the protection of wild bees.

1 Together with the various Secretaries of State and, more recently, the National Assemblies of Scotland, Wales and Northern Ireland.
2 The Importation of Bees Order 1997 SI 1997 No. 310.
3 The Bee Diseases Control Order 1982 and the Bee Diseases Control Order (Northern Ireland) 1998.
4 The Protection of Animals (Scotland) Act 1912 introduced similar provisions.
5 The Wildlife (Northern Ireland) Order 1985 is applicable in that province.
6 There is no detailed definition of 'animal' within the 1981 Act.

BIRDS AND EGGS

See also Falconry; Game Birds; Killing Birds and Animals; Lead Shot; Northern Ireland

Wild birds are defined by the Wildlife and Countryside Act 1981[1] as 'any bird of a kind which is ordinarily resident in, or is a visitor to Great

Britain in a wild state, but does not include poultry or, with exceptions, game birds'.[2] Extensive protection is afforded wild birds by this Act, which prohibits:

(a) the intentional killing, injuring or taking[3] of any wild bird;
(b) taking, damaging or destroying the nest of any wild bird while it is in use or is being built;
(c) the taking or destroying of any egg of a wild bird;
(d) the possession of any live or dead wild bird including any part of such a bird, or anything derived from it;[4]
(e) the possession of any egg of a wild bird or any part of such an egg;[5]
(f) the disturbance of any wild bird included in Schedule 1 while it is building a nest;
(g) the disturbance of a wild bird included in Schedule 1 in, on or near a nest containing eggs or young birds;
(h) the disturbance of the dependent young of any wild bird included in Schedule 1;
(i) selling, offering or exposing for sale any live wild bird other than one included in Schedule 3, Part 1;
(j) selling, offering or exposing for sale the egg of a wild bird or any part of such an egg;
(k) the possession or transportation of any live wild bird for the purposes of sale;
(l) the publication of any advertisement likely to be understood as conveying that live wild birds or their eggs are bought or sold.

Further prohibitions extend to the unlawful showing of live wild birds for the purposes of any competition and to the methods by which wild birds may be killed or captured.

Exceptions to these prohibitions include the killing or taking of quarry species outside the close season for that bird, actions authorised by the Minister of Agriculture, Fisheries and Food, anything done in pursuance of the Animal Health Act 1981 and acts of mercy. Actions necessary for the preservation of public health, air safety, to prevent the spread of disease or the prevention of serious damage to livestock, crops, vegetables, fruit, growing timber or fisheries are also excluded. In addition, licences may be issued for scientific or educational purposes, for the purpose of ringing or marking any wild bird, for conserving wild birds, for falconry or aviculture, taxidermy and photography.

Police officers have been granted extensive powers to enforce the various prohibitions. If a constable suspects with reasonable cause that any person is committing or has committed an offence under the relevant provisions of the 1981 Act, he may without warrant:

(a) stop and search that person if he suspects that evidence is to be found;
(b) search or examine anything which that person may then be using or have in his possession;
(c) arrest that person if he fails to give a satisfactory name and address;
(d) seize and detain anything which may be evidence of the commission of the offence;
(e) enter any land other than a dwelling-house for the purpose of exercising his powers.

Schedules 1–3 to the Wildlife and Countryside Act 1981 list those birds subject to special protection, birds that may be killed or taken, birds which may be sold and those which must be registered and ringed if kept in captivity.

Schedule 1 Birds which are protected by special penalties

Part 1 At all times

Common name	Scientific name	Common name	Scientific name
Avocet	*Recurvirostra avosetta*	Eagle, White-tailed	*Haliaetus albicilla*
Bee-eater	*Merops apiaster*	Falcon, Gyr	*Falco rusticolus*
Bittern	*Botaurus stellaris*	Fieldfare	*Turdus pilaris*
Bittern, Little	*Ixobrychus minutus*	Firecrest	*Regulus ignicapillus*
Bluethroat	*Luscinia svecica*	Garganey	*Anas querquedula*
Brambling	*Fringilla montifringilla*	Godwit, Black-tailed	*Limosa limosa*
Bunting, Cirl	*Emberiza cirlus*	Goshawk	*Accipiter gentilis*
Bunting, Lapland	*Calcarius lapponicus*	Grebe, Black-necked	*Podiceps nigricollis*
Bunting, Snow	*Plectrophenax nivalis*	Grebe, Slavonian	*Podiceps auritus*
Buzzard, Honey	*Pernis apivorus*	Greenshank	*Tringa nebularia*
Chough	*Pyrrhocorax pyrrhocorax*	Gull, Little	*Larus minutus*
Corncrake	*Crex crex*	Gull, Mediterranean	*Larus melanocephalus*
Crake, Spotted	*Porzana porzana*	Harriers (all species)	*Circus*
Crossbills (all species)	*Loxia*	Heron, Purple	*Ardea purpurea*
Curlew, Stone	*Burhinus oedicnemus*	Hobby	*Falco subbuteo*
Divers (all species)	*Gavia*	Hoopoe	*Upupa epops*
Dotterel	*Charadrius morinellus*	Kingfisher	*Alcedo atthis*
Duck, Long-tailed	*Clangula hyemalis*	Kite, Red	*Milvus milvus*
Eagle, Golden	*Aquila chrysaetos*	Merlin	*Falco columnarius*

A–Z OF COUNTRYSIDE LAW B

Common name	Scientific name	Common name	Scientific name
Oriole, Golden	*Oriolus oriolus*	Shorelark	*Eremophila alpestris*
Osprey	*Pandion haliaetus*	Shrike, Red-backed	*Lanius collurio*
Owl, Barn	*Tyto alba*	Spoonbill	*Platalea leucorodia*
Owl, Snowy	*Nyctea scandiaca*	Stilt, Black-winged	*Himantopus himantopus*
Peregrine	*Falco peregrinus*	Stint, Temminck's	*Calidris temminckii*
Petrel, Leach's	*Oceanodroma leucorhoa*	Swan, Bewick's	*Cygnus bewickii*
Phalarope, Red-necked	*Phalaropus lobatus*	Swan, Whooper	*Cygnus cygnus*
Plover, Kentish	*Charadrius alexandrinus*	Tern, Black	*Chlidonias niger*
Plover, Little Ringed	*Charadrius dubius*	Tern, Little	*Sterna albifrons*
Quail, Common	*Coturnix coturnix*	Tern, Roseate	*Sterna dougallii*
Redstart, Black	*Phoenicurus ochruros*	Tit, Bearded	*Panarus biarmicus*
Redwing	*Turdus iliacus*	Tit, Crested	*Parus cristatus*
Rosefinch, Scarlet	*Carpodacus erythrinus*	Treecreeper, Short-toed	*Certhia brachydactyla*
Ruff	*Philomachus pugnax*	Warbler, Cetti's	*Cettia cetti*
Sandpiper, Green	*Tringa ochropus*	Warbler, Dartford	*Sylvia undata*
Sandpiper, Purple	*Calidris maritima*	Warbler, Marsh	*Acrocephalus palustris*
Sandpiper, Wood	*Tringa glareola*	Warbler, Savi's	*Locustella luscinioides*
Scaup	*Aythya marila*	Whimbrel	*Numenius phaeopus*
Scoter, Common	*Melanitta nigra*	Woodlark	*Lullula arborea*
Scoter, Velvet	*Melanitta fusca*	Wryneck	*Jynx torquilla*
Serin	*Serinus serinus*		

Part 2 Birds which are protected by special penalties during the close season

Common name	Scientific name
Goldeneye	*Bucephala clangula*
Goose, Greylag [6]	*Anser anser*
Pintail	*Anas acuta*

Schedule 2 Birds which may be killed or taken

Part 1 Outside the close season

Common name	Scientific name	Common name	Scientific name
Capercaillie	*Tetrao urogallus*	Moorhen	*Gallinula chloropus*
Coot	*Fulica atra*	Pintail	*Anas acuta*
Duck, Tufted	*Aytha fuligula*	Plover, Golden	*Pluvialis apricaria*
Gadwall	*Anas strepera*	Pochard	*Aythya ferina*
Goldeneye	*Bucephala clangula*	Shoveler	*Anas clypeata*
Goose, Canada	*Branta canadensis*	Snipe, Common	*Gallinago gallinago*
Goose, Greylag	*Anser anser*	Teal	*Anas crecca*
Goose, Pink-footed [7]	*Anser platyrhynchos*	Wigeon	*Anas penelope*
Mallard	*Anas platyrhynchos*	Woodcock	*Scolopax rusticola*

BIRDS AND EGGS 17

Part 2 Birds which may be killed or taken by authorised persons at all times

Common name	Scientific name	Common name	Scientific name
Crow	*Corvus corone*	Magpie	*Pica pica*
Dove, Collared	*Streptopelia decaocto*	Pigeon, Feral	*Columba livia*
Gull, Great Black-backed	*Larus marinus*	Rook	*Corvus frugilegus*
Gull, Herring	*Larus argentatus*	Sparrow, House	*Passer domesticus*
Gull, Lesser Black-backed	*Larus fuscus*	Starling	*Sturnus vulgaris*
Jackdaw	*Corvus monedula*	Woodpigeon	*Columba palumbus*
Jay	*Garrulus glandarius*		

Schedule 3 Birds which may be sold

Part 1 Alive at all times if ringed and bred in captivity

Common name	Scientific name	Common name	Scientific name
Blackbird	*Turdus merula*	Linnet	*Carduelis cannabina*
Brambling	*Fringilla montifringilla*	Magpie	*Pica pica*
Bullfinch	*Pyrrhula pyrrhula*	Owl, Barn	*Tyto alba*
Bunting, Reed	*Emberiza schoeniclus*	Redpoll	*Carduelis flammea*
Chaffinch	*Fringilla coelebs*	Siskin	*Carduelis spinus*
Dunnock	*Prunella modularis*	Starling	*Sturnus vulgaris*
Goldfinch	*Carduelis carduelis*	Thrush, Song	*Turdus philomelos*
Greenfinch	*Carduelis chloris*	Twite	*Carduelis flavirostris*
Jackdaw	*Corvus monedula*	Yellowhammer	*Emberiza citrinella*
Jay	*Garrulus glandarius*		

Part 2 Dead at all times

Common name	Scientific name
Pigeon, Feral	*Columba livia*
Woodpigeon	*Columba palumbus*

Part 3 Birds which may be sold dead from 1 September to 28 February

Common name	Scientific name	Common name	Scientific name
Capercaillie	*Tetrao urogallus*	Pochard	*Aythya ferina*
Coot	*Fulica atra*	Shoveler	*Anas clypeata*
Duck, Tufted	*Aytha fuligula*	Snipe, Common	*Gallinago gallinago*
Mallard	*Anas platyrhynchos*	Teal	*Anas crecca*
Pintail	*Anas acuta*	Wigeon	*Anas penelope*
Plover, Golden	*Pluvialis apricaria*	Woodcock	*Scolopax rusticola*

1   The Wildlife and Countryside Act 1981 does not apply to Northern Ireland. The Wildlife (Northern Ireland) Order 1985 provides corresponding protection for birds and their eggs.
2   Birds bred in captivity are not included.
3   This means 'capturing'.
4   In the case of *Robinson* v *Everett and W&FC Bonham & Son Ltd (1988)* this was held to include a golden eagle after it had been stuffed and mounted.
5   No offence under (d) or (e) is committed if the bird or egg was legally killed or taken or had been legally sold.
6   In the Outer Hebrides, Caithness, Sutherland and Wester Ross only.
7   In England and Wales only.

BRIDLE-WAYS

See also Access – A Right to Roam; Bulls and Cattle; Footpaths; Green Lanes; Highways and Roads; Land; Nuisances; Trespass

A bridle-way is a highway over which the public have a right to pass and re-pass on foot, on horseback or when leading a horse.[1] In some instances there is also a right to drive cattle and these routes may be known as drift-ways. Bicycles may be ridden on bridle-ways where an appropriate order has been made by a local authority and subject to the requirement that they accord precedence to pedestrians or persons on horseback.[2] Bridle-ways offer a right of passage and nothing else. The land underneath a bridle-way remains private property and any departure from the course of a bridle-way is likely to constitute a trespass. Once dedicated this right to pass and re-pass is well protected, however, and local authorities are under a general duty to protect such rights of way. They also have responsibility for maintaining the routes and, as a result of the Countryside Act 1968, ensuring that they are clearly marked where they leave a carriageway. In some cases local authorities may move or divert a bridle-way, but it is rare that the right of passage is extinguished.

Under the provisions of the Highways Act 1980, the minimum width of a bridle-way, which is not a field-edge path, should be 2m, although it may be up to a maximum of 3m. A field-edge bridle-way should have a minimum width of 3m.[3] Gates crossing bridle-ways must be of sufficient width[4] to facilitate their use by horses and must be maintained in a safe condition and to a reasonable standard of repair so as to prevent interference with the rights of a person using the bridle-way. If an owner or occupier fails to maintain the gates then the local authority is empowered to complete the maintenance and may pass on any costs incurred to the owner of the land.

It is a public nuisance to obstruct the public highway and this applies equally to bridle-ways. Obstructions do not need to be permanent or even stationary to be actionable; shooting on a bridle-way or allowing bulls to wander near one may be sufficient. As the land beneath a bridle-way remains private they may be subject to the needs of agriculture. This may involve them being ploughed up where it is not reasonably convenient to avoid disturbing the surface of the path. This is permissible under the Rights of Way Act 1990 provided that the surface is made good again, either within 14 days where the disturbance is the first for a particular crop,[5] or within 24 hours in any other case.[6] This does not apply to field-edge ways.

The use of motor vehicles along bridle-ways is prohibited[7] and any trial or event involving motor vehicles which uses or crosses a bridle-way requires both the landowner's permission and that of the local authority.

1 Includes ponies, mules and asses.
2 The Countryside Act 1968; Cycle Tracks Act 1984.
3 The Highways Act 1980 as amended by the Rights of Way Act 1990.
4 The Highways Act 1980 stipulates 5ft.
5 For example, when the crop is sown.
6 The local authority may extend this period for up to 28 days.
7 The Road Traffic Act 1988.

BULLS AND CATTLE

See also Cruelty to Animals; Disease; Livestock; Nuisances; Straying

A familiar sight and an integral part of life in the countryside, bulls and cattle actually account for one or two deaths a year and the law has long recognised that they may present a real danger unless competently controlled or enclosed. Local authorities are empowered by the Public Health (Amendment) Act 1907 to restrict which streets and the manner in which cattle[1] may be driven to market or to any railway siding or wharf.

The provisions of the Highways Act 1835,[2] the Town Police Clauses Act 1847,[3] the Licensing Act 1872[4] and the Highways Act 1980[5] further restrict:

(a) the driving of cattle on any footpath at the side of any road;
(b) which side of the road cattle should be kept to in order to avoid any obstruction of vehicles;[6]
(c) furious driving of cattle in any street;[7]
(d) leading cattle on any footway in any street;[7]
(e) any exposing of them for sale or show in any street;[7]
(f) cleaning cattle in any street;[7]
(g) turning them loose in any street;[7]
(h) being drunk whilst in charge of any cattle;
(i) allowing cattle to stray or lie at the side of a highway.[8]

Bulls allowed to roam freely in any field or enclosure through which a footpath or bridle-way runs may present a particular danger to people exercising their right to pass. An occupier of any field or enclosure crossed by a right of way is liable if they permit a bull to be at large in that field or enclosure. However, this prohibition does not apply to bulls under 10 months of age or any bull other than a recognised dairy breed provided that it is at large with cows or heifers. Recognised dairy breeds include Ayrshire, British Friesian, British Holstein, Dairy Shorthorn, Guernsey, Jersey and Kerry.

When infectious diseases, such as foot and mouth or cattle plague break out, the Minister for Agriculture, Fisheries and Food has the power to make orders prohibiting or restricting the movement of cattle where it is necessary to control the spread of the disease.

As domesticated animals, bulls and cattle are subject to the same controls that apply to livestock generally and are also protected from cruel acts under the terms of the Protection of Animals Act 1911.[9]

1   Defined by the Animal Health Act 1981 as meaning bulls, cows, steers, heifers and calves.
2   (a) and (b) (as listed on p.21).
3   (c), (d), (e) and (f) (as listed on p.21).
4   (h) (as listed on p.21).
5   (i) (as listed on p.21).
6   Cattle should be kept to the near side. The Act refers to 'carriages' and this now includes bicycles and motor cars.
7   This must be to the obstruction, annoyance or danger of residents or passengers.
8   No offence is committed where the highway passes over any common, waste or unenclosed ground and this section does not operate to prejudice any right of pasture at the side of a highway. There is a liability on the part of the owner to pay the reasonable costs of their removal.
9   The Protection of Animals (Scotland) Act 1912.

CANALS

See also Agencies; Bridle-ways; Footpaths; Highways and Roads

British Waterways is the public body[1] created under the Transport Act 1968 to operate the majority of the country's canals and has responsibility for more than 2000 miles of canals and navigable rivers. This responsibility extends to include conservation, regeneration, leisure, recreation and tourism. Over half of all canals are designated as cruising waterways.

Bye-laws regulate the access and use of these waterways and with few exceptions,[2] these controls apply to every canal or inland navigation owned by the Board or under its control. The bye-laws regulate the construction of vessels using the waterways, their maintenance and use as well as use of the tow-paths that run alongside many canals. The regulation of vessels on canals requires that:

(a) vessels[3] should be fit for their use on a particular canal;
(b) vessels should be clearly marked with name and index number,[4] owner or port of registration, together with any other such plates as required;[5]
(c) vessels should be equipped with fenders;
(d) goods and equipment are stowed to avoid unnecessary projections over the sides and secured;
(e) inflammable spirits are stored safely;
(f) the crew is adequate and competent.

The use of vessels at night is also regulated and they are required to display the appropriate lighting for the waterway the vessel is using. Care and consideration is required when any vessel is navigating on any canal and it is an offence against the bye-laws to endanger the safety of other vessels or to obstruct their passage. Speed limits are enforced and pleasure craft should accord precedence to other vessels.[6] Further bye-laws provide detailed dos and don'ts in relation to the operation of locks and movable bridges.

Towing paths running alongside navigable rivers and canals do not confer any right of way for people on foot unless designated as a footpath or bridle-way. In the vast majority of cases these paths are private and access is permitted only subject to the Board's bye-laws. Generally, these state that no person unless authorised by the Board or otherwise legally entitled to do so shall:

(a) ride or drive any animal or vehicle over any towing path;
b) obstruct any towing path or interfere with the authorised use; or
(c) leave open any gate or rail used as a fence or part of a fence alongside, across or on any way leading to a towing path.

An offence is committed by any person who wilfully, wantonly or maliciously damages or otherwise interferes with any hedge, post, rail, wall or other fencing alongside a towing path or on any way leading to a towing path. Further prohibitions apply to turning any vessel adrift, throwing rubbish into a canal, unauthorised bathing, navigating vessels while drunk, shooting on or across canals or otherwise causing any nuisance.

1. British Waterways is a statutory consultee on any planning applications submitted to local planning authorities that may affect canals.
2. Lee and Start Navigation, Gloucester and Sharpness Canal and the River Severn Navigation.
3. This term includes any ship, boat, barge, lighter, raft and any other description of craft.
4. Issued by the Board.
5. Gauge plates, draught marks etc.
6. Includes any yacht, launch, houseboat, randan, wherry, skiff, gig, dinghy, shallop, punt, canoe or float.

CARAVANS AND CAMPING

See also Town and Country Planning; Vagrants

Problems with the siting of caravans[1] and the proliferation of caravan sites in the 1950s resulted in the introduction of the Caravan Sites and Control of Development Act 1960 to control development and reduce any negative impact on the countryside. This Act constrains the creation of unlicensed caravan sites and subjects licensed sites to conditions imposed by local authorities. These conditions are able to restrict:

(a) the number of caravans present on a site;
(b) the occasions when they may be parked on site;
(c) the size and type of caravan permitted; and
(d) their positioning on the site.

Exceptions to the requirement to obtain a licence include the siting of any caravan within the curtilage of a dwelling-house,[2] circumstances where the use of the caravan is for no more than two nights, use by agricultural and forestry workers, building sites and where occupied by travelling showmen.

Individual caravans are also subject to legal controls regarding their siting on any land, depending on whether the caravan is parked with the permission of the landowner, or whether its presence constitutes a trespass.[3] The Criminal Justice and Public Order Act 1994 provides local authorities with powers to direct[4] that occupied caravans on any land forming part of a highway, or any other unoccupied land, or on any occupied land without the consent of the owner be removed. Any person, who fails to comply with such a direction, commits an offence.[5] If a direction is not complied with, a magistrate may make an order under the Caravan Sites Act 1968 allowing the local authority to enter onto the land[6] and take such steps as may be necessary to remove the caravan.

In the case of mass trespass the police have extensive powers[7] where they believe that two or more people are present for the purpose of residing for any period and that reasonable steps have been taken by the occupier of the land to ask them to leave. If the trespassers have caused damage to the land or to any property, or have used any threatening, abusive or insulting words or behaviour towards the occupier, his family or agent, or the trespassers have six or more vehicles between them then the police may direct them to leave.

Setting up camp on a highway or road is an offence under the Highways Act 1980 and this includes footpaths, bridle-ways, causeways, pavements and bridges. In Scotland, the Trespass (Scotland) Act 1865 prohibits camping on or near any turnpike road, statute labour road or other highway. It is also an offence under this Act to camp on or near any private road or enclosed cultivated land or in or near any plantation without the consent of the owner or occupier.

1   Defined as any structure designed or adapted for human habitation, which is capable of being moved from one place to another whether by being towed or by being transported on a motor vehicle or trailer.
2   But see Town and Country Planning.
3   The siting of residential caravans for permanent occupation is beyond the scope of this book.
4   Humanitarian issues must be considered before any direction is made.

5   Defences include illness, breakdown or other emergency.
6   Subject to 24 hours notice.
7   The Criminal Justice and Public Order Act 1994.

CHILDREN

See also Air Weapons; Damage; Horses; Quarries and Mines; Trespass

The ability of young people to get themselves into trouble is legendary and the countryside offers massive temptation. Unfortunately, serious accidents involving farming equipment still regularly occur and legal restrictions have been introduced in an attempt to reduce these incidents. The Agriculture (Safety, Health and Welfare Provisions) Act 1956 prohibits the causing or permitting of a child to ride on or drive any vehicle, machine or agricultural implement in contravention of regulations made under this Act. These currently include requirements that children under 14 years old wear protective headgear when riding on any agricultural vehicle,[1] and when riding a horse on any road.[2]

While criminal law offers a punitive approach to child protection, the civil law adopts a more reactive perspective to situations that result in damage or injury. However, the liability of an owner or occupier of land is not always clearly determined and may depend on the status of the injured party and the nature of their access on to the land. While owners and occupiers are required[3] to take reasonable steps to prevent injury to anyone coming on to their land, regardless of whether the entry was by any right or permission or as a trespass, the level of care required may be different. In cases where the injured party was on the land as of right, easement or invitation the duty of care owed to them may be more easily established than if the injured person was a trespasser. A duty to a trespasser will arise if the occupier is aware of a danger, aware that the trespasser is either in the vicinity of the danger, or may come to it and the risk is one that an occupier of land ought reasonably to protect a trespasser from.[4] It will be a matter for the courts to decide whether sufficient care had been taken, although it may be necessary for the injured party to establish that they were actually owed a duty of care. Punishment is not the objective of civil law; its purpose is to compensate the victim and any contributory negligence on the part of the injured party is likely to affect the level of any compensation awarded by the court.

Generally, the level of care offered to children must always be higher than that offered to an adult, although it may be expected that parents will exercise some reasonable control for their children's safety.

1 The Agriculture (Avoidance of Accidents to Children) Regulations 1958.
2 The Horses (Protective Headgear for Young Riders) Act 1990.
3 The Occupier's Liability Act 1957. 'The common duty of care is a duty to take such care as in all the circumstances of the case is reasonable to see that the visitor will be reasonably safe…'
4 The Occupier's Liability Act 1984. This legislation replaces the common law 'duty of common humanity'.

CLAY TARGET SHOOTING

See also Firearms and Shooting; Lead Shot; Noise; Shotguns; Town and Country Planning

An occasionally controversial country pastime due to the noise levels that may be generated, clay target shooting has a long history[1] and a large following in the UK with competitions occurring at both international and Olympic level.

The sport makes use of shotguns and participants are generally required to hold shotgun licences under the terms of the Firearms Act 1968.[2] While any unlicensed possession of a shotgun is a serious criminal offence the legislation specifically exempts clay target shooting clubs provided that they are registered with their local police force. This exception allows non-licence holders to shoot while at the club but is limited to that place and a shotgun cannot be in the possession of an unlicensed person outside that approved ground. Through this exemption, people are able to 'have a go' without needing to commit themselves to the conditions that are required to obtain a licence.

Clay target shooting grounds generally fall into two categories. The first, are businesses operating with the appropriate planning permission on approved ground owned by the business. These are subject to any controls made out by their planning authority but are not necessarily limited in the times during which shooting may take place.

The second category is less formalised and is often represented by small, member-led clubs operating on farmland and subject to the landowner's permission. These can be sited quite close to built-up areas and occasional noise problems may occur as a result. However, these clubs are not generally subject to the control of a local planning authority as the land on which they shoot has changed its use only temporarily from whatever form of agricultural activity it was being put. Temporary use offers an opportunity for some activities to take place on a limited basis without the need for planning permission under the Town and Country Planning (General Permitted Development) Order 1995.[3] Clay target shooting clubs only make temporary use of the land provided that they do not shoot on more than 28 days within each year. The availability of this exception has led to a large number of small clay target clubs shooting on a fortnightly basis, often on Sunday mornings.

Where noise is a problem, clay target shooting can be made subject to abatement orders served by a local authority. Lead pollution has not, as yet, been a major issue in respect of clay target shooting grounds, but new legislation on the use of lead shot on wetlands may have an impact on any clay target shooting grounds either falling within or shooting over an SSSI.

---

1 The Inanimate Bird Shooting Association held its first championship in 1893. The Clay Pigeon Shooting Association was formed in 1928.

2 The licensing arrangements for Northern Ireland are slightly different.

3 This Order was created under the Town and Country Planning Act 1990.

COCKFIGHTING

See also Cruelty to Animals; Dogs

The fighting of animals was once a widespread practice and fights between cocks were traditionally performed in a pit in front of a gambling audience utilising the birds own territorial and fighting instincts, while supplementing their natural weapons with the addition of long, steel spurs strapped to their feet. A criminal offence relating to the keeping of pits for the purpose of cockfights is enshrined in the Town Police Clauses Act 1847.[1] Offences of using or acting in the management of any house, room, pit or other place for the purpose of fighting are included and the legislation provides powers of entry to facilitate investigation by the police. Any person found in a place used for fighting animals is liable to a penalty of £2500. The Protection of Animals Act 1911[2] makes it an offence for any person to:

(a) cause, procure or assist at the fighting of any domestic or captive animal, including cocks;

(b) keep, use, manage or act or assist in the management of any premises or place for the purpose of fighting any animal;

(c) permit any premises to be so kept, managed or so used;

(d) receive, cause or procure any person to receive money for the admission of any person to such premises or place;

(e) be present at a fight without a reasonable excuse for being there;

(f) advertise any fight between animals.

The Cockfighting Act 1952 states that if any person has in his possession any instrument or appliance designed or adapted for use in connection with the fighting of any domestic fowl, he shall be guilty of an offence. This includes steel spurs.

---

1 The Metropolitan Police Act 1839 and the City of London Police Act 1839 contain similar prohibitions.

2 In Scotland the Protection of Animals Act 1912 applies. These offences may be punishable by six months' imprisonment and a fine of up to £5000.

COMMON LAND

See also Caravans and Camping; Highways and Roads; Village Greens

Rights in common are an ancient and intricate area of land law that still apply to more than one million acres of land in this country. These rights exist in different forms including rights of pasture, rights to take wood, rights to take peat, soil or gravel and rights to take fish. Initially obtained through custom or grant, many date back to medieval times when the need to survive gave added importance to any opportunity to enjoy the produce of the land. Whilst the land remained owned as part of a larger estate, access was often permitted to areas deemed 'manorial waste', and from long use this access changed from being permissive to being a right for the individual, family or village concerned. Similar in concept to rights of way, the land itself is not owned by those who possess the right but remains private. The landowner is, however, restrained and cannot prevent the right from being exercised.

Time has in many cases blurred the nature of these rights and rendered uncertain the ownership of the land. As a result the Metropolitan Commons Act 1866, the Commons Act 1876 and the Commons Registration Act 1965 have all been implemented in an attempt to identify ownership and determine the boundaries of those rights that still exist. The 1965 Act also placed a duty on local authorities to create and maintain registers of common land and rights of common to include who exactly holds what right and where that right may be exercised. While local authorities have had only partial success in achieving this register, its existence reinforces the fact that common land does not necessarily create any right of access to the general public. In the majority of cases access to common land is limited to a specific individual or group and general access is only possible on footpaths or bridle-ways or where permission has been granted by the landowner.

An exception to this occurs where a statute has created an urban common.[1] Examples of such legislation include the Metropolitan

Commons Act 1866, the Law of Property Act 1925, the Commons Act 1899 and the Dartmoor Commons Act 1985. Bye-laws are used to control the right of access to any urban common and these are unlikely to permit driving, camping or caravaning.

Other legislative measures:

(a) make it an offence[2] to graze any animal on common land in contravention of restrictions imposed by a meeting of all the holders of those rights in common;

(b) provide powers for local authorities to search for, dig out and carry away sand, stone or other material from waste or common land for the purpose of repairing any highway maintainable at public expense;[3] and

(c) impose a legal liability on the person who has the right to take rabbit, hares or vermin from common land for any damage caused to trees.[4]

---

1   This includes any metropolitan common (i.e. in the London area) within the meaning of the Metropolitan Commons Acts 1866 to 1898, or manorial waste, or a common, which is wholly or partly situated within a borough or urban district.

2   Commons Act 1908.

3   Highways Act 1980.

4   The right holder will be deemed to be the occupier. Under the Forestry Act 1967, the Forestry Commission is able to seek the return of any costs involved in the protection of trees or tree plants from occupiers.

CONSERVATION

See also Agencies; National Parks

Responsibility for conservation and habitat protection within the UK falls to a number of nature conservation agencies together with the Department of the Environment, Transport and the Regions and the Ministry of Agriculture, Fisheries and Food. The statutory nature conservation agencies are English Nature, Scottish National Heritage and the Countryside Council for Wales. The Environment and Heritage Service (Northern Ireland) is an executive agency within the Department of the Environment for Northern Ireland and operates with similar effect for the conservation needs of the province. In addition, the Secretary of State for the Environment and the Secretary of

State for Agriculture have responsibilities and powers aimed at conservation measures and their departments operate to coordinate and enforce much of the legislation. Some of the functions and responsibilities of these agencies and departments will inevitably cross. European directives and international agreements place further obligations on the British Government to actively protect sites of European and world importance. The Countryside Agency has now been formed from a merger between the Countryside Commission and the Rural Development Commission with the aim of both promoting and conserving the countryside.

The primary conservation initiatives operated by these various departments and agencies are discussed below.

Areas of Outstanding Natural Beauty (AONBs)

The Countryside Agency has responsibility for designating these sites in England and Wales with 41 having been designated since the scheme was first set up in 1949.[1] Nine sites are so designated in Northern Ireland and fall under the responsibility of the Environment and Heritage Service (Northern Ireland).[2] The objective of designating an area as an AONB is to preserve its natural beauty although the land remains private and the every day administration of the scheme rests with local authorities. AONBs include some of the coastal areas designated as Heritage Coasts while the larger inland areas, which have opportunities for extensive outdoor recreation, have been designated as National Parks.

Community Forests

The relatively low proportion of tree cover in the UK has prompted government interest in the establishment of community forests in partnership with the Forestry Commission. The Countryside Agency is involved in the planting and development of 12 community forests including the Forest of Avon, Tees Forest, Forest of Mercia, Great North Forest, the Great Western, Marston Vale, the Greenwood, Mersey Forest, Red Rose Forest, South Yorkshire Forest, Thames Chase and Watling Chase. As with other conservation areas, these may encompass private property and access will be restricted unless an access agreement has been made with the Agency.

Country Parks

Established by the Countryside Act 1968 for the purposes of recreation and exercise, these parks offer free access to members of the general public while still, in many instances, being managed with conservation in mind. Many of these parks include areas subject to SSSI status and are managed by local authorities and the Environment and Heritage Service (Northern Ireland).

Environmentally Sensitive Areas[3]

Introduced to help safeguard areas of countryside of particular importance, this scheme encourages farmers to adapt their farming practices and offers payments to compensate for any losses or costs incurred. Although it is a voluntary scheme, once an agreement has been entered into it lasts for 10 years and is binding on any successors in title. The Ministry of Agriculture, Fisheries and Food and the Department of Agriculture in Northern Ireland operate these schemes.

Local Nature Reserves

Owned or controlled by local authorities, local nature reserves are set up following consultation with the nature conservation agencies and may include some SSSI designated sites. Protected by bye-laws, access to these reserves is dependent on local rules and any rights attached to ownership of that site or adjoining sites.

Marine Nature Reserve

Declared as such by the Secretary of State for the Environment, Transport and the Regions,[4] there are currently only three marine nature reserves in the UK. The purpose of these reserves is to conserve marine flora and fauna or geological or physiographical features of special interest. The legislation allows for the creation of bye-laws to assist with the protection of these sites, which are managed by the nature conservation agencies.

National Nature Reserves

Declared as such by one of the statutory nature conservation agencies[5] under their legislative powers,[6] national nature reserves are either owned, leased or managed by one of the agencies or by an approved wildlife trust. In many cases nature reserves are also designated as SSSIs. Covering everything from salt marshes to meadows, cliffs to woodland there is no general right of access, although entry is possible to the majority of these reserves.

National Scenic Areas

This is a statutory designation for landscapes in Scotland. Local planning authorities are required to consult Scottish Natural Heritage about any development applications within one of these areas. Development is permitted but the consultation arrangement promotes sympathetic and complementary development.

Nature Conservation Orders

Nature Conservation Orders may be issued by the Department of the Environment, Transport and the Regions[7] and operate to increase the protection available to SSSIs by increasing the penalties available to enforce the limitations placed on restricted operations.[8] Nature Conservation Orders are likely to be made where conservation of the site is necessary for the purpose of securing the survival in Great Britain of any animal or plant or for the purpose of conserving its flora, fauna or geological or physiographical features.

Ramsar Sites

An international agreement commonly known as the Ramsar Convention was signed by the British government in 1973,[9] and provides for the designation of wetlands under its full title of the Convention on Wetlands of International Importance Especially as Waterfowl Habitat. A wetland is defined as including any area of fen, marsh, peatland or water, whether natural or artificial, permanent or temporary, with water that is static, flowing, brackish or salt. This also includes areas of marine water that are not more than 6m deep at low tide. Once designated, the Government is obliged to treat a wetland with due care and to stem any encroachment across its borders. The Convention also encourages the Government to prevent the loss of further wetlands.

Sites of Special Scientific Interest (SSSIs)[10]

Where one of the nature conservation agencies is of the opinion that any area of land is of special interest, by reason of any of its flora, fauna, geological or physiographical features, that fact will be notified to the Secretary of State, the local planning authority and the owner or occupier of that land.[11] The relevant agency is obliged to hear and consider any objections to its notification and must confirm the SSSI status of a site within 9 months of the original designation. Once confirmed, the effect of SSSI status is to limit certain operations taking place on that site, require consultation to take place where such operations are proposed[12] and require that prior written consent is obtained before any such operation is carried out.[13] While many of these sites are owned by the Forestry Commission, the Crown Estates, the Ministry of Defence or some other voluntary conservation body, there is no general right of access and the majority of sites remain in private hands. The status of an SSSI indicates to local planning authorities that care needs to be taken when considering any plans likely to affect the site and notification removes any presumption that may otherwise favour development. The ability to preserve these sites remains limited, however, and the Government is due to make proposals to enhance the powers currently available to the conservation agencies.

Special Areas of Conservation

Designated under the European Communities Council Directive on the Conservation of Natural Habitats and of Wild Fauna and Flora and generally known as the Habitats Directive,[14] these sites are of European nature conservation importance. The Directive requires Member States to maintain or restore natural habitats through the establishment of a management plan. The Directive also lists animals and plants whose habitats require special protection. These sites, together with the Special Protection Areas, will eventually form part of the 'Natura 2000' European conservation initiative.

Special Protection Areas

Special protection areas were created under the EU Council Directive on the Conservation of Wild Birds and the UK Government is obliged to designate these areas in order to conserve the habitat of rare, vulnerable and listed migratory birds. Conservation is to be achieved by restricting disturbance, pollution and site deterioration.

1   The National Parks and Access to the Countryside Act 1949.
2   The Amenity Lands Act (Northern Ireland) 1965 and the Nature Conservation and Amenity Lands (Northern Ireland) Order 1985.
3   The Ministry of Agriculture, Fisheries and Food / Department of Agriculture Northern Ireland.
4   Or the Department of the Environment for Northern Ireland.
5   English Nature, the Countryside Council for Wales, Scottish National Heritage or the Environment and Heritage Service (Northern Ireland).
6   The National Parks and Access to the Countryside Act 1949 and the Wildlife and Countryside Act 1981 for England, Wales and Scotland. The Nature Conservation and Amenity Lands (Northern Ireland) Order 1985 applies to Northern Ireland.
7   Or the Department of the Environment for Northern Ireland.
8   The Wildlife and Countryside Act 1981.
9   Ratified in 1976, the Convention gets its name from the place where it was held, Ramsar in Iran.
10 In Northern Ireland these are referred to as Areas of Special Scientific Interest.
11 The Wildlife and Countryside Act 1981 applies to England, Wales and Scotland and the Nature Conservation and Amenity Lands (Northern Ireland) Order 1985 for Northern Ireland where they are referred to as Areas of Special Scientific Interest.
12 The operations that are to be limited are listed on the notice.
13 The work may proceed if the approving body has received written notification of the proposal but has failed to respond within 4 months (Wildlife and Countryside (Amendment) Act 1985).
14 Implemented through the Conservation (Natural Habitats, etc.) Regulations 1994.

COURSING

See also Cruelty to Animals; Hares; Killing Birds and Animals; Rabbits; Wild Mammals

Coursing is a traditional form of hunting hares using dogs, where the dogs rely on sight rather than scent. Coursing is either organised formally by clubs operating under the rules of the National Coursing Club, or informally involving the use of dogs in an unregulated field or enclosure. Unlike many other methods of hunting, organised coursing involves a competitive element whereby the dogs are awarded points according to their skills and a series of knockout competitions are used to identify a winner. Under National Coursing Club rules events are held in open countryside with ample opportunity for the hares to escape. Hares may be driven to the coursing ground by beaters or 'walked up' by dogs and the coursing ground itself is an area bordered only by ordinary hedges or fences, again allowing ample opportunity for the hare to escape. The dogs, usually in pairs, are unleashed only when a hare is 26m (80 yards) or more away and points are awarded by a judge on the basis of speed, agility and the ability to turn the hare from its path. Although not dictated by legislation, the National Coursing Club operates a voluntary close season between 11 March and 14 September to allow an undisturbed breeding season.

Unregulated coursing may use both hares and rabbits and it is the 'kill' rather than any skill on the dog's part that is the arbiter of success. This sport is often referred to as 'lurching' and is subject to a voluntary code of conduct issued by the British Field Sports Society. Although unenforceable this code recommends adherence to the same close season as for organised events.

Coursed hares are wild animals and are, therefore, not generally protected by the provisions of the Protection of Animals Act 1911,[1] which concerns itself with domestic and captive animals. The release of previously captured hares is not officially condoned under National Coursing Club rules, and the 1911 Act specifically excludes the hunting or coursing of any captive animal unless the animal is liberated in an injured, mutilated or exhausted condition. If a captive hare or rabbit was released in such a condition then an offence would be committed. The Act requires that the animal should have an adequate opportunity to escape from any enclosure that it is being coursed within.

Coursing is not a prohibited method of taking or killing wild animals under the Wildlife and Countryside Act 1981 or the Wildlife (Northern Ireland) Order 1985.

1   The Protection of Animals (Scotland) Act 1912 applies to Scotland, while the Welfare of Animals Act (Northern Ireland) 1972 covers the province.

CROPS AND GRAIN

See also Bridle-ways; Damage; Footpaths; Highways and Roads; Nuisances; Pests; Theft; Weeds

The successful production of fruit, grains and other crops involves a constant struggle with adverse weather, disease and pests as well as against the encroachment of other plant species. The law can do little about UK weather but has attempted to create a balance between the protection of wildlife and indigenous plants and the interests of commerce and food production. The balance achieved is an uneasy one and is subject to constant debate, as recent controversies regarding genetically modified food demonstrate. While the Wildlife and Countryside Act 1981[1] offers protection to a large number of wild animals, it also seeks to balance its controls with the needs of farmers by exempting certain prohibited acts provided that these are done in pursuance of a requirement by the Minister of Agriculture, Fisheries and Food. As a result, no liability will arise where a protected animal is killed or taken if that action was necessary for the purpose of preventing serious damage to crops, vegetables, fruit or growing timber. The uprooting or destruction of otherwise protected plants is similarly excused where it occurs as an incidental result of an otherwise lawful action that could not reasonably have been avoided. Ploughing would be an example of such a lawful action.

Laws concerning crops include:[2]

(a) the Agriculture and Horticulture Act 1964: this empowers ministers to make regulations defining grades of quality and forms of labelling for fresh horticultural produce;

(b) The Cereals Marketing Act 1965: establishes the Home Grown Cereals Authority, which is empowered to recommend the imposition of levies and has duties with regard to corn returns;[3]

(c) The Plant Health Act 1967: this provides for the promotion of healthy crops, trees and bushes. Orders subordinate to this enactment include the Plant Health (Great Britain) Order 1993 and the Plant Health (Forestry) (Great Britain) Order 1993;

(d) the Agriculture (Miscellaneous Provisions) Act 1976: this restricts the use of male hop plants;

(e) the Horticultural Produce Act 1986: this contains measures designed to control the movement of horticultural produce where grading requirements have not been met.

Grain quality is also subject to a number of legislative controls including the Agricultural Produce (Grading and Marking) Act 1928, the Plant Varieties and Seeds Act 1964, the Agriculture and Horticulture Act 1964, the Horticultural Produce Act 1986 together with a mass of European Union regulations and directives.

From a criminal perspective, commercial crops, fruit and foliage may be damaged or stolen. The exceptions in both the Criminal Damage Act 1971 and the Theft Act 1968 only concern damage to, or the taking of, mushrooms, flowers, fruit or foliage of any plant growing wild on any land. Where any cultivation or care has taken place these are no longer 'wild' and are protected as private property. Compensation for any damage caused may be sought through the civil courts. An invasion of weeds may also be actionable as an interference that disturbs an owner's or occupier's ability to use their land for crops.

Where crops are grown, other than grass, they should not impinge on the line of any highway; if they do so then the occupier of the land may be committing an offence under the Highways Act 1980. There is a duty to take such steps as may be necessary to prevent any encroachment and the term 'highway' includes both footpaths and bridle-ways.

Ploughing across footpaths and bridleways is also subject to legal controls.

1   The Wildlife (Northern Ireland) Order 1985.
2   This list is able to provide only a flavour of the myriad of current bureaucratic control over the production of crops. The full extent of these controls lies beyond the scope of this book.
3   The Corns Returns Act 1882 as amended by the Agriculture (Miscellaneous Provisions) Act 1943, the Agriculture Act 1970 and the Corn Returns (Delegation of Functions) Order 1981 requires that purchases of British corn by dealers are recorded.

CROSSBOWS AND ARCHERY

See also Air Weapons; Knives

As a result of a number of incidents in the mid-1980s in which injuries were caused by the use of crossbows to both people and wild animals, the Crossbows Act 1987 was passed. Previously uncontrolled, this Act brought the possession of crossbows[1] into line with the limited restrictions placed on air weapons. The Crossbows Act 1987 creates offences based solely on age and bans certain acts in relation to a person under 17 years of age. These are:

(a) the selling to, letting or hiring to such a young person any crossbow or part of a crossbow;[2]
(b) the buying or hiring of any crossbow or part of a crossbow by such a young person;
(c) having with him a crossbow which is capable of discharging a missile;
(d) having with him parts of a crossbow which together[3] can be assembled to form a crossbow capable of discharging a missile.

It remains possible for a person under 17 years to possess a crossbow provided that there was no purchase and the crossbow has been borrowed or received as a gift. No offence is committed under (c) or (d) where the young person is supervised by someone who is 21 years or older.

The police have powers to stop and search anyone they reasonably believe to be under 17 years and in possession of a crossbow. They also have the power to enter on to any land[4] in order to exercise this power.

While target archery continues to be popular as a sport, the use of the bow as a hunting weapon was severely curtailed by the Wildlife and Countryside Act 1981.[5] This legislation makes it an offence for any person to use, for the purpose of killing or taking any wild animal,[6] any bow or crossbow. Both longbows and crossbows may be deemed to be offensive weapons for the purposes of the Prevention of Crimes Act 1953 depending upon their intended use.[7] The Grand National Archery Society is the governing body for the sport of archery in Great Britain and Northern Ireland.

1 For the purposes of this legislation, a crossbow is defined as having a draw weight of at least 1.4kg.
2 It is a defence for the seller or hirer to show that he believed the person to be of or over the age of 17 and that he had reasonable cause for such a belief.
3 And without the need for any other parts.
4 But not a dwelling-house.
5 The Wildlife (Northern Ireland) Order 1985 contains the same prohibitions in respect of bows.
6 In any proceedings for an offence of using a bow to kill or take any wild animal any such animal will be assumed by the court to have been wild unless the contrary is shown.
7 This enactment defines an offensive weapon as something that is made, adapted or intended to cause injury.

CRUELTY TO ANIMALS

See also Cockfighting; Coursing; Dogs; Killing Birds and Animals; Traps and Trapping; Wild Mammals

Cruelty to animals, wild or domestic, is not a recent phenomenon and laws offering protection have been enacted regularly since bull and bear baiting was outlawed in 1835. The Protection of Animals Act 1911[1] is the primary enactment protecting domestic and captive[2]

animals and legislates against cruelty, which is defined as any 'unnecessary suffering'. The Act makes it an offence for any person to:

(a) cruelly beat, kick, ill-treat, over-ride, over-load, torture, infuriate, or terrify any animal, or cause or procure, or being the owner,[3] permit any animal to be so used, or by wantonly or unreasonably doing or omitting to do any act, or causing or procuring the commission or omission of any act, cause any unnecessary suffering, or being the owner, permit any suffering to be so caused to any animal;

(b) convey or carry, or cause or procure, or, being the owner, permit to be conveyed or carried, any animal in such manner or position as to cause that animal any unnecessary suffering;[4]

(c) cause, procure, or assist at the fighting or baiting of any animal; or keep, use, manage, or act or assist in the management of, any premises or place for the purpose, or partly for the purpose, of fighting or baiting an animal, or permit any premises or place to be so kept, managed or used, or receive, or cause or procure any person to receive, money for the admission of any person to such premises or place;

(d) wilfully, without reasonable cause or excuse, administer or cause or procure, or being the owner, permit such administration of any poisonous or injurious drug or substance to any animal, or wilfully, without any reasonable cause or excuse, cause any such substance to be taken by any animal;

(e) subject, or cause or procure, or being the owner, permit to be subjected, any animal to any operation which is performed without due care and humanity;

(f) tether any horse, ass or mule under such conditions or in such manner as to cause that animal unnecessary suffering.

The 1911 Act specifically excludes anything lawfully done under the Animals (Scientific Procedures) Act 1986, in the preparation of any animal as food or to the coursing or hunting of any captive animal.[5] Trapping wild animals with spring traps is excluded as a cruel practice under this legislation provided that the traps are regularly checked.

The Wildlife and Countryside Act 1981[6] deals extensively with wild animals, and while it contains a myriad of protective provisions, cruelty is not specified. Controls are included which limit the means and circumstances in which wild animals may be killed or captured and the effect is to reduce the potential for cruel treatment. The Wild Mammals (Protection) Act 1996 offences relate to the mutilation, kicking, beating, nailing, impaling, stabbing, burning, stoning, crushing, drowning, dragging or asphyxiating of any wild animal[7] with intent to inflict unnecessary suffering. This Act exempts mercy killing in the case of disabled or injured mammals or in cases where the action is a reasonable and humane manner of dispatch in the course of lawful shooting, hunting, coursing or pest control. The lawful use of traps, snares, dogs or birds is also excluded.

Abandonment of domestic or captive animals in circumstances likely to cause unnecessary suffering is defined as cruelty under the provisions of the Abandonment of Animals Act 1960.

Generally, offences of cruelty are punishable at a magistrates' court with a maximum of 6 months imprisonment and a £5000 fine. Courts also have the power to seize and, if necessary, destroy animals and to prohibit a guilty person from keeping any other animal[8] or being concerned in any business involving animals.

1 The Protection of Animals (Scotland) Act 1912 applies to Scotland. The Welfare of Animals (Northern Ireland) Act 1972 applies similar offences to both captive and wild animals.

2 In the case of the *Crown Prosecution Service* v. *Barry (1989)*, 'animal' for the purposes of the 1911 Act was held to mean any domestic or captive animal. 'Captive' includes any animal (not being domestic) of whatever kind or species and whether a quadruped or not, including any bird, fish or reptile, which is in captivity or confinement or which is maimed, pinioned or subjected to any appliance or contrivance for the purpose of hindering or preventing its escape from captivity or confinement.

3 An owner shall be deemed to have permitted cruelty if he fails to exercise reasonable care and supervision in respect of the animal.

4 The Animal Health Act 1981 provides powers for ministers to make such orders as they think fit for the purpose of protecting animals from unnecessary suffering during transit.

5 See p.37 for the details of this exemption. In *Rowley v. Murphy (1964)*, a stag, temporarily unable to escape, was held not to be in confinement for the purposes of the 1911 Act.

6 The Wildlife (Northern Ireland) Order 1985.

7 Defined as not 'domestic' or 'captive' within the meaning of the Protection of Animals Act 1911.

8 Protection of Animals (Amendment) Act 1954.

CYCLES

See also Access – A Right to Roam; Bridle-ways; Common Land; Footpaths; Green Lanes; Highways and Roads; Trespass

The introduction of cycles capable of tackling the type of rougher terrain found away from metalled roads and tracks has brought about an increase in the recreational use of pedal cycles in the countryside, both on-road and off-road. As a road vehicle, the design and use of cycles has long been subject to legislative controls. Design and construction are the subject of British Standards and offences may be committed when cycles are supplied that fail to meet those standards,[1] which include the effectiveness of cycle braking systems. The use of cycles on highways and roads is regulated and prohibitions under such enactments as the Highways Act 1835, Licensing Act 1872, and the Road Traffic Act 1988 include:

(a) the dangerous, careless or inconsiderate use of any cycle on a carriageway;
(b) reckless or furious riding;
(c) failing to conform to traffic signals;
(d) riding without adequate lighting;
(e) being drunk in charge of a pedal cycle;
(f) cycling on a footway.[2]

The transportation of cycles also has legal implications following the introduction of elaborate brackets designed to fit on the rear of cars or on their roof racks. The Road Vehicles (Construction and Use) Regulations 1986 require that loads are secure and their weight, distribution, packing and adjustment are such that no danger is caused or likely to be caused to any person. Storage on the tailgate or boot of a motor car must be in such a fashion so as not to obstruct the driver's view to the rear.

Legal off-road uses include cycling along some footpaths, bridle-ways and other highways as well as on land with the permission of its owner. Footpaths are highways for the use of foot passengers only[3] and cycling may take place only where the local authority has used its powers under the Cycle Tracks Act 1984 to designate a footpath, or part of it, as a cycle track. A bridle-way is a highway with a right to walk, ride or lead horses and, in some cases, drive cattle. The Countryside Act 1968 creates the right for bridleways to be used by bicycles, subject to any local authority bye-laws and a requirement that cyclists using a bridle-way accord precedence to any pedestrians or horse riders that they encounter. Whereas local authorities are under a duty to maintain highways, there is no corresponding obligation under this Act for them to maintain bridle-ways in a condition suitable for cycles. The right of access along bridle-ways does not extend to motor cycles or to cycles other than those with two wheels.

Other highways that may be used by cyclists include Byways Open to All Traffic (BOAT) and Roads Used as a Public Path (RUPP). RUPPs are likely to be reclassified as bridle-ways if government proposals are given legal effect.

Access to any other land is subject to permission. This may require the specific permission of an individual landowner or occupier, a general licence such as those found in National or Country Parks, or the permission of the Waterways Board or that of another controlling body. In many cases any permission granted will be subject to conditions or bye-laws. Land designated as common land does not necessarily confer any right of access to the general public and permission may still be required before cyclists are able to use common land. Cycling across any land without permission or in contravention of any conditions, regulations or bye-laws may amount to trespass. If damage is caused by the use of cycles on land the landowner has a remedy at civil law and may seek compensation.

---

1   The Pedal Bicycles (Safety) Regulations 1984 and the Pedal Cycles (Construction and Use) Regulations 1983. This latter legislation provides police officers with powers to test pedal cycles.

2   A footway is the path situated at the side of a road consisting of a carriageway. This may now be dealt with through the issue of a fixed penalty ticket.

3   The Highways Act 1980.

DAMAGE

See also Access – A Right to Roam; Bridle-ways; Conservation; Footpaths; Highways and Roads; Pollution; Trespass

The demand for increased access to the countryside was resisted in recent parliamentary debates partly on the basis of landowner's rights and partly over fears for the potentially detrimental effects on a fragile environment. The exercise of any right of access, particularly to farmland, needs to be coupled with respect for the property of others and reckless or thoughtless actions may result in damage being caused and losses incurred. Damage in rural areas may fall into four areas:

(a) pollution and erosion where the fabric of the countryside is destroyed or damaged;
(b) damage affecting wildlife and plants;
(c) criminal and malicious damage to property;
d) damage resulting in civil action for compensation.

Pollution and erosion are the concerns of the Department of the Environment, Transport and the Regions as well as the various conservation agencies. Acts that result in pollution are likely to attract criminal sanctions as well as monetary compensation sufficient to rectify the damage caused.

Wild animals are not 'property' and cannot, therefore, be 'damaged'. However, the Criminal Damage Act 1971 includes in its definition of property:

(a) wild creatures which have been tamed or are ordinarily kept in captivity; and
(b) any other wild creature or their carcasses if, but only if, they have been reduced into possession which has not been lost or abandoned or are in the course of being reduced into possession.

Mushrooms growing wild on any land or flowers, fruit or foliage of a plant growing wild on any land are not property and cannot be criminally damaged.

Under the 1971 Act criminal damage[1] occurs where, without lawful excuse, property belonging to another is destroyed or damaged either intentionally or recklessly. For example, the removing, moving or climbing of fences or other barriers, if not done carefully, may result in criminal damage. Damage caused by the intentional or reckless use of fire is arson.[2] These offences are serious matters and the available penalties range between 10 years and life imprisonment. As a result the police have extensive powers to investigate alleged offences and to arrest suspects. It will be a defence under the Act to show that the damage was caused in the genuine belief that the owner would have consented to the damage had they known of the circumstances, or that the damage was caused as a reasonable means of protecting other property. If a person trespasses in any building intending to cause damage then the offence is that of burglary.

A civil action may be available to anyone who has suffered any damage as a result of any trespass to property, even though no criminal offence is made out. Such action will be to seek compensation rather than punishment.

Generally, owners can damage their own property although if they do so in such a way as to endanger others an offence will be committed. An exception to this general rule occurs under the Planning (Listed Buildings and Conservation Areas) Act 1990 in the case of damage caused to any listed building.

1   In Scotland criminal damage is an offence both at common law and under the Criminal Law (Consolidation) (Scotland) Act 1995. There is little difference between the two and the statute provides for similar elements as those under the 1971 Act.
2   Wilful, culpable or reckless fire-raising is a common law crime in Scotland.

DANGEROUS AND DESTRUCTIVE ANIMALS

See also Pests; Vermin

Ownership and possession of dangerous wild animals is regulated through a licensing process operated by local authorities under powers granted by the Dangerous Wild Animals Act 1976.[1] It is an offence under the legislation to possess any of a long list of exotic species[2] without holding a licence.[3] Local authorities will not grant licences unless satisfied that:

(a) it is not contrary to the public interest on the grounds of safety, nuisance or otherwise;
(b) the applicant is a suitable person;
(c) that the animal will at all times –
   (i) be held in secure accommodation which the animal cannot escape from and which is suitable as regards construction, size, temperature, lighting, ventilation, drainage and cleanliness;
   (ii) be supplied with adequate and suitable food, drink and bedding material and will be visited at suitable intervals;
(d) appropriate steps will be taken for the protection of any animal in cases of fire or other emergency;
(e) all reasonable precautions will be taken to prevent and control the spread of infectious diseases;
(f) the animal's accommodation is such that it can take adequate exercise.

Conditions attached to a licence provide for veterinary inspection, controls over the movement of an animal and suitable insurance policies that to allow for adequate compensation should any damage arise as a result of the animal's presence.

The Wildlife and Countryside Act 1981 and the Wildlife (Northern Ireland) Order 1985 regulate the release into the countryside of any non-indigenous species. It is an offence to release or allow to escape[4] into the wild any wild animal which is of a kind not ordinarily resident in or is not a regular visitor to Great Britain or Northern Ireland or which is included in the Schedules[5] to the legislation.

Muskrats are subject to the Destructive Imported Animals Act 1932, which restricts importation and provides for the destruction of any muskrat discovered at large.

1 This Act does not apply to Northern Ireland.
2 The Act includes most carnivores, monkeys, reptiles such as alligators and crocodiles, poisonous snakes, spiders and scorpions as well as larger mammals such as elephants and rhinoceroses. Wild boars are also included. The courts are inclined to take a practical view with hybrids and have held,

for example, that a dog with more than 1 per cent of wolf gene could not be described as a dog (*Wilden* v. *Rotherham Metropolitan Borough Council (1997)* and *Walker-Coates* v. *Sedgefield Borough Council (1998)*).

3   Exceptions extend to zoos, circuses and pet shops which are subject to separate control.
4   It is a defence to show that all reasonable steps and all due diligence were exercised to avoid any escape.
5   These include muntjac deer, gerbils, grey squirrels and budgerigars, some of which are already established, as well as many wilder, exotic and dangerous species.

DEER

See also Cruelty to Animals; Game Dealers; Killing Birds and Animals; Pests; Poaching

Wild deer are a traditional quarry species that may be hunted during their open seasons. The oldest form of hunting may be the chase, and while this is still permitted the opportunities for hunts are increasingly limited and as a result stalking with a high-powered rifle has become the favoured method of killing these animals. Deer are a particularly valuable quarry and, at the same time, a potentially expensive pest capable of inflicting great damage to crops, woodland and pasture, and current legislation reflects both these perspectives while attempting to achieve a balance between protection and control. The Wildlife and Countryside Act 1981 lays down general restraints on the methods by which all wild animals may be killed or taken, but is not specifically concerned with deer. This falls to the Wildlife (Northern Ireland) Order 1985, the Deer Act 1991 and the Deer (Scotland) Act 1996. Other legislation may apply where these animals are farmed[1] or are kept permanently or temporarily captive.[2]

Northern Ireland

The Wildlife (Northern Ireland) Order 1985 makes it an offence for any person to:

(a) intentionally kill, injure or take any fallow, red or Sika deer during the prescribed close season for that deer;

(b) intentionally kill, injure or take any deer between the first hour after sunset and the last hour before sunrise;

(c) use any firearm or ammunition of the following descriptions –

 (i) any smooth-bore gun or cartridge for a smooth bore gun,

 (ii) any rifle having a calibre of less than .236 inches (6mm),

 (iii) any pistol, revolver or other type of hand-gun other than a slaughtering instrument,[3]

 (iv) any air-gun, air-rifle or air-pistol,

 (v) any weapon that discharges a missile by means of a gas propellant,

 (vi) any cartridge or load for use in a rifle other than a cartridge or load so designed that when fired in a rifle the bullet discharged has a muzzle energy of not less than 1700ft lbs

 (vii) any bullet for use in a rifle other than a bullet weighing not less than 100 grains (6.48g) or an expanding bullet designed to deform in a predictable manner and thereby increase its effective diameter upon entering tissue.

(d) discharge any firearm or discharge or project any missile from any mechanically propelled vehicle at any deer;

(e) take or remove any live deer;

(f) mark, or attach any tag, ring, collar or other device to, any live deer.

Exceptions to the above include acts done by a veterinary surgeon or practitioner in the course of treatment, acts done in order to protect any person in danger from any deer, acts of mercy and the licensed acts of an authorised person for the purpose of protecting crops, pasture, vegetables, fruit, growing timber or other forms of property. Licences may also be granted for scientific and educational purposes or in order to move deer from one area to another.

It is an offence of poaching for any person to enter on to any land without the consent of the owner or occupier or other lawful authority in search or pursuit of any deer with the intention of killing, injuring or taking it. A person who, while on any land, intentionally kills, injures or takes any deer or who searches for or pursues any deer for such a purpose without consent commits a similar offence.[4] Owners, occupiers and those who hold the right to take deer have powers under this legislation to demand a suspect's name and address and require him to quit the land. Any failure will amount to a further offence. The Wildlife (Northern Ireland) Order 1985 also makes provision for any dealing in venison.

Scotland

The importance of stalking to the rural economy of Scotland has been recognised in the Deer (Scotland) Act 1996, which has consolidated all previous Scottish deer legislation. This provides Scotland with its own Deer Commission which has the remit to further the conservation, control and management of deer while taking into account the size and density of its deer population, the impact on Scotland's natural heritage and the interests of landowners and occupiers. Offences included under the Act are similar to those under the law in Northern Ireland although some differences are apparent. The Scottish Act creates offences of:

(a) killing, injuring or taking any deer during the prescribed close season for that deer;

(b) taking or killing deer without permission, without legal right or from a person having such a right;

(c) removing any deer carcass from land without legal right or the permission of a person having such a right;

(d) wilfully killing or injuring any deer otherwise than by shooting;

(e) wilfully killing or injuring deer at night;

(f) using a vehicle to drive deer on any land with the intention of taking, killing or injuring them;[5]

(g) discharging any firearm, or discharging or projecting any missile, from any moving vehicle at any deer;[6]

(h) possession of an illegally obtained deer.

Restrictions on firearms for killing deer are based on ammunition and muzzle velocity. It is lawful under the Deer (Firearms, etc.) (Scotland) Order 1985 to use a rifle capable of firing the following lawful ammunition:

(a) for shooting deer of any species – a bullet of an expanding type designed to deform in a predictable manner of not less than 100 grains (6.48g) with a muzzle velocity of not less than 2450ft per second and a muzzle energy of not less than 1750ft lbs; or

(b) for shooting Roe deer – a bullet of an expanding type designed to deform in a predictable manner of not less than 50 grains (3.24g) with a muzzle velocity of not less than 2450ft per second and a muzzle energy of not less than 1000ft lbs.

Where an occupier of agricultural land or of enclosed woodland[7] has reasonable grounds for believing that serious damage will be caused to crops, pasture, trees or human or animal foodstuffs if the deer are not killed, it shall be lawful to use a shotgun with a gauge of not less than 12 bore which is loaded with the following ammunition:

(a) for shooting a deer of any species – a single-rifled non-spherical projectile weighing not less than 380 grains; or

(b) for shooting a deer of any species – a cartridge purporting to contain not less than 550 grains of shot, none of which is less than 0.268 inches in diameter; [8] or

(c) for shooting Roe deer – a cartridge purporting to contain not less than 450 grains of shot, none of which is less than 0.203 inches in diameter.[9]

Rifle sights will only be lawful if they are not light-intensifying, heat-sensitive or some other special sighting device for night shooting. The Deer Commission is granted wide powers to cull deer where they present a danger to any unenclosed woodland, to the interests of public safety or to the natural heritage generally. These powers are not restricted by the close seasons that otherwise limit the taking or killing of any deer. Dealing in venison is also controlled and the legislation generally restricts the sale of venison to licensed venison dealers. Anyone who knowingly sells venison from a beast killed in contravention of any provision of the Act commits an offence and licensed dealers are required to keep records of their transactions in venison.

England and Wales

The Deer Act 1991 regulates the hunting of deer by placing restrictions on the means by which they may be killed or taken, and the times and seasons in which they may be hunted. This Act reflects the general provisions of the Wildlife and Countryside Act 1981 and makes it an offence for any person to:

(a) use or put in place any trap, snare, or poisoned or stupefying bait calculated to cause bodily injury to any deer, or any net;

(b) use any firearm which is a smooth-bore gun,[10] rifle with a calibre of less than .240 inches or a muzzle energy of less than 1700ft lbs, or any air rifle, air-pistol or air-gun, any ammunition for a smooth-bore gun or any ammunition other than a soft-nosed or hollow-nosed bullet;

(c) use any arrow, spear or similar missile;

(d) use any missile carrying or containing any poison, stupefying drug or muscle-relaxing agent;

(e) discharge any firearm or project any missile, from any mechanically propelled vehicle or use such a vehicle to drive any deer.[11]

Further prohibitions include the taking or intentional killing of any deer at night and the taking or intentional killing of any deer during their close season. Once again exceptions apply to acts of mercy, the protection of crops and to acts done under licence[12] or in pursuance of a requirement by the Minister of Agriculture, Fisheries and Food.

The close seasons for deer are listed in the table below.

	England, Wales and Northern Ireland	Scotland[13]
Red deer (*Cervus elaphus*)		
Stags	1 May – 31 July*	21 October – 30 June*
Hinds	1 March – 31 October	16 February – 20 October
Fallow deer (*Dama dama*)		
Buck	1 May – 31 July	1 May – 31 July
Doe	1 March – 31 October	16 February – 20 October
Roe deer (*Capreolus capreolus*)		
Buck	1 November – 31 March	21 October – 31 March
Doe	1 March – 31 October	1 April – 20 October
Sika deer *(Cervus nippon)*[14]		
Stags	1 May – 31 July	21 October – 30 June
Hinds	1 March – 31 October	16 February – 20 October

*All dates are inclusive

To assist in the investigation of offences the police have been given wide-ranging powers to stop and search people and vehicles and may enter onto any land[15] in order to exercise their powers.

1 For example, the Deer (Scotland) Act 1996 excludes farmed deer from its provisions except in that shooting remains the only permitted method of dispatch. Farmed deer are defined as those kept on agricultural land enclosed by a deer-proof barrier and kept as livestock.

2 A hunted stag, temporarily unable to escape, has been held not to be 'in captivity' for the purposes of this Act even though it was then taken and killed by its pursuers. *Rowley* v. *Murphy (1964)*.

3 Within the meaning of the Firearms Order (Northern Ireland) 1981.

4 It is a defence to show that the act was done in the reasonable belief that the consent of the owner or occupier would have been granted if they had known of the circumstances.

5 The Deer Commission may authorise the acts under (d) and (e). Night shooting may be authorised where it is necessary for the protection of crops or woodland and no other means of control would be adequate. Driving deer with a vehicle is permissible where it is done for the purposes of deer management (not sporting activity).

6 Nothing under (d), (e) or (f) is to be construed as prohibiting a person having a legal right to take deer on any land or a person having permission in writing from any such person.

7 Includes arable land, improved permanent pasture (other than moorland) and land which has been regenerated so as to be able to make a significant contribution to the productivity of a holding which forms part of that agricultural land.

8 Size SSG.

9 Size AAA.

10 No offence is committed if the smooth-bore gun is a slaughtering instrument of at least 12 bore, with a barrel less than 24 inches and is using at least AAA shot. A further exemption applies to 12 bore shotguns using either AAA shot or a single non-spherical projectile weighing not less than 350 grains (see exemptions concerned with the protection of crops, p.52).

11 No offence (for (e) only) will be committed if the act is done with the written authority of the occupier of any enclosed land where deer are usually kept.

12 Involving the moving of deer or taking them for scientific or educational purposes.

13 The Deer (Close Seasons) (Scotland) Order 1984.

14 Red / Sika deer hybrids share the close season of Sika deer.

15 But not into a dwelling-house.

DISEASE

See also Agencies, Bees; Dogs; Rabies

Animals, livestock and crops are all subject to legislation aimed at reducing the risk, or controlling the spread of disease. The Animal Health Act 1981 provides powers to facilitate this aim by enabling Ministers[1] to make Orders:

(a) for rabies control;
(b) for the creation of eradication areas;
(c) to restrict the movement of animals;[2]
(d) to restrict animal imports and exports;
(e) to require the compulsory dipping of sheep as a remedy for sheep scab.

Other than rabies, the enactment specifically makes mention of cattle plague, pleuro-pneumonia, foot-and-mouth disease, swine fever and the diseases of poultry.[3] It is a criminal offence for any person in possession of, or in charge of, an animal infected with one of these diseases to fail to keep the animal separate or to fail to report the matter to the police who, together with local authority inspectors, are provided with extensive powers of enforcement. These include powers to enter buildings, pens or other premises, vehicles and vessels for the purposes of inspection. If any person obstructs the exercise of any of these powers they may be arrested and charged with a further offence.

In any case where a disease has established itself, the Minister of State is empowered to make an order requiring the destruction of wild animals within that area where such action is necessary to eliminate or reduce the spread of the disease. Before an order of this type can be made, however, the Minister is required to consult with the appropriate conservation agency.

---

1 In particular, the Minister of State for Agriculture, Fisheries and Food.
2 Generally defined as any cattle, sheep, goats, other ruminating animals and swine, the list can be extended on the order of a Minister of State.
3 Defined as domestic fowl, turkeys, geese, ducks, guinea fowl, pigeons, pheasants and partridges.

DOGS

See also Badgers; Bridle-ways; Coursing; Cruelty to Animals; Damage; Footpaths; Foxes and Fox Hunting; Highways and Roads; Killing Birds and Animals; Poaching; Poison

Canis familiaris is descended from hunting stock and the instincts of his ancestors remain strong enough for the domesticated dog to have a hunting role in the modern countryside. This may be as part of a pack as found in fox hunting, or as a part of a smaller group used for walked-up or driven shooting. Different breeds take separate roles: greyhounds being used for speed to pursue hares; spaniels to flush game birds; and the retriever breeds that use sight and scent to find dead game. Current legislation has little regard for these legal pursuits. The law is far more concerned with dogs when the hunting instinct occurs or is used inappropriately.

The Dogs (Protection of Livestock) Act 1953[1] is concerned with the worrying of livestock by dogs and makes it an offence for any dog to worry livestock on any agricultural land. Liability lies with the owner of an offending dog or the person in charge of it at the time and occurs where a dog:

(a) attacks any livestock;
(b) chases any livestock in such a way as may reasonably be expected to cause injury or suffering or, in the case of females, abortion or loss of or diminution in their produce, for example less milk;
(c) is at large[2] in a field or enclosure in which there are sheep.

Livestock for these purposes include cattle,[3] sheep, goats, swine, horses[4] and poultry,[5] while agricultural land means any arable, meadow or grazing land or land used for the purposes of poultry farming, pig farming, market gardens, allotments, nursery grounds and orchards. Exceptions include police dogs, guide dogs, trainee sheep dogs, working gun dogs and packs of hounds. A dog's owner will not be liable in circumstances where the livestock are themselves trespassing at the time the worrying takes place provided that the dog is not deliberately set on the livestock. Sheep worrying in particular may result in horrific injuries and drastic action by the owner of sheep or other livestock is permissible where necessary for their protection. This may result in the killing of any dog found worrying livestock.[6] Any dog that is shown to have injured cattle or poultry or to have chased sheep may be dealt with under the Dogs Act 1906[7] as a 'dangerous dog'. This legislation empowers a court to direct the owner of a dog to keep it under proper control or in some cases to order its destruction.[8]

In addition to criminal sanctions, the owner of any livestock that have been injured or killed is able to seek compensation from the dog's owner through the civil courts.

Allowing or causing a dog to pursue game may be a criminal trespass punishable as poaching.

Other legislation provides for:

(a) any stray dog to be seized and handed to the police;[9]
(b) an offence to be committed where any dog is on a highway[10] without a collar containing the owner's name and address;[11]
(c) an offence where a person uses or permits the use of a guard dog at any premises unless the dog is under the control of a handler. This will not apply if the dog is so secured that it is not at liberty to go freely about the premises;[12]
(d) an offence where a person uses or permits the use of a guard dog at any premises unless warning notices are clearly exhibited at each entrance to those premises;
(e) an offence where any dog is dangerously out of control in a public place.[13]

Exceptions to (b) apply to packs of hounds, dogs being used for sporting purposes, any dog being used for the capture or destruction of vermin and dogs being used for the driving or tending of cattle. Sheep dogs, police dogs or dogs being used in emergency rescue work or any registered guide dog are also generally exempt.

The right to pass and re-pass along a footpath or bridle-way does not include any right to permit a dog to stray onto adjoining land. If any damage is caused as a result, the owner of the dog, or person in charge of it, may be liable at civil law.

Dogs, as domesticated animals, are protected by the provisions of the Protection of Animals Act 1911[14] and may not be subjected to cruel treatment. They are also 'property' for the purposes of the Criminal Damage Act 1971, which creates a criminal liability on anyone who intentionally or recklessly kills or injures them.[15] In addition, one rather obscure legal section exists for the protection of dogs that may be on land. The Dogs Act 1906 makes it an offence for any person to knowingly and without reasonable excuse permit the carcass of any head of cattle[16] belonging to him, or under his control, to remain unburied in a field or other place to which dogs can gain access.

1   As amended by the Wildlife and Countryside Act 1981.
2   That is, not on a lead or under close control. No offence is committed if the dog is owned by, or in the charge of the occupier of the field or enclosure or the owner of the sheep.
3   Bulls, cows, oxen, heifers and calves.
4   Including asses and mules.
5   Domestic fowl, turkeys, geese and ducks.
6   There is a requirement that the police must be informed within 48 hours of the killing of any dog.
7   Dogs Act 1871 in Scotland.
8   Dangerous Dogs Act 1989.
9   The Dogs Act 1906 and the Environmental Protection Act 1990.
10 This includes both footpaths and bridle-ways.
11 The Animal Health Act 1981 and also the Control of Dogs Order 1992. A lead will also be required on certain roads designated by a local authority under the Road Traffic Act 1988.
12 Guard Dogs Act 1975.
13 Dangerous Dogs Act 1991.
14 The Protection of Animals (Scotland) Act 1912.
15 This may not be the case where an action is taken to protect other property such as livestock.
16 Including horses, mules, asses, sheep, goats and swine.

DRIVING – OFF-ROAD

See also Bridle-ways; Common Land; Damage; Footpaths; Green Lanes; Highways and Roads; Trespass; Village Greens

It is an offence under the Road Traffic Act 1988 for a person without some lawful authority such as the permission of the landowner, to drive a motor vehicle:

(a) on to or on any common land, moorland or land of any description not being land forming part of a road; or

(b) on any road being a footpath or bridle-way.

Offenders are liable to a fine of up to £1000. However, no offence will be committed if a vehicle is driven on to some land merely for the purpose of parking, and provided that it remains within 15 yards of a road on which a motor vehicle may lawfully be driven. Further exceptions extend to emergency vehicles and any other vehicles driven off the road for the purpose of saving life, extinguishing fire or meeting any other like emergency.

Rights of access along footpaths and bridle-ways are limited and, while pedal cycles have been given access to bridle-ways there is no similar right for motor vehicles to use these routes. These highways are rights of passage that sit on private land. The same is true of common land and the majority of common land is owned. What makes them 'common' are the limited rights held in common by one person, or an identifiable group of people. Due to the need for an historical period of use before such rights may be recognised the use of off-road vehicles for recreation is unlikely to have become established as of right.[1] It, therefore, follows that any such use of footpaths, bridle-ways, common or private land without the permission of the landowner will be a trespass. If damage occurs as a result of any illegal driving off-road, the offenders may, in addition to criminal sanctions, be liable to pay damages for any losses incurred by the landowner. In the case of footpaths and bridle-ways the permission of the local authority may also be required, for example, in the case of motor vehicle trials or competitions taking place on land crossed by either of these highways.

1   But see Village Greens, p.196, for details of how a right might be established by 20 years' use.

ESTUARIES AND FORESHORE

See also Common Land; Fish and Fishing; Trespass

The foreshore is the area of our coastline that lies between the high and low water marks of ordinary spring tides and although access is rarely opposed, this strip of land is generally private property[1]. As with all private property there is no automatic right of access either to or along the foreshore unless some footpath or other highway is in existence or permission has been granted. Where permission has been granted it is often subject to bye-laws or other limitations. There are, however, two rights of common that apply to everyone: those of navigation and fishery. A general right of navigation preserved by international law provides for the passage of vessels and this will include access over the foreshore when the sea at high tide covers it. There is also a general right to fish in tidal waters.[2] This right permits fishing from the foreshore when it is covered by the sea but does not include a concurrent right to gain access to the foreshore across any private land lying behind it. Access may therefore require a boat.

Scotland differs slightly from the rest of the UK in that there is a general right of recreation along the foreshore that permits access by the general public to it. Once again this is limited by the absence of an associated right of access to the foreshore across any private land lying behind it.

An unauthorised crossing of any private land without the owner's permission is a trespass unless some footpath or other highway provides access to the foreshore.

1 Generally owned by large estates or leased to local authorities, 50 per cent is managed by the Crown Estates on behalf of the Crown.
2 This includes the tidal reaches of river estuaries to the limit where the sea flows and re-flows.

FALCONRY

See also Birds and Eggs; Cruelty to Animals; Killing Birds and Animals

As the sport of taking wild quarry in its natural state and habitat by means of trained hawks,[1] falconry has a long and noble history and these birds remain popular at country fairs where displays of their skills are regular features. The restrictions imposed by the Wildlife and Countryside Act 1981 and the Wildlife (Northern Ireland) Order 1985 only allows the possession of birds of prey that have been bred in captivity[2] and that are both registered and ringed. When captive the provisions of the Protection of Animals Act 1911 apply with regard to cruel acts. As wild birds, the 1981 and 1985 legislation includes falcons, hawks and eagles within their protective sections and many remain safeguarded by special penalties.[3]

Schedule 1 Birds which are protected by special penalties

Part 1 At all times

Common name	Scientific name	Common name	Scientific name
Buzzard, Honey	*Peris apivorus*	Kite, Red [8]	*Milvus milvus*
Eagle, Golden	*Aquila chrysaetos*	Merlin	*Falco columbarius*
Eagle, White-tailed	*Haliaetus albicilla*	Osprey	*Pandion haliaetus*
Falcon, Gyr [4]	*Falco rusticolus*	Owl, Barn	*Tyto alba*
Goshawk	*Accipiter gentilis*	Owl, Long-eared [9]	*Asio otus*
Harriers (all species) [5]	*Circus*	Owl, Short-eared [10]	*Asio flammeus*
Hawk, Sparrow [6]	*Accipiter nisus*	Owl, Snowy [11]	*Nyctea scandiaca*
Kestrel [7]	*Falco tinnunculus*	Peregrine	*Falco peregrinus*

Schedule 3 Birds which may be sold

Part 1 Alive at all times if ringed and bred in captivity[12]

Common name	Scientific name
Owl, Barn	*Tyto alba*

FALCONRY 61

Schedule 4 [13] Birds which must be registered and ringed if kept in captivity

Common name	Scientific name
Falcons (all species)	Falconidae
Hawks, true[14]	Accipitridae
Osprey	Pandion haliaetus

1 British Falconers Club definition.
2 A licence is required for the breeding and rearing of birds in captivity.
3 The standard offence of taking or killing wild birds is subject to a maximum fine of £1000. Those birds listed under Schedule 1 to both the 1981 Act and the 1985 Order are protected by fines of up to £5000.
4 Not included under the Wildlife (Northern Ireland) Order 1985.
5 The 1985 Order only includes hen and marsh harriers.
6 Included in the 1985 Order but not the 1981 Act.
7 Included in the 1985 Order but not the 1981 Act.
8 Not included in the 1985 Order.
9 Included in the 1985 Order but not the 1981 Act.
10 Included in the 1985 Order but not the 1981 Act.
11 Not included in the 1985 Order.
12 This Part is not included within the Schedules to the 1985 Order.
13 Schedule 4 of the 1985 Order only deals with birds shown for competitive purposes.
14 That is to say, buzzards, eagles, harriers, hawks and kites. All species in each case.

FARMING AND CONSERVATION

See also Forestry

It is generally well known that farmers are able to receive payments under a wide variety of schemes operated by the Ministry of Agriculture, Fisheries and Food. These currently include the Beef Special Premium Scheme,[1] Hill Livestock Compensatory Allowances,[2] Suckler Cow Premium Scheme,[3] Sheep Annual Premium Scheme and the Arable Area Payments Scheme.[4] While these payments support the farming community they are generally beyond the scope of this book except in so far as a Scheme provides some benefit to other countryside users. The Ministry of Agriculture, Fisheries and Food, in addition to its support of farmers, has responsibilities to consider environmental and conservation[5] matters and to seek out ways of improving access to the countryside for the general public. This has seen the attachment to some schemes of conditions that facilitate improved conservation and increased access. The following offer some advantage to the countryside.

The Arable Area Payments Scheme provides for farmers to 'set-aside' land rather than producing unwanted cereals and, providing certain conditions are met, compensate them for doing so. Some of this set-aside land is usable within the Countryside Access Scheme. The aim of the Countryside Access Scheme is to promote public access to suitable set-aside land for walking and quiet enjoyment. This Scheme is voluntary and is reliant on the landowner's permission with no permanent rights of way being created. Under the terms of this Scheme, farmers agree to enter the land into guaranteed set-aside for a period of 5 years, to provide adequate means of entry and maintain the area in a tidy and safe condition. Current payments are in addition to any monies provided under the Arable Area Payments Scheme and amount to £90 per km for access routes, and £45 per hectare for open field sites.

The Countryside Stewardship Scheme offers payments to farmers and landowners who are prepared to adopt enhancement and conservation practices. Ancient meadows, orchards and pastures, chalk and limestone grasslands, coastline, field boundaries and margins, historic landscapes, lowland heaths, upland areas, waterside and the countryside surrounding urban areas are all eligible. Where a Scheme is agreed it usually lasts for 10 years and although many of these provide for public access it is not a mandatory condition within the Scheme. Payment is dependent upon the type of land and ranges between £15 per hectare per year for the regeneration of heather moorland to £280 for turning cultivated land back to grassland. Hedge restoration starts at £2 per metre and other capital work can reach £550 for bracken control. The base payment for new access is £150 per year, with footpaths at 15p per metre and bridle-ways at 30p.[6]

The Environmentally Sensitive Areas Scheme pays agreement holders an annual sum provided that they adopt conservation and landscape enhancement measures. Designated in four stages since its inception in 1987, this Scheme includes such areas as the Norfolk Broads, the Pennine Dales, the South Downs, the Avon valley, Lake District, Dartmoor and the Shropshire Hills.[7] Farmers and landowners enter into a ten-year management agreement[8] prescribing the agricultural practices that must be adopted. Project officers manage each Scheme. Access for members of the public is not an objective of this Scheme which is concerned primarily with conservation, although there is an optional public access tier within the payment rates amounting to £170 per hectare of land covered by an access route.[9]

Farm Woodland Premium Schemes were introduced in 1992[10] to encourage the conversion of agricultural land to woodland. Offering payments of between £60 and £300 per hectare per year depending upon the type of land being converted, Schemes operate for either 10[11] or 15[12] years. The object of these Schemes is the enhancement of the environment[13] and landscape.

The Habitat Scheme seeks to enhance and preserve valuable habitats. Piloted since 1994 these Schemes are set to be incorporated into the Countryside Stewardship Scheme. Designated areas include Slapton Ley, the Upper Avon and the Yorkshire Derwent and involve management agreements for either 10 or 20 years.[14]

Moorland Schemes have existed since 1995 with the aim of conservation and the protection of the upper moorland environment through improved management and grazing regimes. Annual payments are based on the removal of ewes[15] and the erection of temporary fencing[16] in order to protect heather regeneration areas. Bracken control is also eligible for annual payments.[17] Again there are proposals to merge these Schemes with that of the Countryside Stewardship arrangement.

The Nitrate Sensitive Areas Scheme is still operating although no new agreements have been entered into since 1998. Aimed at the protection of drinking water supplies this voluntary scheme will continue to compensate agreement holders until existing agreements have ended.

1   Introduced in 1993 and funded by the EU, the Beef Special Premium Regulations 1993 and the Integrated Administration and Control System Regulations 1993 are the operative legislation. Payment is for male cattle and can be claimed twice, once after the animal is 8 months of age and again at 21 months.
2   These are payments made on breeding sheep and cattle and are aimed at supporting farms in Less Favoured Areas. These are sub-divided into Disadvantaged Areas and Severely Disadvantaged Areas. This allowance is partly funded by the EU.
3   Suckler Cow Premium Regulations 1993, Sheep Annual Premium and Suckler Cow Premium Quotas Regulations 1993. This is EU-funded.
4   This was introduced in 1992 to compensate farmers for a reduction in some cereal prices.
5   Agriculture Act 1986.
6   To date 143 055 hectares are subject to this type of scheme.
7   Over 1 149 208 hectares are currently designated although only 9201 agreements have been made covering some 469 121 hectares.
8   With an option to terminate after 5 years.
9   Providing for a 10m-wide strip.
10 Revised in 1997.
11 For conifer woodland.
12 For broad-leaved woodland.
13 The scheme is closely associated with the Woodland Grant Scheme operated by the Forestry Commission. This offers grants for the establishment of new woodland.
14 Two options are still operative. The water fringe option can operate for 10 or 20 years; the salt marsh option only operates across a 20-year period.
15 At £30 for each one removed.
16 At the rate of £1.20p per metre.
17 Between £110 and £120 per hectare.

FENCES, GATES AND STILES

See also Bridle-ways; Children; Footpaths; Hedges and Hedgerows; Highways and Roads; Land; Quarries and Mines; Trespass

Fencing has two main purposes: the identification of an enclosed area of land and the prevention of unauthorised access. As a demarcation of ownership, boundary fences should accurately reflect the borders identified in the title deeds as disputes are a regular occurrence that may only be resolved by reference to the deeds or the Land Registry. The modern Register is a computerised record of over thirteen million titles to land held at thirteen district land registries but is not an infallible system as a large amount of the total land area of the UK remains unregistered. In such cases a detailed examination of the history of a site may be the only way to determine the exact boundary of a property.

The erection of a fence in or across any highway which comprises of a carriageway is a criminal offence under the Highways Act 1980.

Where the purpose is to prevent access to land, then the nature and type of fence or barrier may be an issue in law. Fences made with barbed wire[1] or having any barbed wire on or in it, may be a nuisance if it affects access along any highway, footpath or bridle-way or is likely to injure any animals or people using the route. In such circumstances a local authority may require the occupier of the land to abate the nuisance within a set time limit identified within a notice served on him.[2] If the occupier fails to deal with the nuisance then the authority may complete whatever work is necessary and recover their costs through the courts. If damage or injury arises as a result of the type of fencing used the landowner may also be liable in any action for compensation pursued through the civil courts by the injured party.

In addition to the prevention of trespass, there may also be a duty on a landowner to prevent access where the land or premises presents some particular danger such as a disused quarry or old mine workings. Where such land is inadequately fenced off, the local authority may complete the work and recover their costs from the occupier. If any damage or injury has occurred due to the failure on the part of the occupier or landowner to erect suitable fencing, a civil action for negligence may result. Such action will seek compensation for the losses or injury incurred.

Gates and stiles allow for access to land through fences and, where the access is part of a highway, footpath or bridle-way, these must be maintained by the landowner[3] in a safe condition and to a standard necessary to prevent any unreasonable interference with users. Any gate across a highway with a carriageway needs to be of a minimum width of 10ft (3.05m). Where the highway is a bridle-way the width must be a minimum of 5ft (1.52m).[4]

1 Defined by the Highways Act 1980 as any wire with spikes or jagged projections.
2 Being not less than 1 month, or more than 6 months from the date of service.
3 The landowner may be able to recover up to one-quarter of the costs involved from the local authority which is liable for the maintenance of the highway.
4 Highways Act 1980.

FIREARMS AND SHOOTING

See also Air Weapons; Deer; Killing Birds and Animals; Northern Ireland; Poaching; Rifles; Shotguns

Although the possession and use of firearms has been the subject of regulation since 1920, the statistical evidence still indicates that there is a firearm-owning population of over 500 000 people in England and Wales alone. The majority of these make active use of their weapons for hunting and clay target shooting and, while dramatic reductions have been seen in the level of ownership in recent years, the evidence still shows a strong link between the possession of guns and traditional countryside pursuits. This is in spite of the current Firearms Acts introduced between 1968 and 1997 that now severely restrict the ability of members of the public to own dangerous firearms. Generally these laws fall into two main categories: those that control ownership and possession; and those that restrict the use of firearms.

The public outcry following the massacres at Hungerford and Dunblane resulted in a tightening of the circumstances in which a firearm may be owned, and the types of firearm that may be possessed. The effect is such that the only licensed firearms now likely to be seen in our countryside are rifles and shotguns. Pistols,[1] together with many automatic and semi-automatic firearms, are now almost totally prohibited, requiring the Home Secretary's permission before a Chief Officer of Police is able to issue a licence. Firearms certificates[2] may still be issued for rifles[3] but these are usually the subject of stringent conditions as to where the rifle may be used and how it must be stored. Shotguns[4] are more common, but while the power of the police to restrict ownership is more limited than in the case of rifles, applicants are still subject to scrutiny and are required to keep the weapon in secure storage. Northern Ireland has a stricter licensing regime under the Firearms Order (Northern Ireland) 1981 than that applied in the rest of the UK, including the use of one certificate for both shotguns and other firearms.

While the Acts and Regulations issued between 1989 and 1997 have made adjustments to the scope of licensing and have introduced limitations on the type of firearm that may be included on a certificate, the primary legislation remains the Firearms Act 1968. This prohibits:

(a) the possession of an unlicensed firearm or shotgun;
(b) operating as an unregistered firearms dealer;
(c) the illegal shortening of any shotgun barrel;
(d) possession of any 'prohibited' firearm;[5]
(e) possession of any firearm, including air weapons, with intent to endanger life or cause serious damage to property;
(f) the use of any firearm in order to resist or prevent an arrest;
(g) the committing of specified offences;[6]
(h) having a firearm with intent to commit an indictable offence;[7]
(i) carrying of a loaded shotgun or air weapon in a public place;

(j) carrying of any other firearm, whether loaded or not, in a public place together with ammunition suitable for use in that firearm;

(k) having a firearm while entering a building or part of a building as a trespasser;

(l) having a firearm when entering on any land[8] as a trespasser;

(m) the possession by certain categories of person based on age or previous history such as, for example, having been sentenced to a term of imprisonment.

In addition to its prohibitions, the 1968 Act also provides police officers with considerable powers to stop people suspected of being in possession of a firearm, to search them and to demand their certificates. Failure to produce the appropriate certificate may result in seizure of the firearm.

Further offences are created by other legislation. Under the Highways Act 1980 it is an offence for any person, without lawful authority or excuse, to discharge a firearm within 50ft (15m) of the centre of the carriageway of a road and, as a result, a user is injured, interrupted or endangered. The culpable and reckless discharge of a firearm may be the subject of a common law complaint in Scotland, while in England and Wales it is a criminal offence to wantonly discharge a firearm in any street to the obstruction, danger or annoyance of residents or passengers.[9] It is also an offence to be drunk in possession of a firearm under the Licensing Act 1872.[10]

The legal use of a firearm is further restricted by the Wildlife and Countryside Act 1981. This prohibits the use of automatic or semi-automatic weapons or any shotgun with a barrel diameter exceeding $1^{3}/_{4}$ inches,[11] for the purpose of killing or taking any wild bird. No automatic or semi-automatic weapon may be used to kill or take any wild animal.

The levels of restriction imposed by these laws suggest that licensed firearms owners in the UK are the most scrutinised in Europe.

1 This does not apply to air pistols.

2 Issued by the local police force on application and payment of a fee. For more information on the licensing process, see Rifles and Shotguns.

3   Referred to as a Section 1 certificate.
4   Section 2 certificates.
5   Listed under section 5. This now includes the majority of different types including machine-guns, military-style firearms and pistols.
6   Including abduction, arson, assault, burglary, taking a motor vehicle and theft. This applies in Scotland to such common law offences as abduction, administration of drugs, housebreaking with intent, theft, etc.
7   This is a serious offence only triable at a Crown Court.
8   Includes land covered in water.
9   Town Police Clauses Act 1847.
10 In a public place the Civic Government (Scotland) Act 1982 makes out a similar offence.
11 Internal dimensions at the muzzle.

FIRES AND SMOKE

See also Damage; Nuisances; Pollution

Stubble burning had been used as an effective method of crop clearance prior to re-ploughing for many years but is now restricted by regulations made under the Environmental Protection Act 1990. The Crop Residues (Burning) Regulations 1993 prohibits the burning of a wide range of crop residues including cereal straw and stubble although some limited burning is still permitted.[1] Other restrictions control the timing of crop residue burning and the safe distances required in order to protect hedgerows and roads. As a pollutant, smoke is also subject to environmental restrictions.[2]

Smoke is a particular problem when fires are lit near to roads as visibility may be reduced and accidents occur as a result. The Highways Act 1980 makes it an offence[3] for any person to light a fire on any land,[4] or to direct or permit a fire to be lit on any such land, which results in any user of a highway[5] being injured, interrupted or endangered. It will be a defence however to show that, at the time the fire was lit, the offender was reasonably satisfied that the fire was unlikely to have such a result and that he took all reasonable precautions to prevent such a result. A similar offence is made out under the Trespass (Scotland) Act

1865, which prohibits the lighting of any fire on or near any turnpike road, statute labour road or other highway. This enactment also prohibits the lighting of a fire on or near any private road or enclosed, cultivated land or in or near any plantation without the consent and permission of the owner or occupier.

Damage or nuisance resulting from a fire is actionable depending upon the nature of its ignition. If a fire starts as a result of carelessness or some irresponsible behaviour then action for recovery of any losses incurred is possible through the civil courts. If, however, a fire is started with an intention to destroy or damage property or is started recklessly or with a disregard to the potential consequences, the matter is a criminal one that may be dealt with as arson. Both fire officers and police officers have powers[6] to enter any premises or place[7] where a fire is reasonably believed to have broken out in order to take whatever steps are necessary to extinguish the fire or protect other property.

1 The Heather and Grass Burning (England and Wales) Regulations 1986 apply similar controls under the auspices of the Hill Farming Act 1946.
2 See p.150.
3 This is a criminal offence punishable by a maximum fine of £5000.
4 Not forming part of a highway, which consists of or comprises a carriageway.
5 Which does consist of or comprise a carriageway.
6 The Fire Services Act 1947 and the Police and Criminal Evidence Act 1984.
7 By breaking in, if necessary.

FISH AND FISHING

See also Bridle-ways; Estuaries and Foreshore; Footpaths; Highways and Roads; Northern Ireland; Poaching; Protected Animals; Salmon and Trout; Theft

As with many other rights, that of fishing is severely restricted as the vast majority of rivers and streams are maintained as private fisheries. A general right to take fish occurs only in tidal waters, over the foreshore and within the tidal section of any estuary or river.[1] The existence of a right does not necessarily mean that fishing in tidal areas is also unregulated, and local committees enforce sea fisheries legislation.[2]

Inland waters are private property. A right of navigation along rivers, canals or other waterways is not automatically accompanied by any right to fish[3] and the existence of footpaths alongside waterways merely provide rights of passage. As with other private land and rights, the right to fish a particular stretch of water can only be conveyed by deed[4] and, unless specifically passed on by sale, lease or otherwise, the right of fishery is likely to be in the possession of the owner of the adjacent land.

While inland waters are private, the status of the fish they contain is more ambiguous. Unless they are particularly constrained in some way, the fish in our rivers and streams are wild and not owned by the person who has the right to fish. It is possible to steal them, however. While not defined as 'property' for the purposes of theft, there is an offence under the Theft Act 1968 that applies to any person who unlawfully takes[5] or destroys any fish other than by angling in the daytime, in water which is private property or in which there is any private right of fishery.[6] Daytime angling whereby a person unlawfully takes or destroys any fish in water which is private property, or in which there is any private right of fishery, is also an offence.[7]

The conservation of freshwater fish, salmon and trout, is principally regulated by the Salmon and Freshwater Fisheries Act 1975[8] and control is achieved by placing prohibitions on the means by which fish may be killed or taken, licensing requirements and through the imposition of close seasons. Limitations are also placed on the implements that may be involved in the killing or taking of freshwater fish,[9] including prohibitions on the use of:

(a) any firearm;
(b) an otter lath or jack,[10] wire or snare;
(c) a crossline[11] or setline;[12]
(d) a spear, gaff,[13] stroke-haul, snatch[14] or other like instrument;
(e) any light.

Mere possession of any of these with the intention that it will be used for the killing or taking of any freshwater fish is an offence, as is the throwing or discharging of any stone or other missile with that intention. Other prohibitions on the methods that may be employed to take freshwater fish encompass the use of fish roe, explosive substances, poisons or other noxious substances and any electrical devices. The use of lead weights by anglers is subject to controls on their importation and supply under the Pollution (Angler's Lead Weights) Regulations 1986.[15] These Regulations do not restrict the use of lead weights for fishing although they are likely to be banned by local bye-laws.

Close seasons[16] in which freshwater fish cannot be killed or taken are generally identified by the legislation but subject to change by local bye-laws. The minimum required by law is 93 days and, subject to any bye-laws, the annual close season for freshwater fish will be the period between 14 March and 16 June.[17] Contravention of the close seasons is a criminal offence. However, no offence is committed if the actions are done for the purpose of artificial propagation or for some scientific purpose, provided the written permission of the National Rivers Authority has first been obtained. Additionally, no offence will occur where local bye-laws have changed the general close seasons or where a fishery is solely for the preservation of salmon and trout and the killing or taking is restricted to eels, freshwater fish or rainbow trout. Fishing for eels by rod and line in any inland water during the close season for freshwater fish is prohibited.

Fishing licences are issued by the National Rivers Authority and distributed through post offices and tackle shops. These licences may restrict the method that can be used for a particular species, the areas within which they can be fished and the periods during which fishing is permissible. Details of any limitations are contained on the licence.[18] Any person or association entitled to an exclusive right of fishing in any inland waters may be granted a general licence to fish in those waters subject to any conditions agreed between the water authority and the licensee. This general licence entitles the licence holder and any person authorised by him in writing to fish. Unlicensed fishing is a criminal offence. Water bailiffs[19] are deemed to be constables by the 1975 Act and are granted extensive powers to examine instruments and baits, as well as boats and other vessels in order to enforce the regulations. As an alternative to prosecution, bailiffs may issue fixed penalty notices in a similar way to traffic wardens. Bailiffs have powers to apprehend any person found fishing illegally at night, found on or near any waters with intent to illegally kill or take freshwater fish or eels, or found in possession of a prohibited instrument for the capture of such fish. Any obstruction of a water bailiff is an offence in itself.

Some species of fish are protected by the Wildlife and Countryside Act 1981.[20]

Schedule 5 Animals which are protected

Common name	Scientific name
Burbot	*Lota lota*
Goby, Couch's	*Gobius couchii*
Goby, Giant	*Gobius cobitis*
Shad, Allis [21]	*Alosa alosa*
Shad, Twaite [22]	*Alosa fallax*

1 Subject to a few exceptions where private rights were granted either prior to 1215 or by specific legislation.

2 Such as the enforcement of minimum size limits.

3 *Smith* v. *Andrews 1891*.

4 *Halse* v. *Alder 1874*.

5 This will include any attempt to commit the offence. The mere keeping of a fish in a keep-net for later return remains sufficient to complete the offence.

6 Punishable by a maximum of 3 months' imprisonment and a fine of £1000. There is an accompanying power of arrest whereby any person may arrest a suspected offender found committing an act contrary to this section.

7 Subject to a maximum fine of £200.

8 The Salmon and Freshwater Fisheries (Protection) (Scotland) Act 1951 applies similar provisions to Scotland together with other *ad hoc* legislation that results in a similar system of protection and conservation. The rivers Solway and Tweed are subject to some localised rules contained in enactments dating from 1804 and 1857.

9   Defined as any fish living in fresh water but not including salmon, trout (including char) or eels (including elvers and fry) or any fish which migrate to and from tidal waters.

10 Includes any small boat or vessel, board, stick or other instrument, whether used with a hand line, or as auxiliary to a rod and line, or otherwise for the purpose of running out lures, artificial or otherwise.

11 This is a fishing line reaching from bank to bank and having attached one or more lures or baited hooks.

12 A fishing line left unattended in water and having attached one or more lures or baited hooks.

13 Does not include a plain metal hook without a barb used as auxiliary to angling with rod and line.

14 Includes any instrument or device, whether used with a rod and line or otherwise, for the purpose of foul hooking any fish.

15 These Regulations apply only to England, Wales and Scotland.

16 Coarse fish are not subject to close season control in Scotland except for brown trout when a close season operates between 6 October and 15 March.

17 The close season for lakes and reservoirs is determined by the owner.

18 Children under 12 do not require a licence.

19 Those appointed by a water authority but not those privately employed by the owner of a fishery or angling club.

20 The Wildlife (Northern Ireland) Order 1985 does not include fish under its Schedules.

21 Protection extends only to the intentional killing, injuring or taking of this fish and to the damaging or destruction of any place it uses for shelter or protection.

22 In this case, protection extends only to a prohibition on any damage or destruction of any place this fish uses for shelter or protection.

FLOODS AND FLOODING

See also Damage; Monuments and Archaeological Sites; Nuisances; Protected Animals

Floods are a natural phenomenon capable of inflicting massive damage to property lying near rivers or the sea and the Environment Agency[1] is the statutory body responsible for flood warnings in England and Wales. In Scotland the task falls to local authorities and in Northern Ireland to the Rivers Agency. These bodies compile flood risk maps and identify potentially high risk areas, and are able to issue flood warnings to properties within areas of high risk via an automated voice messaging system or through their network of local flood wardens. Rivers that are likely to rise quickly may also be equipped with sirens. Other areas subject to some risk may be warned through the national and local media or by the police. Flood warnings are based on three categories of alert:

- yellow – flooding liable to roads and low-lying farmland;
- amber – flooding likely to isolated properties, roads and larger areas of farmland;
- red – flooding affecting many properties, roads and farmland.

Unlike a natural flood, a flooding operation is a deliberate covering of land with water often as part of some works connected with the land. In circumstances where a deliberate or reckless act of flooding causes damage to property or adjoining land two actions may be possible. First, where the damage or destruction was the specific intention then an offence of criminal damage may have been committed. Secondly, in cases where there was no intention to inflict damage, a civil action may be pursued to obtain compensation for any damage actually caused. While either of these may apply to general flooding operations, the law seeks to offer particular liability where flooding take place in areas of special interest or where such works may damage or impede conservation or habitat protection measures.

The Ancient Monuments and Archaeological Areas Act 1979 makes it an offence[2] for any person to execute or cause or permit to be executed, any unauthorised[3] flooding of land in, on or under which there is a scheduled monument. Flooding operations affecting designated areas of archaeological importance require notice to be served on the local authority before the work is carried out.

The Wildlife and Countryside Act 1981[4] and the Conservation (Natural Habitats, etc.) Regulations 1994 are examples of legislation that seeks to protect the resting and breeding sites of a number of protected species. Any deliberate act, including flooding, that damages or destroys such habitats may leave the person responsible liable to criminal sanctions.

1 The National Rivers Authority is now a part of this Agency.
2 It is a defence to show that all reasonable precautions were taken, and due diligence was exercised to avoid or prevent damage to the monument. It is also a defence to prove that the works were urgently necessary in the interests of safety or health and that a written notice had been served on the Secretary of State as soon as reasonably practicable.
3 Authorisation requires the written consent of the Secretary of State and the work is executed in accordance with any conditions attached.
4 The Wildlife (Northern Ireland) Order 1985.

FLY TIPPING

See also Bridle-ways; Footpaths; Highways and Roads; Litter

Figures published by the Country Landowners' Association in 1999 conclude that in excess of 60 000 tons of rubbish is illegally dumped in England and Wales every year, blighting and polluting the countryside.[1] Often referred to as 'fly tipping', the dumping of household, industrial and commercial waste[2] is dealt with by the Refuse Disposal (Amenity) Act 1978, the Highways Act 1980 and the Environmental Protection Act 1990. The 1978 Act places a duty on local authorities to provide places for the disposal of non-business refuse and creates offences for any person without some lawful authority, to:

(a) abandon on any land in the open air, or on any other land forming part of a highway, a motor vehicle or part of a motor vehicle;[3] or
(b) abandon on any such land any thing other than a motor vehicle, being a thing which was brought to the land for the purpose of abandoning it there.[4]

The Highways Act 1980 creates offences committed by anyone depositing:

(a) any dung, compost or other material for dressing land and/or other rubbish either on or within 15 ft from the centre of a made up carriageway;
(b) anything on a highway that interrupts or obstructs its use or injures or endangers any user.

The Environmental Protection Act 1990 prohibits the:

(a) depositing[5] of controlled waste in or on land for which no waste management licence is in force or otherwise than in accordance with the conditions of such a licence;[6]

(b) treatment, keeping or disposal[7] of controlled waste in or on land without holding a current waste management licence or otherwise than in accordance with the conditions of such a licence; and

(c) treatment, keeping or disposal of controlled waste in a manner likely to cause pollution of the environment or harm to human health.

Licence holders are under a duty to ensure that any controlled waste does not 'escape' from their control and must take all reasonable steps to prevent the commission of any of the offences under the 1990 Act.

Where matter has been dumped, a notice may be served on the occupier of that land requiring that the waste be removed and that any consequence of the deposit be eliminated or reduced. It is an offence to fail to comply with such a notice, although the occupier has 21 days in which they may appeal. Appeals may include the assertion that the occupier did not deposit the material nor permit its deposit. In cases where an appeal is successful or where the occupier fails to comply with a notice the local authority may deal with the problem and may recover its costs from the occupier where appropriate. Local authorities also have powers to remove articles under the 1978 Act, which places the authority under a duty to remove any motor vehicles unlawfully abandoned on any land in the open air. Other legislation similarly provides local authorities with powers to issue notices or to remove rubbish, including the Public Health Act 1961, the Town and Country Planning Act 1990 and the Highways Act 1980.[8]

1 The severity of the fly tipping problem is such that the Environment Agency has now set up a 24 hour 'hot-line' to take reports of fly tipping that is in progress or likely to pose a pollution threat (0800 807060).

2 Referred to as 'controlled waste' by the 1990 Act.

3 Where it was removed in the course of dismantling the vehicle on the land.

4 Punishable by up to a £2500 fine and 3 months' imprisonment.

5 And knowingly causing or knowingly permitting its deposit. Knowingly causing will also include the driver controlling any motor vehicle from which the controlled waste was deposited.

6   Household waste is exempt provided that it is treated, kept or disposed of within the curtilage of that dwelling and with the permission of the owner but this does not apply to asbestos, chemicals or mineral oils.

7   This term includes the deposit in or on land as a means of disposal as well as knowingly causing or knowingly permitting the treatment, keeping or disposal.

8   These are not applicable to Scotland, which has similar legislation in place; e.g. the Town and Country Planning (Scotland) Act 1997.

FOOTPATHS

See also Access – A Right to Roam; Bridle-ways; Crops and Grains; Driving – Off-Road; Fences, Gates and Stiles; Green Lanes; Highways and Roads; Trespass

Defined by the Highways Act 1980, a footpath is a highway[1] over which the pubic have a right of way on foot only.[2] Arising from historic usage, dedicated by willing landowners or created by a local authority, footpaths are to be found all over the countryside. As a right, however, a footpath is distinct from the land that it crosses and that land remains, generally, private. Footpaths, therefore, provide only a limited right of access to and across land and their sole purpose is to allow people to pass and re-pass. There is no accompanying right to ride any horse or cycle[3] or other vehicle,[4] or drive cattle,[5] or to camp, picnic, play football on or to let dogs wander across adjoining land or to use a footpath as a means of disrupting any lawful act, such as a hunt or shoot. This is to exceed the right to pass and re-pass in such a way as to render the user a trespasser.[6] However, once these limitations are recognised it should be noted that the right of passage is available to everyone and it is also well protected, although in Scotland footpaths can fall into disuse and may be lost.

Almost anything done which impedes the exercise of that right along a footpath will be a criminal offence. Offences under the Highways Act 1980 include:

(a) the wilful obstruction of a footpath or the deposit of anything, including rubbish and manure on a footpath that interrupts the free passage along that highway;

(b) allowing any filth, dirt, lime or other offensive matter to run or flow on to a footpath from any adjoining premises;

(c) camping on a footpath by any itinerant trader or hawker, or the pitching of any booth, stall or stand on a footpath;

(d) depositing anything on a footpath in consequence of which a user is injured or endangered;

(e) playing football or any other game on a footpath to the annoyance of a user of that footpath;

(f) placing a rope, wire or other apparatus across a footpath in such a manner as to be likely to cause danger to any user of the route.

Stiles, gates or similar structures that cross a footpath are there for the benefit[7] of the landowner and must be maintained by them in a safe condition and to a reasonable standard of repair. Local highways authorities have responsibility to ensure that the right of passage is preserved and protected[8] and any failure to maintain any stile or gate may result in the authority completing the work and recovering its costs from the owner or occupier of that land.

If a footpath crosses a field rather than following its edge, it may be difficult for the farmer to make effective use of that land unless he is able to plough across that highway. Ploughing up such a footpath[9] is permitted provided that the ploughing is in accordance with the rules of good husbandry, or it is not reasonably convenient to avoid disturbing the surface of the path. Where ploughing has taken place, the footpath must be returned to its original condition either within 14 days, in the case of the first disturbance for a particular crop or, in any other case, within 24 hours.[10] Crops, other than grass, should not encroach on to a footpath.

Highway authorities and magistrates' courts have the power to make orders temporarily stopping-up, extinguishing or diverting any footpath, and footpaths may also be temporarily closed if they fall within an area being used for military manoeuvres.[11] Land development may affect a footpath and local planning authorities have powers under the Town and Country Planning Acts to stop-up or divert paths where it is considered necessary in order to enable the development to be carried out. The Countryside Act 1968 also requires local authorities to signpost public footpaths unless such signs are unnecessary. The erection of any sign containing false or misleading information likely to deter the use of any footpath is an offence under the National Parks and Access to the Countryside Act 1949.

1. Determined by the Highways Act 1980 the width of a footpath should be as respects a footpath that is not a field-edge path a minimum of 1m wide. In the case of a field-edge path, the minimum is 1.5m. The maximum in both cases is 1.8m.
2. Not being a footway which is the pavement or way at the side of a road comprising a carriageway.
3. Unless dedicated as a cycle track by the local highways authority under the Cycle Tracks Act 1984.
4. Including motor cycles and four-wheel drive vehicles.
5. Highways Act 1835.
6. *Harrison* v. *Duke of Rutland (1893)*.
7. i.e. as a part of the enclosure of that land.
8. Individuals may by notice require a local authority to meet its obligations in respect of any footpath.
9. This exception does not apply to a field-edge path. The Highways Act 1980 as amended by the Rights of Way Act 1990.
10. Extensions are possible with the permission of the local highways authority.
11. The Manoeuvres Act 1958.

FORESTRY

See also Agencies; Town and Country Planning; Trees

The department responsible for the implementation of Government policy with regard to forests and woodland is the Forestry Commission,[1] which has both duties and powers defined by the Forestry Acts of 1967 and 1979. The 1967 Act charged the Forestry Commission with the promotion of the various interests of forestry, the development of afforestation, the production and supply of timber and the establishment of adequate reserves of growing timber.[2] In order to achieve these aims the Commissioners[3] have been granted extensive powers over the growing and felling of trees, both in its own woodlands and in those that are privately owned, together with legal rights to enter on to any land in order to inspect timber or to assess that land's potential for afforestation.[4]

The Forestry Commission is also the issuing authority for tree felling licences.[5] Such licences are required for the felling of any tree and an unlicensed felling may be punishable by a maximum fine of £2000. Exceptions to this requirement include small trees,[6] fruit trees and those in gardens, orchards or public areas as well as trees that are dead, dangerous or diseased.[7] Following a conviction for an unlawful felling of a tree, the Commission may require the planting, and maintenance, of a suitable replacement.[8] In addition to placing restrictions on the felling of trees, the Commission is also empowered to direct the owner of growing timber to cut it down within a specified period. Any failure to obey such a direction leaves the offender liable to a fine of up to £5000.

The Commission's more recent objectives include the development of woodland recreation, and to this end they now operate woodland parks with access granted to the general public. Such access is subject of conditions and bye-laws which the Commission is empowered to make under the 1967 Act. Generally, these include measures for the protection of trees, plants and wildlife, keeping dogs under control and guarding against the risk of fire. The hunting of deer on Forestry Commission land was banned in 1997.

1 The Commission has two executive agencies: Forest Enterprise, which is responsible for the management of forests and woodland owned by the nation; and Forest Research, which aims to inform both policy and management through scientific research. In addition, the National Forest Company was set up as a non-departmental public body by the Department of the Environment in 1995 to oversee implementation of a new forest site to cover 200 miles lying between Leicestershire and Staffordshire. In Northern Ireland the Forest Service operates as an agency of the Department of Agriculture for Northern Ireland.

2 The Forestry Commission provides grants to encourage the planting of trees and the development of woodland under the Woodland Grant Scheme and the Farm Woodland Premium Scheme.

3 The Queen 'on the recommendation of Ministers' appoints the Board of Commissioners.

4 See also Town and Country Planning regarding exceptions from the requirements of planning permission.

5   The Forest Authority, which issues the licences, is a part of the Commission.
6   Trees which, when measured at a height of 1.3m from the ground, have a diameter of 8cm or less; or, if thinnings, have a diameter of 10cm or less; or, if coppice or underwood, have a diameter of 15cm or less.
7   Lopping, topping, pruning and pollarding are also excepted.
8   Forestry Act 1986.

FOSSIL COLLECTING

See also Bridle-ways; Damage; Highways and Roads; Theft; Trespass

There is no specific legislation aimed at the protection or control of fossils although English Nature has laid out a code of good practice designed to further the study of the fossilised remains of ancient life. This code suggests that only a few representative specimens should be removed from a site as fossils are better examined *in situ*. A record of the exact location should be made in order to assist further evaluation of the site. Significantly, the code mentions the issue of access and ownership and recommends that permission be gained before any collecting takes place. Access onto or across any land for whatever purpose without the express or implied permission of its owner is a trespass. While footpaths and bridle-ways offer routes across land, they do not provide any right to take anything found there and anything that is found remains the property of the landowner. This is the same in the case of land that is in public ownership where access and use are still likely to be restricted. Action to recover compensation for any damage caused to any land or anything on the land may be sought through the civil courts.

FOXES AND FOX HUNTING

See also Crossbows and Archery; Cruelty to Animals; Damage; Dogs; Killing Birds and Animals; Nuisances; Pests; Protected Animals; Protests and Protestors; Traps and Snares; Trespass

Foxes are considered under the law within three overlapping categories: pests, wildlife and as the traditional quarry of hunters. The

Agriculture Act 1947[1] classifies foxes as a pest species and empowers the Minister of Agriculture, Fisheries and Food to make Orders that require specified landowners to take whatever steps are necessary to reduce the fox population within the area under their control. Any failure to comply may leave the landowner liable to a penalty of £500.

The means by which foxes may be killed or taken are subject to the same legislative restrictions that protect all wild animals under the Wildlife and Countryside Act 1981 and the Wildlife (Northern Ireland) Order 1985. Falling within the general protection offered by these enactments, foxes may be killed or taken by any means, but not through the use of any:

(a) self-locking snare;
(b) bow or cross-bow;[2]
(c) explosive, other than ammunition for a firearm; or
(d) live decoy.[3]

To use any of these, or to knowingly cause or permit their use, is a criminal offence. No offence is committed however, if the method is licensed and is either for scientific or educational purposes, for ringing or marking, to conserve foxes or to move them to other areas. Other exclusions include photography, for reasons of public health or safety, to prevent the spread of disease or for the purpose of preventing serious damage to livestock,[4] crops, fruit or fisheries. Licences are issued by the Ministry of Agriculture, Fisheries and Food.[5] Wild foxes are also protected against acts of cruelty by the Wild Mammals (Protection) Act 1996 and, if captive or tamed, the Protection of Animals Act 1911.[6]

Hunting foxes, with or without dogs, is not an unlawful method of killing them and the Protection of Animals Act 1911 specifically excludes from its definition of cruelty the hunting of any captive animal, including foxes, unless the animal is liberated in an injured, mutilated or exhausted condition or hunted within an enclosed area. Fox hunting is, therefore, at least in the eyes of the law, not cruel and, while the traditional pursuit of foxes with hounds has been the subject of numerous attempts in recent years to create legislation aimed at its eradication, none have been successful and no law currently exists restricting this method of control. Hunts do not have an unrestricted right to pursue their quarry across private property, however, and where trespass occurs a hunt may be liable to pay compensation for any damage or nuisance incurred.[7] This may include injury to domestic pets.

The demonstrations that hunts now seem to attract increasingly involve public disorder and are subject to a number of enactments aimed at keeping the peace. These may include trespass, assault, obstruction, violent disorder, harassment and, in some cases, cruelty.

1 The Agriculture (Scotland) Act 1948.
2 The 1985 Order refers only to 'any missile which is not discharged from a firearm, including in particular any arrow or spear'.
3 Also included under the 1985 Order is any 'sound recording'.
4 Defined as any animal kept for the provision of food, wool, skins or fur for the purpose of its use in the carrying on of any agricultural activity, or for the provision or improvement of shooting or fishing.
5 And also the Secretaries of State for Scotland and Wales.
6 The Protection of Animals (Scotland) Act 1912.
7 See p.56 for details of legislation protecting sheep and livestock from dogs and other exemptions affecting hounds.

GAME BIRDS

See also Birds and Eggs; Cruelty to Animals; Deer; Foxes and Fox Hunting; Game Dealers; Game Licences; Game Rights; Hares; Killing Birds and Animals; Lead Shot; Livestock; Northern Ireland; Pests; Poaching; Vermin; Wildfowl

While the Wildlife and Countryside Act 1981 and the Wildlife (Northern Ireland) Order 1985 provide for the protection of many of our wild animals and birds,[1] these do not prohibit the hunting and shooting of traditional quarry species and game birds. These have been legally hunted for hundreds of years and the periods during which they may be killed are limited only by the Game Act 1831 and the

Game (Scotland) Act 1832 for the purpose of protecting these birds during their breeding periods.

Game birds may be killed or taken only during their 'open' season unless such taking or killing is necessary as an act of mercy or where death or injury occurs as an incidental result of an otherwise lawful action. Further legal restrictions apply to the methods by which game birds may be killed or taken,[2] who may do the killing and their subsequent possession.[3] Even the sale of dead game is controlled through a system of licences issued by local authorities. However, no offences will be committed where the Ministry of Agriculture, Fisheries and Food has issued licences in circumstances necessary for the protection of crops or for scientific or educational purposes. Such licences may permit the taking of game birds during their close seasons.

The following dates are the open seasons during which game birds of a particular species may be killed or taken. All dates are inclusive except where stated.[4]

Game	Open season during which game birds may be killed
Black game	20 August – 10 December[5]
Capercaillie	1 October – 31 January
Grouse	12 August – 10 December
Heath or moor game	20 August – 10 December
Partridges	1 September – 1 February[6]
Pheasants	1 October – 1 February[7]
Ptarmigan	12 August – 10 December
Snipe	12 August – 31 January
Woodcock	1 October – 31 January
Woodcock (Scotland)	1 September – 31 January

In addition to the killing these birds during their close seasons, it is also an offence to kill or take any pheasants, partridges, grouse, heath, moor game or black game,[8] snipe or woodcock[9] on a Sunday or Christmas Day.

Orders in respect of Northern Ireland apply special restrictions for the protection of grouse,[10] partridge, red-legged partridges and hen pheasants. The Game Birds Preservation Order (Northern

Ireland) 1999 prohibits the killing or taking of partridges, red-legged partridges and hen pheasants at any time between 30 September 1999 and 30 September 2000.[11]

As wild creatures game birds may not be stolen, although their unlawful killing or taking will amount to poaching. However, in circumstances where they are captive or constrained in some way, these birds may still be property for the purposes of the Theft Act 1968, the subject of cruel treatment under the Protection of Animals Acts and suffer unnecessarily under the Welfare of Animals (Transport) Order 1997.

1   A complete listing of protected wild birds can be found on pp.16–18.
2   The Wildlife and Countryside Act 1981 and the Wildlife (Northern Ireland) Order 1985 apply these controls.
3   The mere carrying or possession of some game birds during their close season will amount to an offence under the Game (Scotland) Act 1772.
4   The principal legislation is the Game (Scotland) Act 1772, the Game Act 1831, the Game Preservation Act (Northern Ireland) 1928 and the Wildlife and Countryside Act 1981.
5   But not in the counties of Somerset or Devon, or in the New Forest, where the open season only operates between 1 September and 10 December.
6   But not in Northern Ireland.
7   Hen pheasants may not be killed or taken in Northern Ireland.
8   The Game Act 1831.
9   The Wildlife and Countryside Act 1981.
10 This renders unlawful the sale of grouse for consumption between 11 August 1999 and 11 August 2000.
11 Exemptions may be granted by the Department of the Environment.

GAME DEALERS

See also Deer; Game Birds; Game Licences; Hares; Northern Ireland; Rabbits; Wildfowl

The buying and selling of game is subject to a requirement under the Game Act 1831[1] that anyone wishing to deal in game should first hold a local authority licence allowing him or her to do so. The Game

Licences Act 1860 additionally requires a dealer to hold an excise licence.

It is an offence under the Game Act 1831 for any person to deal in game without a local authority licence and also for:

(a) any person licensed to kill or take game to sell to an unlicensed dealer;

(b) an unlicensed dealer to buy from anyone other than a licensed dealer;

(c) a licensed dealer to buy game from a person who does not have a licence to kill or take game;

(d) a licensed game dealer to buy or sell game birds more than 10 days after the end of the open season for that bird.[2]

Exceptions include innkeepers selling game for consumption on their premises provided that they have obtained that game from a licensed source. Rabbits are not 'game' for the purposes of the 1831 Act and an excise licence is not required for any dealing in any rabbits, woodcock, or snipe under the 1860 legislation.

The Deer Act 1991 and the Deer (Scotland) Act 1996[3] similarly limit transactions in venison to licensed dealers who are required to keep records of their dealings. These Acts also make out offences that may be committed by:

(a) any person dealing in venison who is not a licensed dealer;

(b) any person who sells to someone other than a licensed dealer;

(c) any person dealing in venison more than 10 days after the end of the open season;[4]

(d) anyone selling, buying, exposing for sale or offering to buy any venison which has been illegally killed;

(e) any licensed venison dealer failing to comply with any condition of the licence.

The Game Birds Preservation Order (Northern Ireland) 1999[5] prohibits the sale or purchase of grouse for consumption in Northern Ireland or elsewhere at any time between 11 August 1999 and 11 August 2000 and the same prohibition applies to partridges, red-legged partridges and hen pheasants at any time between 30 September 1999 and 30 September 2000.[6]

A–Z OF
COUNTRYSIDE
LAW

The Wildlife and Countryside Act 1981 applies to England, Scotland and Wales and effectively bans the sale of geese by not including them in its Schedule of animals that may be sold.

Schedule 3 Birds which may be sold

Part 2 Dead at all times

Common name	Scientific name
Pigeon, Feral	*Columba livia*
Wood pigeon	*Columba palumbus*

Part 3 Birds which may be sold dead from 1 September to 28 February

Common name	Scientific name
Capercaillie	*Tetrao urogallus*
Coot	*Fulica atra*
Duck, Tufted	*Aytha fuligula*
Mallard	*Anas platyrhynchos*
Pintail	*Anas acuta*
Plover, Golden	*Pluvialis apricaria*
Pochard	*Aythya ferina*
Shoveler	*Anas clypeata*
Snipe, Common	*Gallinago gallinago*
Teal	*Anas crecca*
Wigeon	*Anas penelope*
Woodcock	*Scolopax*

The Salmon Act 1986 provides powers for the licensing of salmon dealers.

1   The Game (Scotland) Act 1832
2   This does not include dealing in live birds for the purposes of rearing or exhibition or imported birds.
3   Issued by a council, a venison dealer's licence is valid for three years.
4   This is not an offence under the Deer (Scotland) Act 1996.
5   See p.133 for a full listing of dead wild birds that may be sold.
6   In cases where permission has been granted under the 1928 legislation, the birds may be sold to a licensed game dealer.

GAME DEALERS   **89**

GAME LICENCES

See also Game Dealers; Gamekeepers

Any person wishing to kill or take any game in England, Wales and Scotland is required by the provisions of the Game Licences Act 1860 to be in possession of a game licence before doing so. For the purposes of this Act 'game' means pheasants, partridges, grouse, heath or moor game, black game, hares, woodcock, snipe, rabbits and deer. It is a criminal offence to kill, pursue or aid or assist in any manner in the taking, killing or pursuing by any means whatever, or the using of any dog, gun, net or other engine to take or kill any of these animals without a game licence. There are, however, numerous exceptions and exemptions to this requirement including:

(a) the taking of woodcock and snipe with nets or springes.
(b) the taking or destroying of conies[1] by the proprietor of any warren or of any enclosed ground whatever, or by the tenant either by himself or by his direction or permission;
(c) the pursuing or killing of hares by coursing with greyhounds or by hunting with beagles or other hounds;
(d) the pursuing and killing of deer by hunting with hounds;
(e) the taking and killing of deer in any enclosed lands by the owner or occupier, or by his direction or permission;
(f) the royal family;
(g) any person appointed a gamekeeper for Crown lands on behalf of Her Majesty;
(h) any person aiding or assisting in the taking or killing of any game etc. in the company or presence of a licence holder;
(i) any persons authorised to kill hares by the Hares Act 1848;[2]
(j) employed gamekeepers.

Later legislation[3] further excluded the occupier of any land, or any one other person authorised by him in writing, from the need to obtain a licence in respect of killing or taking hares or rabbits. Game licences are obtainable from a Post Office, which issues four types to cover different periods:

(a) an annual licence operating between 31 July to the following 31 July;
(b) a licence aimed at the grouse season running from 31 July to the 31 October;
(c) 31 October to 31 July;
(d) a 14-day licence.

Any holder of a game licence who is subsequently convicted of an offence of poaching during the daytime will have his licence rendered null and void.[4]

---

1   i.e. rabbits.
2   This includes owners, occupiers and people authorised by them on their land.
3   The Ground Game Act 1880.
4   The Game Act 1831 and the Game (Scotland) Act 1832.

GAME RIGHTS

See also Hares; Pests; Poaching; Rabbits

The issue of who has the right to kill game[1] has been the subject of legal restriction since the Anglo-Saxons first reserved large areas of forest as royal hunting grounds for the king's sole pleasure; a practice continued by the Normans who inflicted severe punishments to enforce these laws. The reservation of hunting rights as a separate right to those attached to ownership or occupation of land continued for many centuries before changes in attitude and royal status saw these laws develop into a set of established principles. Now the right to kill or take game is settled on an owner of land. If the owner leases the land to another, then the tenant has the right unless[2] 'the owner has specifically reserved it for himself',[3] and where the right has been reserved an occupier will be liable[4] if they kill or take any game.[5] A separate and transferable commodity, an owner who reserves the game right may lease it to another who then becomes a shooting tenant. As a result, it may be possible for once parcel of land to be subject to the concurrent rights of a number of different people: the owner; the occupier; and a shooting tenant or tenants. All will have access to the land and all will have the legal right to kill and take ground game. This is the situation that may currently be found in our countryside; a patchwork of shooting estates by shooting syndicates or individuals either hunting or shooting on their own land or another's land as shooting tenants. Any killing or taking of game without some specific right, or the written authority of the right holder will be an offence. If the killing or taking involves any trespass then that will be deemed to be poaching.

The dishonest appropriation of another's property is clearly theft,[6] but the law is more ambiguous in the case of wild animals as they are not owned unless killed or captured and do not qualify as 'property' for the purposes of the law of theft. Furthermore, under the principle of *ferae naturae* such animals are free to roam from one person's land to another's. This applies as equally to truly wild animals as it does to the hundreds of thousands of pheasants and partridge that are bred and released into the wild each year. The poaching laws recognise this free state and their provisions are based on the right to kill or take game. A wild animal legally killed or captured by a person with the right to do so becomes the property of that person and, as property, may be stolen. If a person without such a right takes or kills any game or other animal, that animal then becomes the property of the owners of the game rights.[7]

---

1   The exact definition of this term is unclear as different Acts include different animals.
2   *Coleman v. Bathurst (1871)*.
3   This needs to be in writing.
4   The Game Act 1831.
5   Occupiers retain a right under the Ground Game Act 1880 to kill hares or rabbits as control of these animals is considered necessary to enable an occupier to protect his crops. Crops and woodland may also be protected from other pests and action under a licence issued by the Ministry of Agriculture, Fisheries and Food will exempt an otherwise illegal act.
6   The Theft Act 1968.
7   This may not be the case in Scotland.

GAMEKEEPERS

See also Game Licences; Poaching

Employed for the protection and propogation of game and other quarry species, keepers still manage a total area within the UK equal to the size of Scotland, of which nearly half is made up of conservation and scenic areas. Their efforts to preserve the stocks of game for the enjoyment of their employers is aided by powers granted under a number of game laws. The Night Poaching Act 1828 includes the authority for a gamekeeper to seize and apprehend anyone illegally taking or destroying game or rabbits[1] during the night-time[2] and affords the keeper special protection by providing that if a keeper is assaulted or offered any violence by means of any gun, crossbow, firearm, bludgeon, stick, club or any other offensive weapon, the offender will commit a further criminal offence in addition to that of poaching. Gamekeepers appointed under the Game Act 1831[3] are empowered to seize any dog, net, engine or other instrument for use in the killing or taking of game from any unlicensed person, although this does not include any firearm. Few gamekeepers are now appointed under this legislation, however, as their appointment requires registration with a local authority. Where they are, this Act provides them with additional powers to demand the name and address of anyone found trespassing in the daytime in pursuit of game[4] and to demand that they quit the land. If an offender refuses to provide their details, gives false details or returns to the land after leaving it then the offender may be apprehended and held for up to 12 hours by the gamekeeper in order that they can be taken before a magistrate. Keepers may also seize any game found in the posssession of any trespasser who is in pursuit of game.

In the normal course of their employment a gamekeeper will kill, and more often take,[5] game subject of the game licensing restrictions. The Game Licences Act 1860 accounts for this distinction by providing for a general game licence which may be obtained by the person owning the game rights. This licence covers an employed gamekeeper and is transferable should one keeper leave and another take their place. Provided that the gamekeeper only takes or kills game on the land covered by the general licence there is no requirement for the separate possession of a game licence.[6] The 1860 Act also provides gamekeepers with a power to demand the production of a game licence from any person discovered doing any act requiring a licence. A name and address together with details of the issuing post office may also be demanded. Any failure or refusal is a criminal offence.

1   'Game' includes hares, pheasants, partridge, grouse, heath or moor game and black game.
2   One hour after sunset to one hour before sunrise.
3   Such appointments are restricted to members of royalty, lords of the manor, manorial and royal stewards. The Game (Scotland) Act 1832 applies north of the border.
4   Including woodcock, snipe and rabbits.
5   i.e., capture.
6   If, however, he wishes to pursue game on another person's land then the keeper will require his own licence if not covered by another general licence.

GREEN LANES

See also Access – A Right to Roam; Driving – Off-road; Highways and Roads

The increasing use of four-wheel drive motor vehicles and trail motor cycles designed for off-road use has created controversy in relation to two categories of by-way still found on maps and often referred to as 'green lanes'. These are By-ways Open to all Traffic (BOAT) and Roads Used as Public Paths (RUPP). Rough and unsurfaced, over 2000 miles of BOATs still exist with associated rights of passage by foot, horseback, bicycle or other wheeled vehicle of any kind. RUPPs provide approximately 4000 miles of access of a less determinate nature and local authorities were required by the National Parks and Access to the Countryside Act 1949[1] to review these and reclassify them as either footpaths, bridle-ways or BOATs as appropriate. This enactment also required local authorities to survey all rights of way and record them on to a definitive map for their area so as to clarify the rights of passage that exist for each route.

Unfortunately, the majority of local authorities have failed to achieve this within the time frame set up by the 1949 Act and new legislative proposals are now seeking to remotivate the authorities. The confusion left by the absence of definitive maps has meant that disputes over access still occur regularly between landowners and off-road enthusiasts which may only be resolved either by a prosecution through the courts or through a detailed examination of the historical use of a particular route. Current proposals by the Department of the Environment, Transport and the Regions would automatically reclassify RUPPs as bridle-ways and limit their use to walkers, horse riders and pedal cyclists. This would effectively place responsibility for challenging the status of a green lane upon the off-road enthusiasts who would have to gather and present the evidence necessary to show that there was an existing history of vehicular traffic.

There are no proposals to change the status of BOATs, which are likely to retain their present form. Motor vehicles using a BOAT are using a highway and the legislative controls under the Highways Acts will apply to them.

1   As amended by the Wildlife and Countryside Act 1981.

HARES

See also Common Land; Coursing; Game Dealers; Game Licences; Game Rights; Killing Birds and Animals; Pests; Poaching: Traps and Snares

Hares are perceived as both a traditional quarry species, a destructive pest and part of our wildlife worthy of protection and these perceptions have been reflected in the way in which the law has dealt with these animals since the early eighteenth century. As a quarry animal, the Night Poaching Act 1828 and the Game Act 1831 provide measures to protect the rights of those who own land by prohibiting the poaching of hares and subjecting them to the requirement of a game licence.[1] Hares are also classed as 'game' for the purposes of the Night Poaching Act 1844 and the Poaching Prevention Act 1862.

As a potential pest, hares are included under the Ground Game Act 1880. This allows owners and occupiers[2] of land to protect their crops and grain stores by giving them, or someone authorised in writing,[3] a right to kill or take hares regardless of whether or not they also own or lease the game rights. Where the land is moorland or unenclosed land[4] of more than 25 acres the occupier and the authorised person may only exercise their right to take hares between 11 December and 31 March.[5] The 1880 Act also states that no person who has the right to take or kill game under its provisions or otherwise may use any firearm for the purpose of killing hares at night. However, this restriction has been diminished by the Wildlife and Countryside Act 1981, which now permits shooting at night by occupiers and authorised persons provided the owner of the game rights has given their written consent.[6] Recognition of the needs of owner and occupiers is also found within the provisions of the Hares Act 1848[7] and the Game Licences Act 1860, which both exempt the owners or occupiers[8] of land from the need for a game licence when dealing with hares. Hares may also be subject of a written notice issued by the Minister for Agriculture, Fisheries and Food under the Agriculture Act 1947 requiring any specified person to take such steps as are necessary to kill, take or destroy them on any land.

There is no close season to provide any protection for hares although restrictions ban their killing on Sunday and Christmas Day. The Hares Preservation Act 1892 prohibits the selling of hares, alive or dead, throughout March, April, May, June and July of each year.[9] As wild animals, hares are subject to the general provisions of the Wildlife and Countryside Act 1981[10] as to the acceptable means by which they may be killed, taken or destroyed. This prohibits the use of self-locking snares, bows, crossbows, explosives other than firearm ammunition and live decoys. The use of other types of snare is permitted subject to the requirement that any snare set is checked at least once a day.[11] While the Pests Act 1954[12] provides for the use of approved spring traps for hares, no such traps are currently approved under the provisions of the Spring Traps (Approval) Order 1995 or the Spring Traps (Scotland) (Approval) Order 1996. The use of poisons against hares is prohibited by the Game Act 1831 and the Hares (Scotland) Act 1848.

1   This requirement does not apply to the coursing of hares with dogs.
2   This does not include someone with rights of common.
3   No person may be authorised by an occupier to kill or take hares, except members of his household who are resident on the land, persons employed by him on the land and any one other person employed by him for reward to take and destroy hares and rabbits.
4   Not being arable land.
5   Inclusive – this period is extended to 1 September where the taking of hares does not involve any firearm under the Ground Game (Amendment) Act 1906.
6   Any unauthorised night-time shooting under this right is an offence punishable by a £200 fine. This written authorisation must be produced on demand to the person holding the concurrent rights or to any person authorised to demand the document.
7   The Hares (Scotland) Act 1848 contains similar provisions.
8   Or to one person authorised by them in writing to take or kill hares on the owner's or occupier's land.
9   Any breach of this prohibition is a criminal offence subject to a maximum fine of £200 although this does not apply to foreign (i.e., imported) hares.
10 The Wildlife (Northern Ireland) Order 1985 provides similar provisions for Northern Ireland. Some slight differences do exist and these can be found detailed in the section on pp.110–13.
11 Protection of Animals Act 1911 and the Protection of Animals (Scotland) Act 1912.
12 The Agriculture (Scotland) Act 1948 contains similar provisions.

HEDGES AND HEDGEROWS

See also Conservation; Farming; Trees

The massive clearance of established hedgerows in pursuit of more economical farming methods has changed the traditional appearance of much of our countryside, arguably to its detriment. Such concerns have resulted in legislation aimed at giving local planning authorities powers to oversee the removal of hedgerows and, where the hedge is considered important to prohibit its destruction. The Hedgerows Regulations 1997[1] apply to any hedgerow growing in or adjacent to any common land, protected land or land used for agriculture, forestry or the breeding or keeping of horses, ponies or donkeys if:

(a) it has a continuous length of or exceeding 20m; or
(b) it has a continuous length of less than 20m and, at each end, meets (whether by intersection or junction) another hedgerow.

Removal of such a hedgerow is prohibited by the Regulations unless the local planning authority have been notified and given their written consent.[2] Consent will depend on whether or not a hedgerow is deemed to be 'important' within the definition provided by the Regulations, and this will be the case if it has been in existence for 30 years or more or if it falls within the criteria specified within the Schedules to the Regulations. These include marking the boundary of an historic parish, township, estate or manor, incorporating some archaeological feature, containing specific species of wildlife or the inclusion within the hedge of a variety of woody species. As a result, the majority of countryside hedges still existing are now subject to local planning authority protection. Hedgerows lying within the curtilage or marking the boundary of any dwelling-house are not included for the purposes of the controls. Other exceptions include the making of an opening on to land, obtaining temporary access in an emergency and for the purposes of national defence. Any breach of one of the provisions of the Hedgerows Regulations 1997 may result in a prosecution and fine. Conservation measures are encouraged by the Ministry of Agriculture, Fisheries and

Food through grants under its Countryside Stewardship Scheme that may be made available for the preservation of hedgerows.

The adverse effects that a growing hedgerow may have on any highway, footpath or bridle-way is subject to the provisions of the Highways Act 1980. If a highway having a carriageway is being damaged as a consequence of the exclusions from it of the sun or wind by a hedge or tree then a magistrates' court may order the owner or occupier of the land to cut or prune it. If there is any failure to comply with such an order the local authority may complete the necessary work and recover its costs from the owner or occupier. Cutting and pruning under this law is restricted and may take place only between 31 September and 1 April in order to reduce any potential damage to the habitats and shelter of birds and other hedge-dwelling animals. The courts and local authorities enjoy similar powers where any hedge overhangs a public highway, road or footpath in such a manner as to endanger or obstruct the passage of vehicles or pedestrians, or where a hedge obstructs or interferes with the view of any driver or the light from a public lamp. If a hedge is dead, diseased, damaged or insecurely rooted and is likely to cause any danger by falling onto any highway, road or footpath then it must be cut or felled.

1   Created under the Environment Act 1995.
2   No offence is committed if the local planning authority fail to respond within 42 days of a removal notice being received by them.

HIGHWAYS AND ROADS

See also Access – A Right to Roam; Bridle-ways; Common Land; Firearms and Shooting; Footpaths; Green Lanes

A highway is the general term for a number of rights of way including footpaths, bridle-ways, footways, church-ways, causeways and roads.[1] The term 'right of way' fails to accurately express the importance with which highways should be considered. It has already been established in other sections of this book that land is almost always private and therefore not open for everyone to wander over. Highways are ancient concepts that prevail over private land and allow, as of right, routes around our country. This right of passage applies as equally to a motorway as it does to a footpath. That is not to say that this right is in any way total. As with most rights it is limited. Footpaths may only be used by walkers, bridle-ways by horses and walkers. Even this is not certain as certain footpaths include other rights and bridle-ways may allow for the passage of cattle. In this, highways are akin to rights in common and disputes may be resolved only by an examination of the history of traffic use on the route or the original use for which it was dedicated or established.

Two types of highway encountered in our countryside, footpaths and bridle-ways, are dealt with in depth elsewhere in this book.[2] Highways comprising carriageways are more commonly referred to as roads and the foot-ways that run alongside them as pavements. These will be dealt with in this section together with the more general rules and regulations that concern all highways, including footpaths and bridle-ways.

Sections of the Highways Act 1835 remain in force and make offences out of:

(a) riding on a footpath or causeway at the side of any road, and
(b) driving horses, cattle or carriages along such a footpath or causeway.

Rather more detailed are the 340 sections of the Highways Act 1980 that consolidate all the highways legislation that existed between 1959 and 1971. This enactment now contains the main provisions of law concerned with highways. Generally, the county council or metropolitan district council is deemed to be the 'highways authority' for the purposes of this Act,[3] and has responsibility for the creation and maintenance of all publicly maintainable highways within its area. Highways are created through a mixture of dedication and long use. Where a way over land has been enjoyed by the public as of right and without interruption for a full period of 20 years then that route will be deemed to have been dedicated as a highway by its owner. This will not be the case, however, where there is evidence[4] that the landowner had no such intention regardless of the actual use made of it by people crossing the land; the law does not seek to legitimise trespass. New proposals currently being considered by the Government indicate that the powers of highways authorities may be increased to allow them to create footpaths and bridle-ways. Roads Used as Public Paths (RUPPs) are to be reclassified as bridle-ways as part of the drive towards increased access to the countryside.

Once dedicated, a highway must be maintained. This may be either by the highways authority or by the landowner, and the general criterion appears to be that where the highway is necessary for public use it will be maintainable at public expense. To ease this responsibility, the law prohibits or restricts acts which may damage a highway or interfere with its condition including:

(a) interfering with a highway's drainage;
(b) digging or excavating in any carriageway;
(c) removing soil or turf from a highway;
(d) damaging a highway;
(e) lighting fires, discharging firearms or fireworks within 50ft of the centre of a carriageway, thereby damaging it;
(f) disturbing the surface of any footpath, bridleway or carriageway;
(g) excavating foot-ways;
(h) ploughing footpaths or bridle-ways;[5]
(i) the willful obstruction of free passage along any highway;
(j) allowing crops, other than grass, to encroach on a highway thereby reducing its width;
(k) any unlicensed planting of trees or shrubs within 15ft from the centre of a made up carriageway.

The Act also imposes a general duty upon the authority to maintain all highways in such a condition as is reasonable in light of the type of highway and the amount of traffic expected to use it. Specific duties include the removal of things deposited in such a way as to cause a nuisance and the removal of snow and other obstructions. Where adjoining land causes some problem then the authorities have wide powers under the Act to require landowners to sort the matter out. Should such a requirement be ignored, then, in the majority of cases, the highways authority is empowered to do whatever work is necessary and recover its costs from the landowner through the courts.

It is the clear duty of the highways authority to 'assert and protect the rights of the public to the use and enjoyment of any highway'. This includes highways maintainable at public expense and other highways where a highways authority feels it necessary to protect the right of way. Once created or dedicated, highways are not easily extinguished. Powers do exist, however, allowing the authority to divert, reroute, stop-up or suspend the use of a highway to allow for the development of housing on land[6] or for some other land use.[7] In Scotland lack of use of a highway may result in its loss.

1   Defined by the Road Traffic Act 1988 as meaning 'any highway and any other road to which the public has access'. In Scotland the meaning is defined by the Roads (Scotland) Act. The Highways Act 1835 defined a 'highway' as including 'all roads, bridges (not being county bridges), carriageways, cartways, horseways, bridle-ways, footways, causeways, churchways and pavements'.
2   See pp.94–5 for consideration of Public Byways Open to All Traffic and Roads Used as Public Paths.
3   In some cases the authority may be the Minister for Transport.
4   Signs clearly showing that a path was not to be regarded as a right of way will be sufficient to evidence the landowner's true intention.
5   Rights of Way Act 1990. For exceptions to this, see p.80.
6   Town and Country Planning Act 1990.
7   e.g. mineral extraction under the Open Cast Coal Act 1958.

HORSES

See also Access – A Right to Roam; Bridle-ways; Cruelty to Animals; Green Lanes; Highways and Roads; Livestock

The law recognises the continuing popularity of horses and horse riding from the perspectives of recreational use on the highway, their care and treatment and the requirements of safety.

Bridle-ways[1] are highways for riders and provide a right to pass and re-pass with horses – ridden or being led. Footpaths are the sole preserve of walkers and any riding, driving, leading or tethering of any horse on any footpath or causeway by the side of any road made or set aside for the use of foot passengers is an offence under the Highways Act 1835. Other highways include RUPPs and BOATs as well as the myriad of carriageways that range from motorways to minor country lanes. As with all common rights, access is limited and horse riding may be an acceptable means of travelling the right of way depending upon its history. This is particularly the case on a RUPP although current Government proposals recommend that these routes should be reclassified as bridle-ways. Although the motor car has taken over as the main user of our carriageways, their original purpose was for the use of horse-drawn carriages and horses are still able to travel along them.

As domestic animals, horses are protected from cruel treatment under the Protection of Animals Act 1911.[2] This identifies cruelty as including any circumstances where a horse is beaten, kicked, ill-treated, over-ridden, over-loaded, tortured, infuriated or terrified. Cruel acts may also include the carrying, conveying or tethering of a horse in such a manner or position as to cause that animal unnecessary suffering. The Welfare of Animals (Transport) Order 1997 specifies the physical conditions in which horses may be transported and their treatment during the journey. These include:

(a) the means of transport, receptacles and their fitting shall be constructed, maintained and operated so as to avoid injury and unnecessary suffering and to ensure the safety of the animals during transport, loading and unloading;

(b) the accommodation shall be such as to provide adequate space to lie down[3] and stand;

(c) the means of transport and receptacles shall have sufficient natural or artificial lighting to enable the proper care and inspection of any horse being carried;

(d) a requirement that the animal is not subject to severe jolting or shaking;

(e) clean and disinfected forms of transport;

(f) the provision of adequate ventilation;

(g) effective protection against the weather.

Riding stables are also subject to control under the Riding Establishments Act 1964,[4] which requires that stables are licensed by their local authority and meet any conditions imposed by them. Licences are not issued until a veterinary practitioner has inspected the premises and conditions will require that:

(a) horses are to be in a fit condition for work;
(b) incompetent riders are supervised by someone over 16 years of age;
(c) no person under 16 years may be in sole charge of the establishment;
(d) insurance is held against injury by hirers;
(e) all horses less than 3 years old are registered.

The local authority is empowered to authorise a person to act as an inspector with the power to enter any licensed riding establishment at any reasonable time in order to ascertain that no offences against the Act are being committed. Any wilful obstruction or delaying of an inspector is an offence.[5] Other offences under this legislation include using any horse under 3 years old for paid riding instruction, using any mare heavy with foal[6] and any letting or hiring of a horse which is in such a condition that its riding would be likely to cause it unnecessary suffering. The use of any equipment that is defective in such a way as to cause suffering to the horse or be likely to cause an accident to the rider is prohibited.

Concerns for the safety of inexperienced riders also lie behind the Horses (Protective Headgear for Young Riders) Act 1990. This requires any person under 14 years to wear protective headgear when riding any horse, pony, mule, donkey or other equine animal on a road other than a bridle-way or a footpath that is not associated with a carriageway. Placing liability on any person who causes or permits the child to ride without approved headgear helps to enforce the requirement. Liability rests with both the person who has responsibility for that child as well as the owner of the horse, or whoever has custody or is in possession of it. Where a public highway is ridden on, the 1835 Act requires that those in charge of any horse keep to the left-hand side and avoid obstructing anyone who wishes to pass them. The wilful obstruction of any highway is an offence under the Highways Act 1980. Other safety considerations prohibit furious riding in such a manner as to endanger the life or limb of anyone else and being drunk while in charge of a horse on any highway or other public place.[7] The keeper of any horse found straying or lying at the side of a highway will also commit an offence and is liable for any costs involved in removing the horse.[8]

1   Pedal cyclists are now also allowed to use bridle-ways provided that they give preference to horse riders.
2   The Protection of Animals (Scotland) Act 1912.
3   Unless not necessary having regard for the species of animal or the type of journey.
4   For the purposes of this legislation 'horse' includes any mare, gelding, pony, foal, colt, filly, stallion, ass, mule or jennet.
5   Punishable by a £500 fine.
6   Or within 3 months after foaling.
7   The Licensing Act 1872.
8   This does not include highways passing over any common, waste or unenclosed land nor does this section prejudice any right of pasture at the side of a highway.

HUNTING

See also Coursing; Cruelty to Animals; Deer; Falconry; Fish and Fishing; Killing Birds and Animals; Police; Protected Animals; Protests and Protestors; Traps and Snares; Wild Mammals; Wildfowl

The pursuit of animals for food or sport encompasses many different activities that may fall under the general term 'hunting'. These include:

(a) driven shoots – pheasants, partridges or grouse are driven by beaters across a line of 'guns';

(b) walked-up shoots – the guns act as their own beaters, driving any game in front of themselves;

(c) rough shoots – less formal affairs involving a mixture of driven and walked-up techniques;

(d) stalking – deer shooting;
(e) wildfowling – shooting ducks and geese, often from marshland or coastal mud-flats;
(f) ferreting – using ferrets to drive rabbits into nets or in front of guns;
(g) coursing – pursuing rabbits or hares with dogs;
(h) falconry – using birds of prey;
(i) trapping – the use of traps or snares to catch pest species;
(j) game fishing – hunting for fish with rod and line.

More recently, and in particular from a political perspective, the term hunting has become almost solely associated with the pursuit of animals by dogs and it is this image that continues to generate a good deal of controversy. Hunting in its various guises remains a legal activity, however, and the majority of legislation introduced into Parliament aimed at its prohibition has so far failed to reach the statute books. As a lawful countryside pursuit, hunting in itself is not cruel. The Protection of Animals Act 1911[1] is concerned with acts that cause unnecessary suffering to captive and domestic animals but largely excludes hunting and coursing from its protective measures. This is also the case with the Wild Mammals (Protection) Act 1996 which exempts the killing of any wild mammal provided that it is done in a reasonably swift and humane manner in the course of lawful shooting, hunting, coursing or pest control. Comprehensive conservation and protective measures found in the Wildlife and Countryside Act 1981[2] similarly make no provision to curtail hunting or shooting by proscribing those methods of killing wild animals. Neither does it include any of the game or traditional quarry species in its Schedules, other than to identify some close seasons.

With the present Government appearing unhappy at the prospect of introducing measures that may alienate a large proportion of people living in the countryside, this situation seems unlikely to change in the near future. Fox-hunting is the pastime most likely to suffer legislative control or prohibition although this is by no means certain.

Those opposed to hunting have, however, been subject to more impactive legislative controls than those who hunt. The Criminal Justice and Public Order Act 1994 creates an offence of 'aggravated trespass' that may be committed by hunt saboteurs or other protestors. This Act criminalises any trespass on land in the open air which is intended to intimidate, deter, obstruct or disrupt any person engaging in a lawful activity, including hunting, on that or any adjoining land.[3] Police officers are granted extensive powers to direct offenders to leave the land and they may arrest if there is any refusal or failure to do so. Other implications for protestors arise under the Protection from Harassment Act 1997, which outlines two offences involving some course of conduct that is unreasonable, unlawful and amounts to the harassment of another. If such conduct occurs on at least two occasions and causes some person to fear that violence will be used against him or her then an arrestable offence[4] is committed. Civil remedies are also available under this Act and any person who is being harassed may seek an order from the court preventing the course of conduct from continuing and also seeking damages for any financial loss or anxiety caused. Restraining orders may be granted by the court and any breach of such an order can result in imprisonment.

1   The Protection of Animals (Scotland) Act 1912.
2   The Wildlife (Northern Ireland) Order 1985.
3   Punishable by a maximum of 3 months' imprisonment and a fine of £2500.
4   Punishable by up to 5 years in prison.

INSECTS AND OTHER INVERTEBRATES

See also Killing Birds and Animals; Northern Ireland; Protected Animals

It is generally legal to take insects and other invertebrates from the wild and to possess them. Of approximately 30 000 species of invertebrate found in the countryside or on our coastline, only a few are subject to any legislative control over their taking and killing. Schedule 5 to the Wildlife and Countryside Act 1981[1] identifies those animals that are protected and the extent of the protection. This protection extends to include all of the following prohibitions in respect of 44 species whether alive or dead:

(a) intentional killing, injuring or taking;
(b) possession of live or dead animals;
(c) damage, obstruction or destruction of access to any shelter;[2]
(d) disturbing the animals whilst they are in a shelter;[3]
(e) selling, offering or exposing for sale, or having possession of or transporting for the purposes of sale or publishing or causing to be published any advertisement likely to be understood as being for the purpose of buying or selling.[4]

A further 22 species are protected only to the extent of (e). No offence will be committed where the killing or taking was an act of mercy or an incidental result of an otherwise lawful act or where the animal is part of a collection that pre-dates the legislation. Licences may be issued under the Wildlife and Countryside Act 1981 for the killing or taking of these animals for scientific purposes.

Schedule 5 Animals which are protected

Common name	Scientific name
Anemone, Ivell's Sea	Edwardsia ivelli
Anemone, Starlet Sea	Nematosella vectensis
Apus, Tadpole Shrimp	Triops cancriformis
Beetle	Graphoderus zonatus
Beetle	Hypebaeus flavipes
Beetle	Paracymus aeneus
Bettle, Lesser Silver Water	Hydrochara caraboides
Beetle, Mire Pill [5]	Curimopsis nigrita
Beetle, Rainbow Leaf	Chrysolina cerealis
Beetle, Stag [6]	Lucanus cervus
Beetle, Violet Click	Limoniscus violaceus
Butterfly, Adonis Blue [7]	Lysandra bellargus
Butterfly, Black Hairstreak [7]	Boloria euphrosyne
Butterfly, Brown Hairstreak [7]	Thecia betulae
Butterfly, Chalkhill Blue [7]	Lysandra coridon
Butterfly, Chequered Skipper [7]	Carterocephalus palaemon
Butterfly, Duke of Burgundy Fritillary [7]	Hamearis lucina
Butterfly, Glanville Fritillary [7]	Melitaea cinxia
Butterfly, Heath Fritillary [7]	Mellicta athalia

Common name	Scientific name
Butterfly, High Brown Fritillary [8]	Argynnis adippe
Butterfly, Large Blue [7,8]	Maculinea arion
Butterfly, Large Copper [8]	Lycaena dispar
Butterfly, Large Heath [8]	Coenonympha tullia
Butterfly, Large Tortoiseshell [8]	Nymphalis polychloros
Butterfly, Lulworth Skipper [8]	Thymelicus acteon
Butterfly, Marsh Fritillary [8]	Eurodryas aurinia
Butterfly, Mountain Ringlet [8]	Erebia epiphron
Butterfly, Northern Brown Argus [8]	Aricia artaxerxes
Butterfly, Pearl-bordered Fritillary [8]	Boloria euphrosyne
Butterfly, Purple Emperor [8]	Apatura iris
Butterfly, Silver Spotted Skipper [8]	Hesperia comma
Butterfly, Silver-studded Blue [8]	Plebejus argus
Butterfly, Small Blue [8]	Cupido minimus
Butterfly, Swallowtail [8]	Papilio machaon
Butterfly, White Letter Hairstreak [8]	Stymonida w-album
Butterfly, Wood White [8]	Leptidea sinapis
Crayfish, Atlantic Stream	Austropotamobius pallipes
Cricket, Field	Gryllus campestris
Cricket, Mole	Gryllotalpa gryllotalpa
Damselfly, Southern	Coenagrion mercuriale
Dragonfly, Norfolk Aeshna	Aeshna isosceles
Grasshopper, Wart-biter	Decticus verrucivorus
Hatchet Shell, Northern	Thyasira gouldi
Hydroid, Marine	Clavopsella navis
Lagoon, Snail	Paludinella littorina
Lagoon Snail, De Folin's	Caecum armoricum
Lagoon Worm, Tentacled	Alkmaria romijini
Leech, Medicinal	Hirudo medicinalis
Moth, Barberry Carpet	Pareulype berberata
Moth, Black-veined	Siona lineata
Moth, Essex Emerald	Thetidia smaragdaria
Moth, Fiery Clearwing	Bembecia chrysidiformis
Moth, Fisher's Estuarine	Gortyna borelii
Moth, New Forest Burnet	Zygaena viciae
Moth, Reddish Buff	Acosmetia caliginosa
Moth, Sussex Emerald	Thalera fimbrialis
Sandworm, Lagoon	Armandia cirrhosa
Sea Fan, Pink	Eunicella verrucosa
Sea Mat, Trembling	Victorella pavida
Sea Slug, Lagoon	Tenellia adspersa
Shrimp, Fairy	Chirocephalus diaphanus
Shrimp, Lagoon Sand	Gammarus insensibilis
Slow-worm	Anguis fragilis
Snail, Glutinous	Myxas glutinosa
Snail, Sandbowl	Catinella arenaria
Spider, Fen Raft	Dolomedes plantarius
Spider, Ladybird	Eresus niger

1   As amended in 1992 and 1998. While this Act does not apply to Northern Ireland, Schedule 5 of the Wildlife (Northern Ireland) Order 1985 applies similar controls.

2   This does not include the Atlantic stream crayfish or pink sea fan.

3   As note 2 above.

4   Includes the whole animal or any part of the animal as well as anything derived from it and extends to their immature stages, i.e. eggs, caterpillars or pupae.

5   Only to the extent of protecting its habitat, i.e. destroying, damaging or obstructing access to shelters. Disturbing this creature is not an offence.

6   In respect of selling only.

7   In respect of (e) above only.

8   This is further protected by the Conservation (Natural Habitats, etc.) Regulations 1994 from any disturbance while it is occupying any shelter.

KILLING BIRDS AND ANIMALS

See also Birds and Eggs; Northern Ireland; Poison; Protected Animals; Traps and Snares

The Wildlife and Countryside Act 1981 and the Wildlife (Northern Ireland) Order 1985 include detailed provisions restricting the killing and taking of wild birds and animals. It is an offence for any person to intentionally kill, injure or take any wild bird or to kill, injure or take any wild animal included in Schedule 5 to the Acts.[1] In both cases there are extensive exceptions and not all wild birds and animals are afforded full protection.[2] The legislation also places restrictions on the methods by which wild birds and animals may be killed or taken. These prohibitions are listed below:

Birds

(a) Setting into position[3] of any of the following, being an article which is of such a nature and so placed as to be calculated to cause bodily injury to any wild bird coming into contact with it, that is to say:

   (i)   any springe, trap,[4] gin, snare, hook or line;

   (ii) any electrical device for killing, stunning or frightening;

   (iii) any poisonous, poisoned or stupefying substance.[5]

(b) Using for the purpose of killing or taking any wild bird any such article, whether or not of such a nature or so placed as (a), or any net, baited board, bird lime or similar substance.

(c) Using for the purpose of killing or taking any wild bird:

   (i) any bow or crossbow;[6]

   (ii) any explosive other than ammunition for a firearm;

   (iii) any automatic or semi-automatic weapon;

   (iv) any shotgun of which the barrel has an internal diameter at the muzzle of more than 1 3/4 inches;

   (v) any metal bar, axe, hatchet, cudgel, club, hammer or similar instrument;[7]

   (vi) any device for illuminating a target or any sighting device for night shooting;

   (vii) any form of artificial light or any mirror or other dazzling device;

   (viii) any gas or smoke;

   (ix) any chemical wetting agent.

(d) Using as a decoy, for the purposes of killing or taking any wild bird, any sound recording or any live bird or other animal which is tethered, or which is secured by means of braces or other similar devices, or which is blind, maimed or injured.

(e) Using any mechanically propelled vehicle in immediate pursuit of any wild bird for the purpose of killing or taking that bird.

Animals

(a) Setting into position any self-locking snare which is of such a nature and so placed as to be calculated to cause bodily injury to any wild animal coming into contact with it.

(b) Using for the purpose of killing or taking any wild animal any self-locking snare, whether or not of such a nature or so placed as (a), any bow or crossbow[8] or any explosive other than ammunition for a firearm.

(c) Using as a decoy for the purposes of killing or taking any wild animal, any live mammal or bird whatever.

(d) Setting into position any of the following, being an article which is of such a nature and so placed as to cause bodily injury to any wild animal included in Schedule 6 (see p.154) which comes into contact with it, that is to say:

   (i) any trap or snare;[9]

   (ii) any electrical device for killing or stunning;

   (iii) any poisonous,[10] poisoned or stupefying substance.[11]

(e) Using for the purpose of killing or taking any wild animal in Schedule 6 any of the articles in (d) above or any net.

KILLING BIRDS AND ANIMALS   **111**

(f) Using for the purpose of taking any wild animal in Schedule 6:
   (i) any automatic or semi automatic weapon;
   (ii) any metal bar, axe, hatchet, cudgel, club, hammer or similar instrument;[12]
   (iii) any device for illuminating a target or any sighting device for night shooting;
   (iv) any form of artificial light or any mirror or other dazzling device;
   (v) any gas or smoke;
(g) Using as a decoy any sound recording.
(h) Using any mechanically propelled vehicle in immediate pursuit of any Schedule 6 wild animal for the purpose of driving, killing or taking that animal.

The list of protected wild animals is reinforced by further restrictions under the Conservation (Natural Habitats, etc.) Regulations 1994.[13] These identify 30 animals that may not be killed by the use of:

(a) blind or mutilated animals used as live decoys;
(b) tape recorders;
(c) electrical or electronic devices capable of killing or stunning;
(d) artificial light sources;
(e) mirrors and other dazzling devices;
(f) devices for illuminating targets;
(g) sighting devices for night shooting comprising an electronic image magnifier or image converter;
(h) explosives;
(i) nets or traps which are non-selective;
(j) crossbows;
(k) poisons and poisoned or anaesthetic bait;
(l) gas or smoke;
(m) semi-automatic weapons or automatic weapons with a magazine capable of holding more than two rounds of ammunition.

Restrictions on ammunitions size and firearm types used in the taking of deer and other quarry are dealt with elsewhere in this book.

---

1   The 1981 Act and the 1985 Order both use the same numbers for their Schedules.

2   See Birds and Eggs and Protected Animals for details of the protected species.

3   It is a defence to show that the article was set in position in the interests of public health, agriculture, forestry, fisheries or nature conservation in order to kill or take wild animals that could lawfully be killed and that all reasonable precautions were taken to prevent injury to any wild bird.

4   This does not include a cage trap or net used by an authorised person for the purpose of taking a bird included in Schedule 2, Part 2 (see p.18). Nor does this extend to the use of a cage-trap or net for the purpose of taking any game bird solely for the purposes of breeding. In both cases the defence only extends to nets propelled by hand.

5   The 1985 Order includes any muscle-relaxing agent.

6   The 1985 Order does not refer to bows or crossbows, but includes 'any missile which is not discharged from a firearm, including in particular any arrow or spear'.

7   In Northern Ireland only. See p.130.

8   As note 6 above.

9   The 1985 Order includes any 'springe, trap, gin, snare, hook or line'.

10 For Northern Ireland this includes any muscle-relaxing agent.

11 It is a defence to show that the article was set in position in the interests of public health, agriculture, forestry, fisheries or nature conservation in order to kill or take animals that could lawfully be killed and that all reasonable precautions were taken to prevent injury to any wild animal included in Schedule 6.

12 In Northern Ireland only.

13 See p.154.

KNIVES

These bladed tools are often carried by hunters, shooters, anglers and all types of countrymen and women who, at some time or other, find a particular need to have a knife available while in the countryside. It is unfortunate that criminals also find a need to carry these weapons in their activities as this has led to increasingly tight restrictions on what may now be carried and where it may be carried.

Under the Prevention of Crimes Act 1953 it is an offence for any person without lawful authority or reasonable excuse to have an offensive weapon in a public place.[1] This includes almost any type of article if it is either made[2] or adapted for use in causing injury, or intended by the person having it with him for such a purpose. While this would seem to be an effective measure to prevent the inappropriate carrying of knives it remains arguable whether a particular knife is made to inflict injury or is merely manufactured to cut some inanimate object. As a result the Criminal Justice Act 1988 was introduced to address the possession of knives that may not have been made to cause injury to any person but which were, nevertheless, capable of doing so. This Act prohibits the possession of any bladed or sharply pointed article in any public place[3] other than a folding pocketknife with a cutting edge to its blade not exceeding 3 inches in length. Case law has now removed locking knives from this exception and the effect is to severely limit the size and type of knife that may be carried in a public place without some lawful authority or good reason.[4] Only small, easily folded knives may now be carried.

In Scotland the Criminal Law (Consolidation) (Scotland) Act 1995 provides for the same offences as those found in the Prevention of Crimes Act 1953 and the Criminal Justice Act 1988.

1   The possession of knives on private premises or land is not subject to legislative control.
2   Flick knives, for example, are considered by the courts to be manufactured for the sole purpose of causing injury and will always be deemed an offensive weapon regardless of the intended use.
3   Public place includes anywhere to which the general public have access, whether on payment or otherwise and will include roads, footpaths and other public highways.
4   It is for the person found carrying the offending knife to prove that they had some lawful authority or good reason. These may include use at work or religious reasons.

LAND

See also Common Land; Fires and Smoke; Game Rights; Nuisances; Town and Country Planning; Trespass

Land according to common law is the soil, the rocks that lie beneath it and the air above. The Law of Property Act 1925 is concerned with legal dealings in relation to land and with the rights and interrelationships connected with ownership and possession. This Act identifies only two legal interests in land that will be capable of subsisting or of being conveyed or created under the law:

(a) an estate in fee simple absolute in possession – more commonly known as 'freehold';

(b) a term of years absolute – otherwise known as a lease.

Legal ownership and possession are founded within the law on these estates. The law is complicated, however, by a recognition that people other than owners and tenants may have some legally enforceable rights over land that they do not own or possess (see p.93). The 1925 Act states that certain of these interests or charges are similarly capable of subsisting or being conveyed or created. These include easements, rights and privileges in or over land that are equivalent to either of the two estates. Such interests might be rights of access, rights of way or rights in common.[1]

Ownership of registered or unregistered[2] land is achieved through a transfer of title and this is generally completed by deed. The Land Registry records all transfers as well as listing all covenants and charges.

Effective ownership of land may, however, also be obtained by 'adverse possession', which is occasionally referred to as 'squatter's rights'. While this may eventually mature into full title, the concept is really based on time barring[3] of legal action for the recovery of land after a set period. As a result, in circumstances where a trespasser[4] takes real possession of some land without permission and that possession denies the rights of the owner then no action may be taken to dispossess the trespasser if a period of 12 years has passed.[5] Squatters do not gain full title after 12 years but the law effectively removes any legal remedy from the true owner. Indeed, any other action after that date may amount to harassment.[6]

Although in theory, ownership conveys a right for the owner to do as he wishes with his land, the reality is rather different. Many laws restrict any freedom of action including limitations on mining and mineral extraction, controls over noise and other nuisances, prohibitions on operations that require prior planning permissions and even the type of animals that may be kept on the land. Aircraft can fly overhead and authorised people may enter on to the land[7] and also, in some cases, dig holes in it. A landowner may even be deprived of ownership through compulsory purchase.

In addition, the purchase or renting of land is also likely to be accompanied by restrictions set by predecessors in title that may include easements, profits, covenants and licences. Easements and profits are interests in and over someone else's land. An easement is a right to 'do' something and a profit is the right to 'take' something. A typical example of an easement is a right of passage across another's land in order to gain access to some other area and profits can be found in common land where someone has the right to graze cattle on another's land or take wood. Covenants may place restrictions on subsequent owners and tenants. Modern examples of restrictive covenants ban the operation of businesses from dwelling-houses and restrict the height of fences or buildings.[8] A licence is a permission providing some limited right for someone to do something on or over another's land. Types include a bare licence, which grants temporary permission for some act such as crossing the land to get from A to B. This can be revoked at any time. A licence may also be created by a contract with revocation limited under the terms of that contract. Licences may also be associated with some of the other interests in land mentioned above. For example, where a common right to graze cattle exists over another person's land there is likely to be an accompanying licence for the cattle owner to gain access to them.

Land law is both extensive and intricate and this section can do little more than provide a flavour of a vast array of legislation that includes the Access to Neighbouring Land Act 1992, the Administration of Estates Act 1925, the Commons Registration Act 1965, the Land Charges Act 1972, the Landlord and Tenant Acts 1927, 1954, 1985 and 1988, the Land Registration Acts 1925, 1986, 1988 and the Law of Property Act 1925 and 1969 to name but a few. In Scotland land law remains based largely on feudal systems although the new Scottish Executive is proposing a wide-ranging modernisation of these ancient laws.

1   The Act also recognises that equitable rights may exist.
2   Currently about 30 per cent of all land remains unregistered.
3   Limitations Act 1980.
4   Or trespassers. A succession of different trespassers over the 12-year period may be sufficient to bar action.
5   The adverse possession must be open and cannot be achieved through concealment, fraud or deception.
6   Protection from Eviction Act 1977 and Protection from Harassment Act 1997.
7   Including police officers, employees of the main utilities, forestry inspectors, local authority inspectors and a host of government officials.
8   In some circumstances covenants can fall into disuse and end.

LEAD SHOT

See also Conservation; Fish and Fishing; Shotguns; Wildfowl

The potential effects of ingested lead in wildfowl has been a matter of concern for many years and has led to a gradual change away from the use of lead weights by anglers.[1] It was unlikely that other sources of lead on wetlands would escape control and the Environmental Protection (Restriction on Use of Lead Shot) (England) Regulations 1999 has now brought in restrictions on the use of lead shot[2] of the type used in shotguns.[3] A ban now extends to the use of lead shot for the purpose of shooting with a shotgun:

(a) on or over any area below the high-water mark of ordinary spring tides;
(b) on or over any site of special scientific interest listed in Schedule 1 to the Regulations;[4]
(c) any wild bird included in Schedule 2.

The Act makes it a criminal offence to use lead shot in any of the above circumstances and also to cause or permit another to do so.[5]

The Regulations also include powers for authorised persons[6] to enter any premises[7] at any reasonable time, make any examinations and take any samples necessary for the purpose of determining whether the Regulations are being complied with. In circumstances where entry is refused and the authorised person believes that force may be necessary to gain entry, then that entry can only be made under the authority of a warrant issued by a magistrate. Any intentional obstruction of an authorised person is also an offence.

Schedule 2 to the Regulations (below) lists the wild birds against which lead shot may not be used:

Schedule 2 Wild birds in respect of which the prohibition on shooting with lead shot applies.

Common name	Scientific name
Coot	*Fulica atra*
Ducks, Geese and Swans (all species of each)	Anatidae
Moorhen	*Gallinula chloropus*
Plover, Golden	*Pluvialis apricaria*
Snipe, Common	*Gallinago gallinago*

The prohibition under these Regulations only applies to England, although it is likely to be extended once the new Scottish and Welsh Assemblies have had an opportunity to consider the issue. While the prohibition should reduce the amount of lead shot fired over wetlands and near rivers and streams, it does not stop the use of such shot near those areas when used against other quarry species unless the site is one of those listed in Schedule 1.[8]

1. The Pollution (Angler's Lead Weights) Regulations 1986 bans the importation and supply of lead fishing weights in England, Wales and Scotland.
2. Lead shot is defined as any shot made of lead or any alloy or compound of lead where lead comprises more than 1 per cent of that alloy or compound.
3. Defined as a smooth-bore gun but not including any shotgun chambered for 9mm or smaller rim-fire cartridges.
4. These are identified by criteria and powers under the Wildlife and Countryside Act 1981. See p.35.

5   Punishable by a fine of up to £1000 for any offence.
6   Authorised by the Secretary of State for the Environment, Transport and the Regions.
7   Includes land, vehicles and vessels but not premises used for residential purposes.
8   With 278 sites included in the Schedule, the details of these protected areas are outside the scope of this book.

LIMESTONE PAVEMENTS

See also Conservation

A limestone pavement is an area of limestone that lies wholly or partly on the surface of the ground which has been fissured by natural erosion to give it a paved effect.

In cases where English Nature is of the opinion that any land which comprises a limestone pavement is of special interest by reason of its flora, fauna or geological or physiographical features then the Agency is under a duty placed on them by the Wildlife and Countryside Act 1981[1] to notify that opinion to the local planning authority. While notification initially allows any planning applications to be considered with this status in mind, in cases where the local planning authority[2] believe that the character or appearance of any land containing a limestone pavement would be likely to be adversely affected by the removal of the limestone or by its disturbance in any way whatever, they may make a Limestone Pavement Order designating the land and prohibiting the removal or disturbance of limestone on or in it unless authorised by previously obtained planning permission.

Areas of limestone pavement protected by a Limestone Pavement Order are also designated as priority habitats under the Conservation (Natural Habitats, etc.) Regulations 1994.

1   This Act is not applicable in Northern Ireland.
2   Or the Secretary of State for the Environment.

LITTER

See also Fly Tipping; Highways and Roads; Nuisances; Pollution

Defacement of the countryside by litter is a sad fact of modern life and the sight of plastic bags littering roadside ditches is not uncommon. Under the Environmental Protection Act 1990 it is an offence for any person to throw down, drop or otherwise deposit and then leave, any thing whatsoever in such circumstances as to cause, contribute to or tend to lead to the defacement of that place by litter.[1] Unfortunately, this prohibition is limited and only applies to an 'public open place' to which members of the general public have an entitlement to be in or are permitted access, whether on payment or otherwise.[2] The effect of this limitation is that an offence will only occur when litter is deposited:

(a) in a public open place;
(b) into a public open place;
(c) from a public open place.

No offence is therefore committed under this Act where a person deposits litter from one area of private land on to another. Highways, including footpaths, bridle-ways, roads and other routes maintainable at public expense are protected, however, even where they cross private land and the legislation places a duty on local authorities[3] to ensure that any highway is so far as is practicable kept clean. To assist them in this duty, the Litter Act 1983 empowers local authorities to provide suitable bins as receptacles for litter in streets and other public places. It is an offence for anyone to remove or otherwise interfere with any litter bin.

While the 1990 Act is limited, the Refuse Disposal (Amenity) Act 1978 creates an offence if any person abandons on any land in the open air or on land forming part of a highway:

(a) a motor vehicle;
(b) anything which formed part of a motor vehicle and was removed from it in the course of dismantling the vehicle on the land;

(c) anything other than a motor vehicle which has been brought to the land for the purpose of abandoning it there.[4]

Civil action may also be possible for the recovery of costs in cases where the person leaving the litter can be identified.

1   Fixed penalty notices may be issued for this offence in Northern Ireland under the provisions of the Litter (Northern Ireland) Order 1994 and the Litter (Fixed Penalty) Order (Northern Ireland) 1998.
2   The definition also includes any covered place that is open to the air on at least one side and available for public use.
3   The Secretary of State for Transport in the case of trunk roads.
4   Punishable by a maximum of 3 months' imprisonment and a £2500 fine.

LIVESTOCK

See also Bulls and Cattle; Cruelty to Animals; Disease; Horses

Most often associated with cattle and sheep, the term 'livestock' actually encompasses almost any creature kept for any agricultural purpose[1] including animals kept for wool, food, skin or fur and also deer kept for their antlers in velvet.[2] The Agriculture (Miscellaneous Provisions) Act 1968 is concerned with the general welfare of livestock and makes it an offence for any person:

(a) to cause them unnecessary pain or distress while they are situated on any agricultural land[3] and under his control;
(b) to permit any such livestock to suffer any unnecessary pain or distress.[4]

This Act also provides for Regulations and Orders controlling the conditions under which livestock may be kept and empowers local authority inspectors to gain access to any land in order to check that these controls are being complied with. Authorised veterinary practitioners are able to examine any livestock and take such tests and samples as considered necessary, and any obstruction of an inspector or authorised vet will amount to a criminal offence. If any outbreak of disease occurs the Animal Health Act 1981 enables the Ministry of

Agriculture, Fisheries and Food to impose controls over any movement of livestock while other Regulations allow for the monitoring of livestock when at markets.[5]

The carriage of livestock and poultry is controlled by the Welfare of Animals (Transport) Order 1997, which lays down standards to be achieved where livestock[6] are to be transported from one place to another. General provisions contained in this Order require that no animal is transported in any way that causes or is likely to cause injury or unnecessary suffering to that animal. Subject to slightly differing requirements for different species the standards to be achieved include:

(a) the maintenance of the means of transport and any receptacles in such a condition and so operated as to avoid injury or unnecessary suffering during transport, loading and unloading;

(b) adequate weatherproofing;

(c) accommodation of a sufficient size to allow the animal to lie down;[7]

(d) the construction of the means of transport and any receptacles so as to allow appropriate cleaning and disinfection;

(e) loading only into a means of transport or receptacle that has been thoroughly cleaned and, where appropriate, disinfected;

(f) no undue noise, vibration or severe jolting;

(g) a requirement that the means of transport and any receptacles shall have sufficient natural or artificial lighting to enable the proper care and inspection of any animal being carried; and

(h) being accompanied by sufficient attendants having regard to the number of animals transported and the duration of the journey.

No animal may be transported unless it is fit for the intended journey and suitable provision has been made for its care during the journey and on its arrival at the place of destination.

Artificial insemination techniques used in the breeding of livestock are also controlled and the Animal Health and Welfare Act 1984 allows the Minister of State for Agriculture, Fisheries and Food to create Regulations to control the practice. These powers are wide-ranging and well able to keep up with changes in the techniques. Once again authorised inspectors are empowered to gain access to any premises used in order to check on the livestock and the procedures.

As domesticated animals, livestock are also protected from acts of cruelty by the Protection of Animals Act 1911, although its provisions do not apply to acts lawfully done in the course of destroying livestock for food unless accompanied by the infliction of unnecessary suffering.

1   The Agricultural Statistics Act 1979.

2   The Welfare of Livestock (Deer) Order 1980.

3   This does not apply to any act that is lawfully done as part of licensed scientific research. Punishment may be a fine of up to £2500 and 3 months' imprisonment.

4   Exemptions include acts done under licence for the purposes of scientific research.

5   For example, the Welfare of Calves at Markets Regulations (Northern Ireland) 1998.

6   This Act applies to cattle, sheep, pigs, goats, horses, poultry, domestic birds and domestic rabbits, all other mammals (except man) and birds and also to other vertebrate and cold-blooded animals.

7   The Regulations exclude this requirement where it is unnecessary having regard to the species being carried.

METAL DETECTORS

See also Agencies; Bridle-ways; Damage; Footpaths; Highways and Roads; Monuments and Archaeological Sites; Theft; Treasure Trove; Trespass

The recreational use of metal detectors increased dramatically during the 1970s and 1980s with the introduction of cheaper equipment, the effectiveness of which has required legislation to protect historic sites. The Ancient Monuments and Archaeological Areas Act 1979 makes it an offence for any person:

(a) to use a metal detector in a protected place without the prior and written consent[1] of English Heritage;[2]

(b) to remove any object of archaeological or historical interest found in a protected place through the use of a metal detector.[3]

For the purposes of the Act, a metal detector is defined as any device designed or adapted for detecting or locating any metal or mineral in the ground and protected sites include those of any scheduled monument or any place within an area of archaeological importance.

Two defences are available for any person found using a metal detector on a protected site:

(a) that the detector was being used for a purpose other than detecting objects of archaeological or historical interest; or
(b) that the user had taken all reasonable steps to find out whether the place was protected and that he did not believe that it was.

In addition to the written consent of English Heritage in the case of protected land, access will also require the permission of the landowner or occupier. Footpaths, bridle-ways and other rights of passage across land do not provide any right to use a metal detector along their route. Compensation for any damage caused by unauthorised digging may be sought through the civil courts.

1   Where consent is granted it is liable to be conditional and the user of the metal detector must comply with any conditions imposed.
2   An offender is liable on conviction to a fine of up to £2500. See p.3 for details of the Agencies for Scotland and Wales.
3   Punishable by a fine of up to £5000.

MONUMENTS AND ARCHAEOLOGICAL SITES

See also Floods and Flooding

Ancient monuments of pubic interest due to some historic, architectural, traditional, artistic or archaeological factor are scheduled under the provisions of the Ancient Monuments and Archaeological Areas Act 1979. This provides protection for a large number of buildings and other structures[1] by restricting what may be done with or to them. The 1979 Act places a duty on the Secretary of State for the Environment to compile a schedule of monuments worthy of protection and inform the owners or occupiers of any such site as to its new status. Once notified, owners and occupiers may not start to do any work that may affect the scheduled monument without the prior and written approval of a local authority or the Department of the Environment. This includes any work that may result in the demolition or destruction of a scheduled monument, work that may cause it any damage and also the removal or repair of any part of such a monument. Flooding and tipping operations on the land around the monument are also controlled.

Archaeological areas of public interest can also be designated as sites of importance under the 1979 Act, which provides them with some limited protection. Once an area has been designated, restrictions are placed on the owner's or occupier's ability to do anything to the land which may affect the site. The Act provides that where any work is proposed a notice detailing what is planned must be served on the local authority[2] at least six weeks before the work is due to start. This applies to any tipping operation[3] or work that is likely to disturb or flood the ground and this period of grace allows the potential effects of the proposed work to be fully investigated. Where the local authority then determines that the site is of particular interest they may delay the intended work for a period of up to 6 months in order to allow the site to be excavated and examined.

---

1   'Monument' means any building, structure or work, whether above or below the surface of the land, and also any cave or excavation; any site comprising the remains of any such building, structure or work, cave or excavation and any site comprising, or comprising the remains of, any vehicle, vessel, aircraft or other moveable structure or part thereof which neither constitutes nor forms part of any building, structure or work, etc.
2   Or the Secretary of State for the Environment if it is a local authority that intends to carry out the work.
3   Defined as tipping soil or spoil or depositing building or other materials or matter and including waste materials and refuse on any land.

MUSHROOMS AND FUNGI

See also Plants and Flowers; Theft; Trespass

In 1998 nearly 83 500 tonnes of commercially produced salad mushrooms were sold in this country in addition to those found and picked growing wild in fields and woodlands. Wild mushrooms are not generally afforded any protection by the provisions of the Wildlife and Countryside Act 1981 or the Wildlife (Northern Ireland) Order 1985 and are not defined as 'property' for the purposes of the Theft Act 1968.[1] As a result, wild mushrooms may be picked at any time and by anyone without any criminal offence being committed and this includes picking wild mushrooms on private land.

While the law does not criminalise the picking of wild mushrooms, neither does it does not grant any rights of access and where a person trespasses on any land in order to take any mushrooms they leave themselves open to civil action by the landowner. This may be for compensation where any damage has occurred as a result of the trespass, or to seek an injunction to prevent any repeated trespass by a person searching for wild mushrooms.

Some species of fungi do receive special protection under the 1981 and 1985 legislation. Those protected are listed in the table below.

Schedule 8 Plants which are protected

Common name	Scientific name
Hedgehog fungus	*Hericium erinaceum*
Oak polypore	*Buglossoporus pulvinus*
Royal bolete	*Boletus regius*
Sandy-stilt puffball	*Battarraea phalloides*

1   Cultivated mushrooms are property and may be stolen.

NATIONAL PARKS

> *See also* Access – A Right to Roam, Bridle-ways; Footpaths; Highways and Roads; Town and Country Planning

The concept of conserving areas of particular natural beauty for the enjoyment of the general public was particularly buoyant in the 1930s and 1940s and the National Parks and Access to the Countryside Act

1949 was introduced to provide the powers necessary for the designation of national parks. This did not involve large areas of countryside falling into public ownership but allowed for a Commission to identify extensive tracts of country in England and Wales that it considered worthy of preservation and enhancement. Decisions were to be based on the natural beauty of those areas and the opportunities they would afford for open-air recreation. National Park designation allows the park authorities[1] to influence planning and development matters within the park area and provides them with powers to act against any environmentally damaging activities such as intensive farming or off-road driving. Parkland will also qualify for grants and public funding.

While public bodies such as the National Trust or the Forestry Commission may own large areas falling with a National Park, the land generally remains private and as a result there may be no right of access. The Environment Act 1995 confirmed the original purpose of the 1949 Act as being to conserve areas of natural beauty and wildlife and to promote public enjoyment. General access within the parks, however, remains limited to footpaths and bridle-ways together with any areas over which permissive access has been negotiated with the landowner. The majority of parks were designated between 1951 and 1957, with the Broads receiving similar status under the Norfolk and Suffolk Broads Act 1988. New proposals to be submitted to Parliament in the 1999–2000 session indicate that the South Downs and the New Forest may soon be added to the list. Scotland, which was not included within the 1949 Act, is also actively considering new legislation to allow the designation of National Parks. The Scottish Executive is presently considering adding the areas of Loch Lomond and the Trossachs by 2001 and the Cairngorms by 2002.

Ten National Parks are now established under the National Parks and Access to the Countryside Act 1949; these are listed overleaf.

Park	Established	Size (sq.km)
Lake District National Park	1951	2290
Dartmoor National Park	1951	950
Snowdonia National Park	1951	2176
Peak District National Park	1951	1440
North York Moors National Park	1952	1440
Pembrokeshire Coast National Park	1952	620
Yorkshire Dales National Park	1954	1769
Exmoor National Park	1954	690
Northumberland National Park	1956	1040
Brecon Beacons National Park	1957	1350
Norfolk Broads	1989	300

1   The Local Government Act 1972.

NOISE

See also Nuisances

The tranquillity of the countryside is subject to pressures from modern life, including rising noise levels and the nuisance that these create. Roads, motor vehicles, farm machinery, airports and industrial premises are all found in rural areas and all may have an effect on the enjoyment of residents and visitors alike. Noise pollution is the concern of the Environmental Protection Act 1990 if it emits from any premises, vehicles, machinery or equipment in a street or road in such a manner as to be prejudicial to health or to be a nuisance. A duty to seek out instances of excessive noise is placed onto local authorities who are empowered to issue noise abatement notices to prohibit or restrict noise problems. Any failure to comply with a noise abatement or reduction notice is a criminal offence.[1] The Noise Act 1996 allows local authorities to investigate complaints of excessive noise emanating from dwellings at night and for the issue of warning notices. Authorities also have powers under the Local Government Act 1972 to create bye-laws for the suppression of noise problems within specific areas while the Secretary of State for the Environment is able to make regulations controlling noise emissions from any machinery under the Control of Pollution Act 1974.

Ad hoc Regulations include the Road Vehicles (Construction and Use) Regulations 1986, which apply a mass of controls to the most prolific noise generator in the countryside – the motor car. Offences include:

(a) the use of any vehicle propelled by an internal combustion engine if it has no exhaust system with a silencer through which the exhaust gases must pass before escaping into the atmosphere;

(b) driving any motor vehicle where excessive noise arises from the use of that vehicle on a road and where the noise could have been avoided by the exercise of reasonable care;

(c) the use of any horn when the vehicle is stationary,[2] or moving between 11.30 p.m. and 7.00 a.m.;

(d) the failure by a driver to stop the action of any machinery attached to or forming part of the vehicle so far as may be necessary for the prevention of noise when it is stationary.

However, in the case of (d) no offence will be committed when the vehicle is stationary owing to traffic, to facilitate examination of the machinery or where the machinery is required to be worked for some purpose other than driving the vehicle. This last exception covers tractors and farm vehicles being used to operate other machinery.

---

1 Punishable by a fine of up to £5000 plus £50 for each day the noise continues after conviction.

2 Other than at times of danger due to another moving vehicle on or near the road.

NORTHERN IRELAND

See also Agencies; Birds and Eggs; Conservation; Game Birds; Killing Birds and Animals; Protected Species; Rifles; Shotguns; Traps and Snares

Not all legislation is universally applied within the UK and some differences reflect the different history and needs of Northern Ireland. In the context of countryside law the most obvious examples include the differing procedures concerning the possession of firearms,[1] the restrictions on the taking of some game species and, most notably, the failure of the Wildlife and Countryside Act 1981 to apply to the province. However, the provisions of the Wildlife (Northern Ireland) Order 1985 introduce similar controls with the purpose of offering protection to its flora, fauna and wildlife.

Restrictions on the taking or killing of wild birds and animals are generally the same although some differences in the species listed in the various Schedules can be found. The prohibitions on methods by which some wild animals may be taken or killed are also the same except in that the 1985 Order additionally provides:

(a) a prohibition on the use of any metal bar, axe, hatchet, cudgel, club, hammer or similar instrument for the taking or killing of wild birds or wild animals;

(b) an offence committed by a person who, being the occupier or concerned with the management of any land, permits or suffers another person to use a prohibited method of taking or killing a wild bird or wild animal;

(c) an offence committed by any person who sells, offers or exposes for sale any self-locking snare with a view to its being used for the taking or killing of any wild bird or wild animal; and

(d) a power to make Orders in respect of wildlife refuges prohibiting certain actions such as the killing of wild birds or animals or the taking of eggs within the specified area.

Where other legal differences occur they are noted within the appropriate sections of this book. The commencement of a separate Northern Ireland Assembly with similar legislative powers to those devolved to the other nations within the UK is likely to add further countryside measures to the statute book.

The main schedules of the Wildlife (Northern Ireland) Order 1985 are listed in the following table:

Schedule 1 Birds which are protected by special penalties

Part 1 At all times

Common name	Scientific name	Common name	Scientific name
Bittern	*Botaurus stellaris*	Nightjar	*Caprimulgus europaeus*
Bunting, Corn	*Emberiza calandra*	Osprey	*Pandion haliaetus*
Buzzard	*Buteo buteo*	Ousel, Ring	*Turdus torquatus*
Chough	*Pyrrhocorax pyrrhocorax*	Owl, Barn	*Tyto alba*
Corncrake	*Crex crex*	Owl, Long-eared	*Asio otus*
Crossbill	*Loxia curvirostra*	Owl, Short-eared	*Asio flammeus*
Diver, Red-throated	*Gavia stellata*	Peregrine	*Falco peregrinus*
Dotterel	*Charadrius morinellus*	Petrel, Storm	*Hydrobates pelagicus*
Dove, Turtle	*Stretopelia turtur*	Phalarope, Red-necked	*Phalaropus lobatus*
Dunlin	*Calidris alpina*	Pipit, Tree	*Anthus trivialis*
Eagle, Golden	*Aquila chrysaetos*	Quail	*Coturnix coturnix*
Eagle, White-tailed	*Haliaeetus albicilla*	Redstart	*Phoenicurus phoenicurus*
Fieldfare	*Turdus pilaris*	Ruff	*Philomachus pugnax*
Firecrest	*Regulus ignicapillus*	Scoter, Common	*Melanitta nigra*
Flycatcher, Pied	*Ficedula hypoleuca*	Swan, Berwick's	*Cygnus columbianus*
Garganey	*Anas querquedula*	Swan, Whooper	*Cygnus cygnus*
Godwit, Black-tailed	*Limosa limosa*	Tern, Arctic	*Sterna paradisaea*
Goosander	*Mergus merganser*	Tern, Common	*Sterna hirundo*
Goshawk	*Accipiter gentilis*	Tern, Little	*Sterna albifrons*
Grebe, Black-necked	*Podiceps nigricollis*	Tern, Roseate	*Sterna dougallii*
Greenshank	*Tringa nebularia*	Tern, Sandwich	*Sterna sandvicensis*
Harrier, Hen	*Circus cyaneus*	Tit, Bearded	*Panurus biarmicus*
Harrier, Marsh	*Circus aeruginosus*	Twite	*Carduelis flavirostris*
Hawk, Sparrow	*Accipiter nisus*	Wagtail, Yellow (all races)	*Motacilla flava*
Heron	*Ardea cinerea*	Warbler, Garden	*Sylvia borin*
Kestrel	*Falco tinnunculus*	Warbler, Reed	*Acrocephalus scirpaceus*
Kingfisher	*Alcedo atthis*	Warbler, Wood	*Phylloscopus sibilatrix*
Merlin	*Falco columbarius*	Whimbrel	*Numenius phaeopus*

Part 2 Birds which are protected by special penalties during the close season

Common name	Scientific name	Common name	Scientific name
Gadwall	*Anas strepera*	Pochard	*Aythya ferina*
Goldeneye	*Bucephala clangula*	Scaup	*Aythya marila*
Pintail	*Anas acuta*	Shoveler	*Anas clypeata*
Plover, Golden	*Pluvialis apricaria*	Wigeon	*Anas penelope*

Schedule 2 Birds which may be killed or taken

Part 1 Outside the close season

Common name	Scientific name	Common name	Scientific name
Curlew	*Numenius arquata*	Goose, Greylag	*Anser anser*
Duck, Tufted	*Aythya fuligula*	Goose, Pink-footed	*Anser brachyrhynchus*
Gadwall	*Anas strepera*	Mallard	*Anas platyrhynchos*
Goldeneye	*Bucephala clangula*	Pintail	*Anas acuta*

Common name	Scientific name	Common name	Scientific name
Plover, Golden	*Pluvialis apricaria*	Shoveler	*Anas clypeata*
Pochard	*Aythya ferina*	Teal	*Anas crecca*
Scaup	*Aythya marila*	Wigeon	*Anas penelo*

Part 2 Birds which may be killed or taken by authorised persons at all times

Common name	Scientific name	Common name	Scientific name
Crow, Hooded/Carrion	*Corvus corone*	Pigeon, Feral	*Columba livia*
Gull, Great Black-backed	*Larus marinus*	Pigeon, Wood	*Columba palumbus*
Gull, Herring	*Larus argentatus*	Rook	*Corvus frugilegus*
Gull, Lesser Black-backed	*Larus fuscus*	Sparrow, House	*Passer domesticus*
Jackdaw	*Corvus monedula*	Starling	*Sturnus vulgaris*
Magpie	*Pica pica*		

Schedule 3 Birds which may be sold dead at all times

Common name	Scientific name
Wood pigeon	*Columba palumbus*

Schedule 5 Animals which are protected at all times

Common name	Scientific name	Common name	Scientific name
Badger	*Meles meles*	Cetaceans (all species)	Cetacea
Bats (all species)	Chiroptera	Lizard, Common or Viviparous	*Lacerta vivipara*
Butterfly, Brimstone	*Gonepteryx rhamni*	Marten, Pine	*Martes martes*
Butterfly, Dingy Skipper	*Erynnis tages*	Newt, Common	*Triturus vulgaris*
Butterfly, Holly Blue	*Celastrina argiolus*	Otter, Common	*Lutra lutra*
Butterfly, Large Heath	*Coenonympha tullia*	Seal, Common	*Phoca vitulina*
Butterfly, Marsh Fritillary	*Euphydryas aurinia*	Seal, Grey	*Halichoerus grypus*
Butterfly, Purple Hairstreak	*Quercusia quercus*	Squirrel, Red	*Sciurus vulgaris*
Butterfly, Small Blue	*Cupido minimus*		

Schedule 6 Animals which may not be killed or taken by certain methods

Common name	Scientific name	Common name	Scientific name
Badger	*Meles meles*	Lizard, Common or Viviparous	*Lacerta vivipara*
Bats (all species)	Chiroptera	Marten, Pine	*Martes martes*
Deer, Fallow	*Dama dama*	Newt, Common	*Triturus vulgaris*
Deer, Red	*Cervus elaphus*	Otter, Common	*Lutra lutra*
Deer, Sika	*Cervus nippon*	Seal, Common	*Phoca vitulina*
Hare, Brown	*Lepus europaeus*	Seal, Grey	*Halichoerus grypus*
Hare, Irish	*Lepus timidus*	Squirrel, Red	*Sciurus vulgaris*
Hedgehog	*Erinaceus europaeus*		

Schedule 7 Animals which may not be sold alive or dead at any time

Common name	Scientific name	Common name	Scientific name
Badger	Meles meles	Hedgehog	Erinaceus europaeus
Bats (all species)	Chiroptera	Lizard, Common or Viviparous	Lacerta vivipara
Butterfly, Brimstone	Gonepteryx rhamni	Marten, Pine	Martes martes
Butterfly, Dingy Skipper	Erynnis tages	Mussel, Freshwater	Margaritifera margaritifera
Butterfly, Holly Blue	Celastrina argiolus		
Butterfly, Large Heath	Coenonympha tullia	Newt, Common	Triturus vulgaris
Butterfly, Marsh Fritillary	Euphydryas aurinia	Otter, Common	Lutra lutra
Butterfly, Purple Hairstreak	Quercusia quercus	Seal, Common	Phoca vitulina
Butterfly, Small Blue	Cupido minimus	Seal, Grey	Halichoerus grypus
Fox	Vulpes vulpes	Sea-urchin, Common	Echinus esculentus
Frog, common	Rana temporaria	Squirrel, Red	Sciurus vulgaris

Schedule 8 Plants which are protected[2]

Part 1

Common name	Scientific name	Common name	Scientific name
Avens, mountain	Dryas octopetala	Orchid, Bird's Nest	Neottia nidus-avis
Barley, Wood	Hordelymus europaeus	Orchid, Bog	Hammarbya paludosa
Betony	Stachys officinalis	Orchid, Green-Winged	Orchis morio
Broomrape, Ivy	Orobanche hederae	Orchid, Irish Lady's Tresses	Spiranthes romanzoffiana
Buckthorn, Alder	Frangula alnus		
Bugle, Pyramidal	Ajuga pyramidalis	Orchid, Narrow-Leaved Marsh	Dactylorchis traunsteineri
Campion, Moss	Silene acaulis		
Cat's-ear, Smooth	Hypochoeris glabra	Orchid, Small White	Pseudorchis albida
Centaury, Seaside	Centaurium littorale	Oyster-plant	Mertensia maritima
Cloudberry	Rubus chamaemorus	Pea, Marsh	Lathyrus palustris
Clubmoss, Marsh	Lycopodium inundatum	Pennyroyal	Mentha pulegium
Cowslip	Primula veris	Pillwort	Pilularia globulifera
Cow-wheat, Wood	Melampyrum sylvaticum	Rosemary, Bog	Andromeda polifolia
Cranesbill, Wood	Geranium sylvaticum	Saw-wort, Mountain	Saussurea alpina
Cress, Shepherds	Teesdalia nudicaulis	Saxifrage, Purple	Saxifraga oppositifolia
Crowfoot, Water	Ranunculus fluitans	Saxifrage, Yellow Marsh	Saxifraga hirculus
Fern, Holly	Polystichum lonchitis	Saxifrage, Yellow Mountain	Saxifraga aizoides
Fern, Killarney	Trichomanes speciosum		
Fern, Oak	Gymnocarpium dryopteris	Sea-lavender, Rock	Limonium binervosum
Fleabane, Blue	Erigeron acer	Sedge, Broad-leaved Mud	Carex magellanica
Globe-Flower	Trollius europaeus		
Grass, Blue-eyed	Sisyrinchium bermudiana	Sedge, Few-flowered	Carex pauciflora
Grass, Holy	Hierochloe odorata	Small-reed, Northern	Calamagrostis stricta
Heath, Cornish	Erica vagans	Spike-rush	Eleocharis parvula
Helleborine, Green-flowered	Epipactis phyllanthes	Thistle, Melancholy	Cirsium helenioides
		Violet, Fen	Viola persicifolia
Helleborine, Marsh	Epipactis palustris	Violet, Water	Hottonia palustris
Moschatel, or Town Hall Clock	Adoxa moschatellina	Waterwort, Eight-stamened	Elatine hydropiper
Mudwort	Limosella aquatica	Wintergreen, Serrated	Ramischia secunda
Orchid, Bee	Ophrys apifera	Yellow Bird's-nest	Monotropa hypopitys

Schedule 8 Plants which are protected[3]

Part 2

Common name	Scientific name
Primrose	*Primula vulgaris*

1. For example, the Firearms Act 1968 requirement for a shotgun licence does not apply to the holders of a Northern Ireland firearms certificate, which records both section firearms and shotguns.
2. Protection extends to a prohibition on the intentional picking, removing, uprooting or destruction of any wild plant in Part 1 and also to the selling, offering for sale, possession or transporting of such a wild plant. It is also an offence to uproot any wild plant that is not included in Part 1.
3. Protection extends to a prohibition on an unauthorised person intentionally uprooting or destroying any wild plant in Part 2 and also to the selling, offering for sale, possession or transporting of such a wild plant.

NUISANCES

See also Dangerous and Destructive Animals; Fires and Smoke; Noise

From a legal perspective, nuisances occur at two levels: private and public. A private nuisance arises where there is some unreasonable interference with the use or enjoyment of land. A public nuisance occurs with some act or omission that materially affects the reasonable comfort and convenience of a proportion of the community. While both may give rise to similar civil action for damages, only a public nuisance is a crime at common law. Many public nuisances are now subject to statutory controls such as those that cover smoke and noise pollution.

Instances of actionable private nuisance may occur in any way in which it is possible to interfere with someone's use of their land although the law seeks to achieve a balance by adopting a 'live and let live' approach wherever possible. Emphasis, therefore, lies on the unreasonableness of the interference. Cases have included the overflow of water from one person's land to another,[1] the percolation of noxious chemicals,[2] the encroachment of tree roots[3] and the emission of obnoxious odours.[4] When considering whether or not some interference is unreasonable the courts will have regard to the nature and the locality as well as the period, extent and duration of the nuisance but will not take any regard of a particular sensitivity on the part of the plaintiff.[5] Only those people who have a legal interest in the land concerned can generally pursue an action for private nuisance, although this view appears to be changing.[6] Where some private nuisance continues for a period of 20 years without any action being taken, that period legalises the nuisance. It is no defence, however, for the defendant to claim that the plaintiff came to the nuisance by occupying the land next to it and a nuisance accepted by one neighbour does not have to be accepted by a new neighbour. In addition to any action for damages, an injunction may be sought through the courts that either requires the cessation of the nuisance or places some limitation upon it.

A public nuisance is more general in its effect and is a crime at common law. It may also give rise to damages in cases where a plaintiff suffers some 'particular damage' over and above that sustained by the section of the community generally affected. Statutory nuisances are a development of older common law nuisances and the Environmental Protection Act 1990 now consolidates those that are detrimental to the environment. The 1990 Act identifies a statutory nuisance as occurring from:

(a) any premises that are in such a state as to be prejudicial to health or a nuisance;

(b) smoke emitted from premises so as to be prejudicial to health or a nuisance;

(c) fumes or gases emitted from premises so as to be prejudicial to health or a nuisance;

(d) any dust, steam, smell or other effluvia arising on industrial, trade or business premises and being prejudicial to health or a nuisance;

(e) any accumulation or deposit which is prejudicial to health or a nuisance;

(f) any animal kept in such a place or manner as to be prejudicial to health or a nuisance;

(g) noise emitted from premises so as to be prejudicial to health or a nuisance;

(h) noise that is prejudicial to health or a nuisance and is from or caused by a vehicle, machinery or equipment in a street or road;

(i) any other matter declared by any enactment to be a statutory nuisance.

While the legislation creates numerous exceptions to its own provisions it also places a duty on local authorities to inspect their areas from time to time in order to detect any statutory nuisance. Where found, or having been reported, local authorities are empowered to issue abatement orders to stop or control the nuisance. Individuals may also apply for abatement orders from the court without relying on a local authority provided that they indicate their intention to the person causing the nuisance.

Another area of civil law that may assist in the reduction of nuisances is known as the rule in *Rylands* v. *Fletcher (1868)*. This case actually concerned things escaping from land,[7] although the reasoning should apply equally to some nuisance arising from interference. The ruling clearly identifies that when a person brings on to his land something that is likely to cause mischief if it escapes, then he must keep it at his peril and will be answerable for all the damage which is the natural consequence of its escape. This does not apply to any natural use of the land, however, and has been interpreted as meaning that the thing collected and kept must involve a non-natural use of the land. For example, keeping cattle on land would be a natural use, whereas keeping tigers or other exotic species would appear to be an unnatural use.

1 *Sedley-Denfield* v. *O'Callaghan (1940)*.
2 *Maberley* v. *Peabody & Co (1946)*.
3 *Davey* v. *Harrow Corp. (1958)*.
4 *Bone* v. *Seal (1975)*.
5 *Bridlington Relay Co.* v. *Yorkshire Electricity Board (1965)* involved interference with television signals caused by an electricity cable. The action failed and interference with radio and television signals was held not to be sufficiently substantial to give rise to an action for nuisance.
6 *Hunter* v. *Canary Wharf (1996)*.
7 In this particular case the substance was water.

PESTICIDES

See also Insects and Other Invertebrates; Pests; Poison; Protected Animals; Vermin; Weeds

Indiscriminate use of pesticides is a major cause of losses among protected species as well as being a potential danger to consumers. In order to regulate their use, the Ministry of Agriculture, Fisheries and Food is granted extensive powers under the Food and Environmental Protection Act 1985 to:

(a) protect the health of human beings, creatures and plants;
(b) safeguard the environment; and
(c) secure safe, efficient and humane methods of controlling pests.[1]

Regulations made under this Act can be introduced to control the type of pesticides that may be made available, their sale, importation, storage, possession and use. Current Regulations include the Control of Pesticides Regulations 1986, the Pesticides (Maximum Residue Levels in Crops, Food and Feeding Stuffs) (Amendment) Regulations 1994 and the Plant Protection Products (Basic Conditions) Regulations 1997. The 1985 Act empowers Ministry inspectors to enter and inspect any premises or place in order to enforce the controls and to seize and dispose of unacceptable pesticides. Where necessary, the Ministry may also seize and dispose of any crop believed to contain more pesticide residue than those permitted under the 1994 Regulations. The Control of Pesticides Regulations 1986 requires that the advertising, sale or supply of pesticides is approved and that all persons employed to sell, supply or store pesticides are adequately trained in their use. Certificates of competence are required for storage, sale or supply of pesticides approved for agricultural use,[2] and all employers are placed under a duty to ensure that anyone required to use a pesticide has been fully trained and given sufficient guidance so as to be safe and efficient. Any aerial application is subject to further conditions regarding notification and restrictions on the times and weather conditions during which pesticides may be applied from the air.

The Farm and Garden Chemicals Act 1967 controls substances designed for the destruction or repelling of insects, mites, molluscs, nematodes, fungus, bacterial organisms, viruses or other pests capable of destroying or damaging plants and vegetables. This includes pesticides and poisons for the destruction of weeds or for repelling birds and animals.

1   Defined as 'any organism harmful to plants or to wood or other plant products, any undesired plant and any harmful creature'.
2   Amounts of more than 200kg or 200 litres.

PESTS

See also Birds and Eggs; Conservation; Deer; Foxes and Fox Hunting; Hares; Killing Birds and Animals; Rabbits; Vermin

Not all wild animals and birds are considered to be of benefit to the countryside and the list of those considered to be pests includes, as well as rats and mice, such species as hares, rabbits, deer, foxes, moles and pigeons. The Prevention of Damage by Pests Act 1949 places a duty on all local authorities to take such steps as may be necessary to keep their districts free from rats and mice, to destroy rats and mice on their own land and to enforce the duties of landowners and occupiers. Powers under the Agriculture Act 1947 also allow the Minister of Agriculture, Fisheries and Food to issue notices requiring any person to take whatever steps are necessary for the killing, taking or destruction of specified animals or birds[1] on their land.[2]

The killing or taking of any wild bird or animal is permissible under the Wildlife and Countryside Act 1981[3] where the action taken is licensed by the Ministry,[4] or where necessary to prevent serious damage to livestock, foodstuffs for livestock, crops, vegetables, fruit or growing timber. Authorised persons may also kill those birds listed under Schedule 2 to the Act.

Schedule 2 Birds which may be killed or taken

Part 2 By authorised persons at all times

Common name	Scientific name	Common name	Scientific name
Crow	*Corvus corone*	Magpie	*Pica pica*
Dove, Collared	*Streptopelia decaocto*	Pigeon, Feral	*Columba livia*
Gull, Great Black-backed	*Larus marinus*	Pigeon, Wood	*Columba palumbus*
Gull, Lesser Black-backed	*Larus fuscus*	Rook	*Corvus frugilegus*
Gull, Herring	*Larus argentatus*	Sparrow, House	*Passer domesticus*
Jackdaw	*Corvus monedula*	Starling	*Sturnus vulgaris*
Jay	*Garrulus glandarius*		

An authorised person is:

(a) the owner or occupier, or any person authorised by them, of the land on which the killing is to take place;

(b) any person authorised by the local authority for the area;

(c) any person authorised by one of the nature conservation bodies, water authorities or a district board for a fishery district in Scotland.

1 Or their eggs.

2 Any refusal or failure to comply with a Ministry notice is punishable in a magistrates court by a maximum fine of £500 plus £5 for every day that the refusal or failure continues.

3 The Wildlife (Northern Ireland) Order 1985.

4 In pursuance of a requirement under the Agriculture Act 1947 or the Agriculture (Scotland) Act 1948.

PLANTS AND FLOWERS

See also Northern Ireland

The Wildlife and Countryside Act 1981[1] provides protection to a large number of plants by making it an offence to intentionally uproot any wild plant. While this general prohibition allows for wild plant to be picked, the Act provides extra safeguards for those plant varieties that are rare or in particular need of protection. It is a criminal offence to:

(a) intentionally pick, uproot or destroy any of the plants listed under Schedule 8 to the Act;
(b) sell or offer for sale one of these plants; or
(c) publish any advertisement indicating that such plants are bought or sold.

No offence will be committed where the act occurs as an incidental result of an otherwise lawful operation, provided that the picking, uprooting or destroying could not reasonably have been avoided. Licences are available for scientific and educational purposes, photography, the preservation of public health and public safety and for the purpose of preventing serious damage to livestock, crops, vegetables, fruit, growing timber or any other form of property.

Further protection is afforded by the Conservation (Natural Habitats, etc.) Regulations 1994, which introduces European controls into domestic legislation. Plants which are protected under the Wildlife and Countryside Act 1981[2] are listed in the table below.

Schedule 8 Plants which are protected

Common name	Scientific name	Common name	Scientific name
Adder's-tongue, Least	*Ophioglossum lusitanicum*	Clary, Meadow	*Salvia pratensis*
Alison, Small	*Alyssum alyssoides*	Club-rush, Triangular	*Scirpus triquetrus*
Anomodon, Long Leaved	*Anomodon longifolius*	Colt's-foot, Purple	*Homogyne alpina*
Beech-lichen, New Forest	*Enterographa elaborata*	Cotoneaster, Wild	*Cotoneaster integerrimus*
Blackwort	*Southbya nigrella*	Cottongrass, Slender	*Eriophorum gracile*
Bluebell[3]	*Hyacinthoides non-scripta*	Cow-wheat, Field	*Melampyrum arvense*
Bolete, Royal	*Boletus regius*	Crocus, Sand	*Romulea columnae*
Broomrape, Bedstraw	*Orobanche caryophyllacea*	Crystalwort, Lizard	*Riccia bifurca*
Broomrape, Oxtongue	*Orobanche loricata*	Cudweed, Broad-leaved	*Filago pyramidata*
Broomrape, Thistle	*Orobanche reticulata*	Cudweed, Jersey	*Gnaphalium luteoalbum*
Cabbage, Lundy	*Rhynchosinapis wrightii*	Cudweed, Red-tipped	*Filago lutescens*
Calamint, Wood	*Calamintha sylvatica*	Cut Grass	*Leersia oryzoides*
Caloplaca, Snow	*Caloplaca nivalis*	Deptford Pink[4]	*Dianthus armeria*
Catapyrenium, Tree	*Catapyrenium psoromoides*	Diapensia	*Diapensia lapponica*
		Dock, Shore	*Rumex rupestris*
Catchfly, Alpine	*Lychnis alpina*	Earwort, Marsh	*Jamesoniella undulifolia*
Catillaria, Laurer's	*Catillaria laureri*	Eryngo, Field	*Eryngium campestre*
Centaury, Lender	*Centaurium tenuiflorum*	Feather-moss, Polar	*Hygrohypnum polare*
Cinquefoil, Rock	*Potentilla rupestris*	Fern, Dickie's Bladder	*Cystopteris dickieana*
Cladonia, Convoluted	*Caladonia convoluta*	Fern, Killarney	*Trichomanes speciosum*
Cladonia, Upright Mountain	*Cladonia stricta*	Flapwort, Norfolk	*Leiocolea rutheana*
		Fleabane, Alpine	*Erigeron borealis*
		Fleabane, Small	*Pulicaria vulgaris*

140 PLANTS AND FLOWERS

A–Z OF COUNTRYSIDE LAW

Common name	Scientific name	Common name	Scientific name
Fleawort, South Stack	Tephroseris integrifolia	Lichen, Scaly Breck	Squamarina lentigera
Frostwort, Pointed	Gymnomitrion apiculatum	Lichen, Starry Breck	Buellia asterella
Fungus, Hedgehog	Hericium erinaceum	Lily, Snowdon	Lloydia serotina
Fungus, Oak Polypore	Buglossoporus pulvinus	Liverwort	Petallophyllum ralfsi
Fungus, Royal Bolete	Boletus regius	Liverwort, Lindenberg's Leafy	Adelanthus lindenbergianus
Fungus, Sandy Stilt Puffball	Battarraea phalloides	Marsh-mallow, Rough	Althaea hirsuta
Galingale, Brown	Cyperus fuscus	Marshwort, Creeping	Apium repens
Gentian, Alpine	Gentiana nivalis	Milk-parsley, Cambridge	Selinum carvifolia
Gentian, Dune	Gentianella uliginosa	Moss	Drepanocladius vernicosus
Gentian, Early	Gentianella anglica	Moss, Alpine Copper	Mielichoferia mielichoferi
Gentian, Fringed	Gentianella ciliata	Moss, Baltic Bog	Sphagnum balticum
Gentian, Spring	Gentiana verna	Moss, Blue Dew	Saelania glaucescens
Germander, Cut-leaved	Teucrium botrys	Moss, Blunt-leaved Bristle	Orthotrichum obtusifolium
Germander, Water	Teucrium scordium	Moss, Bright Green Cave	Cyclodictyon laetevirens
Gladiolus, Wild	Gladiolus illyricus	Moss, Cordate Beard	Barbula cordata
Goblin Lights	Catolechia wahlenbergii	Moss, Cornish Path	Ditrichum cornubicum
Goosefoot, Stinking	Chenopodium vulvaria	Moss, Derbyshire Feather	Thamnobryum angustifolium
Grass-poly	Lythrum hyssopifolia		
Grimmia, Blunt-leaved	Grimmia unicolor	Moss, Dune Thread	Bryum mamillatum
Gyalecta, Elm	Gyalecta ulmi	Moss, Flamingo	Desmatodon cernuus
Hare's ear, Sickle-leaved	Bupleurum falcatum	Moss, Glaucous Beard	Barbula glauca
Hare's ear, Small	Bupleurum baldense	Moss, Green Shield	Buxbaumia viridis
Hawk's-beard, Stinking	Crepis foetida	Moss, Hair Silk	Plagiothecium piliferum
Hawkweed, Northroe	Hieracium northroense	Moss, Knothole	Zygodon forsteri
Hawkweed, Shetland	Hieracium zetlandicum	Moss, Large Yellow Feather	Scorpidium turgescens
Hawkweed Weak-leaved	Hieracium attenautifolium	Moss, Millimetre	Micromitrium tenerum
Heath, Blue	Phyllodoce caerulea	Moss, Multifruited River	Cryphaea lamyana
Helleborine, Red	Cephalanthera rubra	Moss, Nowell's Limestone	Zygodon gracilis
Helleborine, Young's	Epipactis youngiana		
Horsetail, Branched	Equisetum ramosissimum	Moss, Rigid Apple	Bartramia stricta
Hound's-tongue, Green	Cynoglossum germanicum	Moss, Round-leaved Feather	Rhyncostegium rotundifolium
Knawel, Perennial	Scleranthus perennis		
Knotgrass, Sea	Polygonum maritimum	Moss, Schleicher's Thread	Bryum schleicheri
Lady's-slipper	Cypripedium calceolus	Moss, Triangular Pygmy	Acaulon triquetrum
Lecanactis, Churchyard	Lecanactis hemisphaerica	Moss, Vaucher's Feather	Hypnum vaucheri
Lecanora, Tarn	Lecanora archarian	Mudwort, Welsh	Limosella australis
Lecidea, Copper	Lecidea inops	Naiad, Holly-leaved	Najas marina
Leek, Round-headed	Allium sphaerocephalon	Naiad, Slender	Najas flexilis
Lettuce, Least	Lactuca saligna	Orache, Stalked	Halimione pedunculata
Lichen, Arctic Kidney	Nephroma articum	Orchid, Early Spider	Ophrys sphegodes
Lichen, Ciliate Strap	Heterodermia leucomelos	Orchid, Fen	Liparis loeselii
Lichen, Coralloid Rosette	Heterodermia propagulifera	Orchid, Ghost	Epipogium aphyllum
		Orchid, Lapland Marsh	Dactylorhiza lapponica
Lichen, Ear-lobed Dog	Peltigera lepidophora	Orchid, Late Spider	Ophrys fuciflora
Lichen, Forked Hair	Bryoria furcellata	Orchid, Lizard	Himantoglossum hircinum
Lichen, Golden Hair	Teloshistes flavicans	Orchid, Military	Orchis militaris
Lichen, Orange Fruited Elm	Caloplaca luteoalba	Orchid, Monkey	Orchis simia
Lichen, River Jelly	Collema dichotomum		

PLANTS AND FLOWERS

Common name	Scientific name	Common name	Scientific name
Pannaria, Caledonia	Pannaria ignobilus	Saxifrage, Tufted	Saxifraga cespitosa
Parmelia, New Forest	Parmelia minarum	Solenopsora, Serpentine	Solenopsora liparina
Parmentaria, Oil Stain	Parmentaria chilensis	Solomon's-seal, Whorled	Polygonatum verticillatum
Pear, Plymouth	Pyrus cordata	Sow-thistle, Alpine	Cicerbita alpina
Penny-cress, Perfoliate	Thlaspi perfoliatum	Spearwort, Adder's Tongue	Ranunculus ophioglossifolius
Pennyroyal	Mentha pulegium	Speedwell, Fingered	Veronica triphyllos
Pertusaria, Alpine Moss	Pertusaria bryontha	Speedwell, Spiked	Veronica spicata
Physcia, Southern Grey	Physcia tribacioides	Spike-rush, Dwarf	Eleocharis parvula
Pigmyweed	Crassula aquatica	Starfruit	Damasonium alisma
Pine, Ground	Ajuga chamaepitys	Star-of-Bethlehem, Early	Gagea bohemica
Pink, Cheddar	Dianthus gratianopolitanus	Stonewort, Bearded	Chara canescens
Pink, Childling	Petroraghia nanteuilii	Stonewort, Foxtail	Lamprothamnium papulosum
Plantain, Floating Water	Luronium natans	Strapwort	Corrigiola litoralis
Polypore, Oak	Buglossoporus pulvinus	Sulphur-tresses, Alpine	Alectoria ochroleuca
Pseudocyphellarial, Ragged	Pseudocyphellaria lacerata	Threadmoss, Long-leaved	Bryum neodamense
Psora, Rusty Alpine	Psora rubiformis	Turpswort	Geocalyx graveolens
Puffball, Sandy Stilt	Battarraea phalloides	Violet, Fen	Viola persicifolia
Ragwort, Fen	Senecio paludosus	Viper's-grass	Scorzonera humilis
Ramping-fumitory, Martin's	Fumaria martinii	Water-plantain, Ribbon Leaved	Alisma gramineum
Rampion, Spiked	Phyteuma spicatum	Wood-sedge, Starved	Carex depauperata
Restharrow, Small	Ononis reclinata	Woodsia, Alpine	Woodsia alpina
Rock-cress, Alpine	Arabis alpina	Woodsia, Oblong	Woodsia ilvensis
Rock-cress, Bristol	Arabis stricta	Wormwood, Field	Artemisia campestris
Rustworth, Western	Marsupella profunda	Woundwort, Downy	Stachys germanica
Sandwort, Norwegian	Arenaria norvegica	Woundwort, Limestone	Stachys alpina
Sandwort, Teesdale	Minuartia stricta	Yellow-rattle, Greater	Rhinanthus serotinus
Saxifrage, Drooping	Saxifraga cernua		
Saxifrage, Marsh	Saxifrage hirulus		

The Conservation (Natural Habitats, etc.) Regulations 1994 lists the following protected species of plants:

Schedule 4 European protected species of plants

Common name	Scientific name	Common name	Scientific name
Dock, Shore	Rumex rupestris	Naiad, Slender	Najas flexilis
Fern, Killarney	Trichomanes speciosum	Orchid, Fen	Liparis loeselii
Gentian, Early	Gentianella anglica	Plantain, Floating-leaved Water	Luronium natans
Lady's-slipper	Cypripedium calceolus		
Marshwort, Creeping	Apium repens	Saxifrage, Yellow Marsh	Saxifraga hirculus

142 PLANTS AND FLOWERS

1   See p.133 for the plant species protected under the Wildlife (Northern Ireland) Order 1985.
2   As amended by the Wildlife and Countryside Act 1981 (Variation of Schedules 5 and 8) Order 1998.
3   In respect of Section 13(2) only, which prohibits the sale, offering or exposing for sale or possession for sale of certain live or dead plants. This prohibition extends to ban any advertisement likely to be understood as conveying that such plants are bought or sold.
4   This applies only in England and Wales.

POACHING

See also Birds and Eggs; Deer; Fish and Fishing; Gamekeepers; Salmon and Trout; Theft

Property can be stolen if it is dishonestly appropriated without the consent of its owner. Wild animals and birds have no owners and cannot therefore be stolen. As a result of this basic rule in criminal law the illegal taking of wild creatures has to be something else and 'poaching' is the term used to cover a number of activities that generally involve a combination of trespass and unlicensed, illegal killing and taking of animals. In modern times these activities have included the taking of livestock which, as they are domesticated, is simply theft. Poaching is regarded somewhat romantically as a sort of traditional game between landowners and their poorer neighbours with gamekeepers employed to safeguard their employer's stocks of pheasant and partridge. The reality has always been a more sordid affair, occasionally involving violence, dating back to the Normans' early attempts to reserve hunting rights for the Crown and this long history is reflected in our current laws that date back to an earlier age.

Although old these laws remain relevant and include the Night Poaching Act 1828, the Game Act 1831, the Game (Scotland) Act 1832, the Night Poaching Act 1844, the Poaching Prevention Act 1862, the Salmon and Freshwater Fisheries (Protection) (Scotland) Act 1951, the Deer (Scotland) Act 1959, the Game Laws (Amendment) Act 1960, the Salmon and Freshwater Fisheries Act 1975, the Deer Act 1991 and the Deer (Scotland) Act 1996. Each of these identifies offences and grants powers of enforcement to landowners, occupiers, gamekeepers, water bailiffs, police officers and, in some cases, licence holders.

The Night Poaching Act 1828 as amended by the Night Poaching Act 1844[1] makes it an offence for any person to unlawfully take or destroy any hares, pheasants, partridges, grouse, heath or moor game, black game or rabbits at night.[2] It is also an offence to enter or to be on any land with any gun, net, engine or other instrument for the purpose of taking or destroying game.[3] The Act also creates an aggravated form of the latter offence where the offender is armed with any firearm, crossbow or other offensive weapon or when in a group of three or more poachers.[4] Owners, occupiers, gamekeepers and other employees are empowered to stop and detain[5] any person found committing these offences. If violence with an offensive weapon is threatened against any owner, occupier or gamekeeper attempting to enforce this provision then a further aggravated offence will have been committed.

Poaching during the daytime is dealt with by the Game Act 1831 and the Game (Scotland) Act 1832, which criminalise any trespass in search of or pursuit of game,[6] woodcock, snipe or rabbits.[7] Aggravated offences occur if five or more people together commit this offence[8] or where five or more people commit the basic offence and any one of them has a gun and violence is offered or threatened to any person lawfully demanding their names and addresses.[9] Any person found in such illegal pursuit during the daytime is required to provide these details to the holder of the game rights, the owner or occupier of the land or their employee or gamekeeper who are also empowered to seize any game that appears to have been recently killed. Any refusal or failure is an offence punishable by a magistrates' or sheriff's court. The 1831 Act also makes it an offence to take eggs from the nests of any game birds, swan, wild duck, teal or widgeon.

Trespassing in pursuit of deer is a poaching offence under the Deer Act 1991 and the Deer (Scotland) Acts 1959 and 1996.[10]

The illegal taking of fish from any water that is private property or in which there is a private right of fishery is deemed to be theft under the Theft Act 1968.[11] Poaching offences under the Salmon and Freshwater Fisheries (Protection) (Scotland) Act 1951 and the Salmon and Freshwater Fisheries Act 1975 are dealt with elsewhere in this book. Water bailiffs have powers to apprehend any person found illegally taking or killing salmon, trout or other freshwater fish or eels at night.

In addition to owners, occupiers, gamekeepers and water bailiffs the police are also able to deal with poachers having been granted wide powers of entry, stop, search and arrest under the Acts. A power of arrest granted by the Police and Criminal Evidence Act 1984 also empowers police officers to arrest where any offence has been committed and the offender's name and address is either not given, believed to be false or insufficient to allow for the service of a summons. Courts, in addition to imposing punishment in the form of fines, imprisonment and being able to cancel game licences, may also forfeit any game or gun found on an offender[12] as well as any cartridges, nets, traps or snares. If the offence committed is one of the aggravated forms under the Game Acts a court may also order the forfeiture of any vehicle used for the purpose of committing the offence.[13] The Deer Acts provide similar powers of forfeiture.

1 The 1844 amendment extends the prohibition to cover any 'public road, highway, or path, or the sides thereof, or the openings, outlets, or gates from any (open or enclosed) land into any such public road, highway or path'.
2 Night is deemed to commence one hour after sunset and finish one hour before sunrise.
3 Both of these offences are punishable by a maximum fine of £1000.
4 The maximum punishment then rises to 6 months' imprisonment together with a fine of £2500.
5 Using only such force as is reasonable in the circumstances.
6 'Game' for the purposes of this legislation includes hares, pheasants, partridges, grouse, heath or moor game and black game.
7 Wild ducks are included under the Scottish enactment.

8   A potential fine of £1000 is increased to £2500 for each person where the aggravated form is committed. If a game licence is lawfully held by any person convicted of an offence under this Act then the court may also cancel that licence.
9   This is punishable by a £5000 fine.
10 These laws are dealt with in depth on pp.49–54.
11 In Scotland theft is a common law offence although a specific statutory offence of taking fish from enclosed waters is made out under the Theft Act 1607.
12 The Game Laws (Amendment) Act 1960.
13 The Criminal Justice and Public Order Act 1994.

POISON

See also Fish and Fishing; Highways and Roads; Insects and Other Invertebrates; Northern Ireland; Pesticides; Protected Animals; Salmon and Trout; Scotland; Vermin

Poisons exist for the eradication of life and their use as pesticides is so massive that detailed regulatory controls have been necessary to limit the dangers that occur to wildlife through both negligent and deliberate use. Negligence probably has the greater destructive effect through indiscriminate spraying or poor storage although the deliberate use of poisons to kill wild animals, particularly birds of prey, still occurs.

The Game Act 1831 restricts the measures by which any game[1] may be taken and it is a criminal offence under the legislation for any person at any time, with intent to destroy or injure any game, to put or cause to be put any poison or poisonous ingredient on any ground where game usually resort, or in any highway. This is extended to all animals by the Protection of Animals Act 1911,[2] which prohibits:

(a) the wilful administration,[3] without any reasonable cause or excuse, of any poisonous or injurious drug or substance to any animal or cause such a substance to be taken by any animal;

(b) the selling or offering or exposing for sale or giving away[4] of any grain or seed which has been rendered poisonous except for *bona fide* use in agriculture;

(c) knowingly putting or placing[5] in or upon any land or building any poison or any fluid or edible matter[6] which has been rendered poisonous.

Exceptions include the use of poisonous gas in rabbit holes and the use of specified poisons for the destruction of grey squirrels and coypus.[7] In the case of (a), no offence is committed if the administration is lawful under the Animals (Scientific Procedures) Act 1986. There is a defence in any proceedings for (c) where it can be shown that the poison was placed for the purpose of destroying insects and other invertebrates,[8] rats, mice or other small ground vermin where such is necessary in the interests of public health, agriculture or in the preservation of other animals. This defence will not be effective where the poison used is prohibited,[9] and a defendant must show that all reasonable precautions were taken to prevent injury to dogs, cats, fowls or other domestic animals and wild birds.

The Wildlife and Countryside Act 1981 deals with the dangers of poisoning to wild birds by making it an offence to set in position any poisonous, poisoned or stupefying substance which is of such a nature and so placed as to be calculated to cause bodily injury to any wild bird coming into contact with it. This Act also prohibits the use of poisons to kill or take wild birds or wild animals and the placing of a poison in circumstances where certain protected animals may have contact with it.[10]

Fish are afforded protection from poisoning under the Salmon and Freshwater Fisheries Act 1975, which makes out an offence for any person to cause or knowingly permit to be put into any waters containing fish[11] any liquid or solid matter to such an extent as to cause the waters to be poisonous or injurious to fish or the spawning grounds, spawn or food of fish. However, no offence will be committed in circumstances where the action is taken in the exercise of some lawful right.

The extensive use of such poisons has an effect on its users too and legislation has been introduced to provide protection for employees using agricultural poisons as part of their working practices. The Agriculture (Poisonous Substances) Act 1952 places a duty on everyone involved in the use of these substances to take reasonable care to avoid anything likely to cause risk to themselves or others.

1   Defined by this Act as including hares, pheasants, partridges, grouse, heath or moor game and black game.
2   The Protection of Animals (Scotland) Act 1912.
3   Or the causing or procuring or, being an owner permitting any wilful administration.
4   Causing or procuring or knowingly being a party to any sale, etc.
5   Causing, procuring, etc.
6   But this does not include sown seed or grain.
7   The Agriculture (Misc. Provisions) Act 1972 and the Grey Squirrels (Warfarin) Order 1973.
8   See p.107 for the protected species.
9   The Animals (Cruel Poisons) Act 1962.
10 i.e. those listed in Schedule 6 to the Act. See p.154.
11 Or into any tributaries of waters containing fish.

POLICE

See also Land; Nuisances; Protests and Protestors; Town and Country Planning; Trespass

The police officers of England, Wales, Scotland and Ireland hold their authority from the Crown and are responsible for maintenance of peace, saving life and property and preventing and detecting crime. Modern police powers are granted by legislation and may be either wide ranging or restricted, depending upon which Act is being relied on. Police officers are also subject to limitations and rules that are aimed at protecting the wide freedoms enjoyed by individuals in this country and officers may only act where they have powers to do so, and only to the extent of those powers.[1]

Civil law is not the territory of the police, who are generally powerless to act in this context. Disputes over boundaries, simple trespass and planning issues are only actionable by the people affected or, in some cases, by local authorities or the various Ministers of State. Public nuisances are usually the concern of local authorities or government departments. Other than ensuring that disputes do not become violent, the police are unable to offer much assistance with these issues. Some areas of countryside law are clearly criminal, however, and theft, damage, poaching and public demonstrations are all issues of concern to the police.[2]

Common law powers of arrest are available to all police officers in the UK. In England and Wales,[3] statutes that grant specific powers under particular circumstances have largely replaced these powers while Scottish officers still use a wide common law power of arrest without warrant.[4] Generally a police officer is likely to make an arrest where he or she suspects a serious offence has been committed, is being committed or is about to be committed. Enactments, such as the Firearms Act 1968 and the various game laws provide particular powers to facilitate enforcement of their sections and these will often empower officers to stop, search and arrest suspects. Minor matters may also lead to arrest where the suspect fails to satisfy an officer as to the correctness or suitability of their name or address. In circumstances where there is no power of arrest or where arrest is inappropriate police officers may report the matter to the courts who will then summon the offender to appear.

Police officers are often called to deal with problems over which they have little or no authority and are only able to maintain some sense of balance between opposing perspectives. This task is an onerous one and unlikely to win the police any friends in circumstances that are often frustrating to both sides. This is particularly the case where both sides consider themselves in the right. However, the police have sufficient powers to assist them in resolving many of the problems that occur in the countryside, and most police forces have now set up countryside liaison offices with the expertise necessary to deal with them. In all cases the police should be able to give advice on the best way of proceeding.

---

1 For example the Codes of Practice to the Police and Criminal Evidence Act 1984 provide a mass of dos and don'ts that police officers are obliged to follow. Rights still include silence and access to legal advice.

2   Where appropriate police powers have been included in the various sections of this book.
3   The Police and Criminal Evidence Act 1984 grants general powers to officers within England and Wales. Arrestable offences include all the most serious of offences and specifically those where the punishment may be 5 years or more imprisonment on first conviction. Arrest may also occur if a suspect fails to provide a name or address that is sufficient to allow the service of a summons.
4   The Criminal Procedure (Scotland) Act 1995 has supplemented the common law in some instances and outlines many police powers.

POLLUTION

See also Agencies; Fires and Smoke; Litter; Noise

Extensive powers have been granted to the Environment Agency[1] to assist in the prevention of instances of pollution and, where pollution does occur, to prosecute offenders.[2] The Environmental Protection Act 1990 defines the environment as consisting of air, water and land, and pollution as pollution due to the release of any substances capable of causing harm to man or any other living organism. The Act provides powers for the Secretary of State to:

(a) proscribe by regulation any process or activity capable of causing pollution;
(b) establish standards, objectives or requirements in relation to any emissions;
(c) establish an authorising mechanism under the Environment Agency to authorise and control any proscribed processes.[3]

An authorisation granted by the Agency is subject of any conditions necessary to ensure that the best available techniques in terms of scientific advances and cost are used to prevent or render harmless any polluting substances. Enforcement notices are used to ensure compliance with any conditions and to stop the continuation of any process involving an imminent risk of serious pollution to the environment. The Agency has sufficient powers to take immediate action to deal with anything in imminent danger of being polluted.

Another of the principal functions of the Environment Agency when it was created was to take over the functions of the National Rivers Authority as well as the responsibilities of waste regulation authorities.

This includes enforcement of the provisions of the Water Resources Act 1991, which among other things controls the entry of potential pollutants into the water system. It is an offence under this Act for any person to cause or knowingly permit any:

(a) poisonous, noxious or polluting matter, or any solid waste, to enter any controlled water;[4]
(b) matter, other than trade effluent, to enter controlled waters by being discharged from a drain or sewer; and
(c) matter whatever to enter any inland freshwater so as to tend to impede the proper flow in a manner leading or likely to lead to a substantial aggravation of pollution or the consequences of pollution.

Authorised persons have the power to enter, examine and investigate as to whether any of the provisions of the pollution control enactments are not being complied with. This power also allows the authorised person to take whatever samples are needed for the purposes of analysis.

Pollution by smoke is dealt with under the Clean Air Act 1993, noise under Part III of the Environmental Protection Act 1990 and pollution by litter, tipping and dumping by a number of Acts including the 1990 Act, the Highways Act 1980 and the Refuse Disposal (Amenity) Act 1978. In addition to its pollution control activities the Environment Agency also has a duty to promote the conservation and enhancement of natural beauty and amenity of inland and coastal waters, the conservation of flora and fauna and the use of such waters for recreational purposes.

---

1 The Environment Agency and the Scottish Environmental Protection Agency were set up by the Environment Act 1995.
2 The Act makes out a number of criminal offences punishable by fines of up to £20 000.
3 New Regulations to bring pollution control systems in line with the requirements of the European Union (EC Directive 96/61/EC) are now likely as a result of the Pollution Prevention and Control Act 1999.
4 This includes coastal waters, inland freshwaters including lakes, ponds and reservoirs which discharge into another controlled water. The definition does not include any public sewer or drain.

PROTECTED ANIMALS

See also Amphibians; Bats; Birds and Eggs; Insects and Other Invertebrates; Killing Birds and Animals; Northern Ireland

Schedule 5 to the Wildlife and Countryside Act 1981[1] lists those animals to which it offers particular protection.[2] This protection may include some or all of the following prohibitions:

(a) intentional killing, injuring or taking;[3]
(b) possession of live or dead animals;[4]
(c) damage, obstruction or destruction of access to any shelter;[5]
(d) disturbing the animals while they are in a shelter;[6]
(e) possession of any parts derived from such an animal for the purpose of sale;[7]

The section numbers have been provided in the endnotes to assist in determining any limitations on the extent of the protection that applies. Where an entry on a Schedule is not annotated by an endnote then they are fully protected. General exceptions to these criminal offences include acts of mercy, the prevention of serious damage to livestock or crops, the incidental results of lawful operations, the destruction of shelters sited within dwelling-houses[8] or anything done in pursuance of a requirement by the Minister of Agriculture, Fisheries and Food. It is a specific defence in respect of (b) to show that the animal had not been killed or taken or that it had been killed or taken otherwise than in contravention of the relevant provisions of the Act[9] or that the animal or other thing in his possession had been sold to him otherwise than in contravention of the relevant provisions of the Act.[10]

Schedule 6 identifies those animals that may not be killed or taken by certain methods.

The Conservation (Natural Habitats, etc.) Regulations 1994 contain lists of scheduled animals and introduced a number of offences relating to their killing, taking, habitats and shelters. The Schedules to the Wildlife and Countryside Act are listed on the following pages.[11]

A–Z OF COUNTRYSIDE LAW

Schedule 5 Animals which are protected

Common name	Scientific name
Adder[12]	Vipera berus
Anemone, Ivell's Sea	Edwardsia ivelli
Anemone, Starlet Sea	Nematosella vectensis
Apus, Tadpole Shrimp	Triops cancriformis
Bats, horseshoe (all species)	Rhinolophidae
Bats, Typical (all species)	Vespertilionidae
Beetle	Graphoderus zonatus
Beetle	Hypebaeus flavipes
Beetle	Paracymus aeneus
Beetle, Lesser Silver Water	Hydrochara caraboides
Beetle, Mire Pill[13]	Curimopsis nigrita
Beetle, Rainbow Leaf	Chrysolina cerealis
Beetle, Stag[14]	Lucanus cervus
Beetle, Violet Click	Limoniscus violaceus
Burbot	Lota lota
Butterfly, Adonis Blue[15]	Lysandra bellargus
Butterfly, Black Hairstreak[15]	Boloria euphrosyne
Butterfly, Brown Hairstreak[15]	Thecia betulae
Butterfly, Chalkhill blue[15]	Lysandra coridon
Butterfly, Chequered Skipper[15]	Carterocephalus palaemon
Butterfly, Duke of Burgundy Fritillary[15]	Hamearis lucina
Butterfly, Glanville Fritillary[15]	Melitaea cinxia
Butterfly, Heath Fritillary[15]	Mellicta athalia
Butterfly, High Brown Fritillary[15]	Argynnis adippe
Butterfly, Large Blue[15]	Maculinea arion
Butterfly, Large Copper[15]	Lycaena dispar
Butterfly, Large Heath[15]	Coenonympha tullia
Butterfly, Large Tortoiseshell[15]	Nymphalis polychloros
Butterfly, Lulworth Skipper[15]	Thymelicus acteon
Butterfly, Marsh Fritillary[15]	Eurodryas aurinia
Butterfly, Mountain Ringlet[15]	Erebia epiphron
Butterfly, Northern Brown Argus[15]	Aricia artaxerxes
Butterfly, Pearl-bordered Fritillary[15]	Boloria euphrosyne
Butterfly, Purple Emperor[15]	Apatura iris
Butterfly, Silver-spotted Skipper[15]	Hesperia comma
Butterfly, Silver-studded Blue[15]	Plebejus argus
Butterfly, Small Blue[15]	Cupido minimus
Butterfly, Swallowtail[15]	Papilio machaon
Butterfly, White Letter Hairstreak[15]	Stymonida w-album
Butterfly, Wood White[15]	Leptidea sinapis
Cat, Wild	Felis silvestris
Cicada, New Forest	Cicadetta montana
Crayfish, Atlantic Stream	Austropotamobius pallipes
Cricket, Field	Gryllus campestris
Cricket, Mole	Gryllotalpa gryllotalpa
Damselfly, Southern	Coenagrion mercuriale
Dolphins (all species)	Cetacea
Dormouse	Muscardinus avellanarius
Dragonfly, Norfolk Aeshna	Aeshna isosceles
Frog, Common[16]	Rana temporaria
Goby, Couch's	Gobius couchii
Goby, Giant	Gobius cobitis
Grasshopper, Wart-biter	Decticus verrucivorus
Hatchet shell, Northern	Thyasira gouldi
Hydroid, Marine	Clavopsella navis
Lagoon Snail	Paludinella littorina
Lagoon Snail, De Folin's	Caecum armoricum
Lagoon Worm, Tentacled	Alkmaria romijini
Leech, Medicinal	Hirudo medicinalis
Lizard, Sand	Lacerta agilis
Lizard, Viviparous[17]	Lacerta vivipara
Marten, Pine	Martes martes
Moth, Barberry Carpet	Pareulype berberata
Moth, Black-veined	Siona lineata
Moth, Essex Emerald	Thetidia smaragdaria
Moth, Fiery Clearwing	Bembecia chrysidiformis
Moth, Fisher's Estuarine	Gortyna borelii
Moth, New Forest Burnet	Zygaena viciae
Moth, Reddish Buff	Acosmetia caliginosa
Moth, Sussex Emerald	Thalera fimbrialis
Mussel, Fan[18]	Atrina fragilis
Mussel, Freshwater Pearl	Margaritifera margaritifera
Newt, Great Crested, or Warty	Triturus cristatus
Newt, Palmate[19]	Triturus helveticus
Newt, Smooth[20]	Triturus vulgaris
Otter, Common	Lutra lutra
Porpoises (all species)	Cetacea
Sandworm, Lagoon	Armandia cirrhosa
Sea fan, Pink[21]	Eunicella verrucosa
Sea mat, Trembling	Victorella pavida
Sea slug, Lagoon	Tenellia adspersa

PROTECTED ANIMALS

Common name	Scientific name	Common name	Scientific name
Shad, Allis [22]	*Alosa alosa*	Spider, Ladybird	*Eresus niger*
Shad, Twaite [23]	*Alosa fallax*	Squirrel, Red	*Sciurus vulgaris*
Shark, Basking	*Cetorhinus maximus*	Sturgeon	*Acipenser sturio*
Shrimp, Fairy	*Chirocephalus diaphanus*	Toad, Common [26]	*Bufo bufo*
		Toad, Natterjack	*Bufo calamita*
Shrimp, Lagoon Sand	*Gammarus insensibilis*	Turtles, Marine (all species)	Dermochelyidae and Cheloriidae
Slow Worm [24]	*Anguis fragilis*		
Snail, Glutinous	*Myxas glutinosa*	Vendace	*Coregorus albula*
Snail, Sandbowl	*Catinella arenaria*	Vole, Water [27]	*Arvicola terrestris*
Snake, Grass [25]	*Natrix helvetica*	Walrus	*Odoberus rosmarus*
Snake, Smooth	*Coronella austriaca*	Whale (all species)	Cetacea
Spider, Fen Raft	*Dolomedes plantarius*	Whitefish	*Coregorus lavaretus*

Schedule 6 Animals which may not be killed or taken by certain methods

Common name	Scientific name	Common name	Scientific name
Badger	*Meles meles*	Hedgehog	*Erinaceus europaeus*
Bats, Horseshoe (all species)	Rhinolophidae	Marten, Pine	*Martes martes*
		Otter, Common	*Lutra lutra*
Bats, typical (all species)	Vespertilionidae	Polecat	*Mustela putorius*
Cat, Wild	*Felis silvestris*	Porpoise, Harbour, or Common	*Phocaena phocaena*
Dolphin, Bottle-nosed	*Tursiops truncatas*		
Dolphin, Common	*Delphinus delphis*	Shrews (all species)	Soricidae
Dormice (all species)	Gliridae	Squirrel, Red	*Sciurus vulgaris*

The Schedules to the Conservation (Natural Habitats, etc.) Regulations 1994 are detailed below.

Schedule 2 European protected species of animals

Common name	Scientific name	Common name	Scientific name
Bats, Horseshoe (all species)	Rhinolophidae	Otter, Common	*Lutra lutra*
		Snake, Smooth	*Coronella austriaca*
Bats, Typical	Vespertilionidae	Sturgeon	*Acipenser sturio*
Butterfly, Large Blue	*Maculinea arion*	Toad, Natterjack	*Bufo calamita*
Cat, Wild	*Felis silvestris*	Turtles, Marine (all species)	*Caretta caretta*
Dolphin, Porpoises and Whales (all species)	Cetacea		*Chelonia mydas*
			Lepidochelys kempii
Dormouse	*Muscardinus avellanarius*		*Eretmochelys imbricata*
			Dermochelys coriacea
Lizard, Sand	*Lacerta agilis*		
Newt, Great Crested	*Triturus cristatus*		

Schedule 3 Animals which may not be killed or taken in certain ways

Common name	Scientific name	Common name	Scientific name
Barbel	*Barbus barbus*	Seal, Grey	*Halichoerus grypus*
Grayling	*Thymallus thymallus*	Seal, Harp	*Phoca groenlandica*
Hare, Mountain	*Lepus timidus*	Seal, Hooded	*Cystophora cristata*
Lamprey, River	*Lampetra fluviatilis*	Seal, Ringed	*Phoca hispida*
Marten, Pine	*Martes martes*	Shad, Allis	*Alosa alosa*
Polecat	*Mustela putorius*	Shad, Twaite	*Alosa fallax*
Salmon, Atlantic [28]	*Salmo salar*	Vendace	*Coregonus albula*
Seal, Bearded	*Erignathus barbatus*	Whitefish	*Coregonus lavaretus*
Seal, Common	*Phoca vitulina*		

1 The Wildlife (Northern Ireland) Order 1985 includes prohibitions and Schedules similar to those contained within the 1981 Act.
2 As amended.
3 Section 9(1).
4 Section 9(2).
5 Section 9(4)(a).
6 Section 9(4)(b).
7 Section 9(5). Includes selling, offering for sale and advertising for sale.
8 See p.12 for restrictions operating on this exception.
9 e.g. not involving a prohibited method of taking etc.
10 i.e., as a registered person under the Wildlife and Countryside (Registration to sell etc. Certain Dead Wild Birds) Regulations 1982, as amended.
11 For details of the offences under these Regulations, see Killing Birds and Animals.
12 In respect of section 9(1) in so far as it relates to killing or injuring and section 9(5) only.
13 In respect of section 9(4)(a) only, i.e., destroying, damaging or obstructing access to shelters but not disturbance.
14 In respect of section 9(5) only.
15 In respect of section 9(5) only.
16 In respect of section 9(5) only.
17 In respect of section 9(1) in so far as it relates to killing or injuring and section 9(5).
18 In respect of sections 9(1), 9(2) and 9(5) only.

19 In respect of section 9(5) only.
20 In respect of section 9(5) only.
21 In respect of section 9(1), 9(2) and 9(5) only.
22 In respect of section 9(1) and 9(4)(a) only.
23 In respect of section 9(4)(a) only.
24 In respect of section 9(1) in so far as it relates to killing or injuring and 9(5).
25 In respect of section 9(1) in so far as it relates to killing or injuring and 9(5).
26 In respect of section 9(5) only.
27 In respect of section 9(4) only.
28 Only in freshwater.

PROTESTS AND PROTESTORS

See also Damage; Theft; Trespass

Increased interest in conservation issues and animal rights have seen an accompanying rise in the number of demonstrations and protests made against the use of animals in scientific research, fur farming, hunting and the construction of roads through the countryside. While the law has long recognised a right of peaceful protest[1] it has also sought to regulate against the type of demonstration that disrupts the normal tranquillity expected in our society. The common law dates back in time to early history and provides for the general peace[2] to be maintained and the courts may deal with any beach of that peace. This ancient law also provides a power of arrest exercisable by any person[3] in circumstances where:

(a) someone is found committing a breach of the peace;
(b) a breach has been committed and a renewal is threatened;
(c) a breach is reasonably believed to be about to be committed.

In Scotland a breach of the peace is a crime at common law and occurs where any person conducts themselves in a riotous or disorderly manner to the alarm, annoyance or disturbance of others. It is deemed to be mobbing and rioting where a number of people assemble and combine for a common purpose. This may involve as few as twelve persons and their assembly for the purposes of intimidating others may be sufficient for a crime to have been committed.

In England and Wales, organised assemblies and protests have resulted in more modern legislation being introduced which seeks to criminalise certain behaviour and provide the police and the courts with sufficient powers to prevent any serious disruption to lawful activity. The Public Order Act 1986 creates a range of offences, including circumstances where:

(a) twelve or more persons are present together and using or threatening unlawful violence for a common purpose, and their conduct is such to cause a person of reasonable firmness to fear for their personal safety;[4]

(b) three or more persons are together and using or threatening unlawful violence, and their conduct is such to cause a person of reasonable firmness to fear for their personal safety;[5]

(c) a person uses or threatens unlawful violence towards another and where the conduct is such to cause a person of reasonable firmness to fear for their personal safety;[6]

(d) a person uses threatening, abusive or insulting words or behaviour or distributes or displays any writing, sign or visible representation which is threatening, abusive or insulting with intent to cause fear of immediate unlawful violence;[7]

(e) a person, with intent to cause harassment, alarm or distress uses threatening, abusive or insulting words or behaviour or distributes or displays any writing sign or visible representation which is threatening, abusive or insulting;[8]

(f) a person uses threatening, abusive or insulting words or behaviour or displays any writing sign or visible representation which is threatening, abusive or insulting within the sight or hearing of a person likely to be caused harassment, alarm or distress.[9]

Police officers may arrest if any of these offences are committed[10] and are also granted powers of stop and search under the provisions of the Criminal Justice and Public Order Act 1994 where they anticipate violence. Any collective and aggravated trespass which interrupts some lawful activity is now dealt with by this Act and provides the police with powers to order trespassers to leave the land and to deal with any failure on their part to do so.

If anyone is assaulted or if damage occurs as a result of any demonstration or protest the normal criminal law is capable of dealing with these offences under enactments such as the Offences Against the Person Act 1861 and the Criminal Damage Act 1971. Although the criminal law is primarily punitive in its approach to dealing with offenders, it is possible for the courts to grant compensation as an alternative to a fine and this may prove an easier course of redress than pursuing an action through the civil courts. Civil action remains an option though in any case of trespass to the person or trespass to property.

The provisions of the common law are not the only powers available to members of the general public and the Police and Criminal Evidence Act 1984 provides for citizen's arrests in cases involving any 'arrestable offence'. This is defined as being any offence where the penalty is fixed by law,[11] where the penalty may be imprisonment for 5 years or more on first conviction or where the offence is included on a list of specified statutes and sections. If any person sees an 'arrestable offence' being committed then they have a power to arrest the offender. This is also the case where they know that an 'arrestable offence' has been committed and they reasonably suspect someone of committing it. Offences for which this general power to detain is applicable include criminal damage, theft, assaults occasioning actual bodily harm as well as (a) and (b) above. Where someone other than a police officer effects an arrest under these powers they should hand over their prisoner as soon as practicable to a police officer. The use of any excessive force to make an arrest may in itself be a criminal offence so care should be exercised before any untrained person effects an arrest and the power should only be used in circumstances where the police are unlikely to arrive in sufficient time to deal with the matter themselves, or where the offender may escape.

1   Footpaths, bridle-ways and other highways and roads only offer a limited right of access; i.e., to pass and re-pass. There is no right to protest on any such highway.
2   The peace is the normal state of society and a breach of the peace occurs when harm is done to a person, or in his presence to his property, or a person is in fear of such harm.
3   This power is not restricted to the police.

158   PROTESTS AND PROTESTORS

4   Punishable by up to 10 years' imprisonment.
5   Punishable by up to 5 years' imprisonment.
6   Up to 3 years' imprisonment.
7   Up to 6 months' imprisonment and a £5000 fine.
8   Once again a maximum of 6 months' imprisonment and a £5000 fine.
9   Six months and a fine of £5000.
10 (f) requires a warning to be given before an arrest may be made.
11 i.e. murder.

QUARRIES AND MINES

See also Children; Nuisances

Accidents at old quarry sites still occur every year and the dangers that these areas hold for inquisitive children and the unwary have led to legislation that seeks to identify who has responsibility for their security. The Mines and Quarries Act 1954 places a duty on quarry owners to make adequate provision to comply with its various controls, which include the fencing of abandoned and disused mines and quarries.[1] The Act identifies as being a statutory nuisance:

(a) any shaft or the outlet of a mine[2] which has not been worked for a period of 12 months, the surface entrance of which is not provided with a properly maintained enclosure, barrier, plug or other device to prevent any person accidentally falling down the shaft;

(b) any shaft or outlet of a mine[3] that is not provided with a properly maintained enclosure, barrier, plug or other device and, by reason of its accessibility from a highway or public place, constitutes a danger to members of the public; and

(c) any quarry[4] which –

   (i) is not provided with an efficient and properly maintained barrier so designed and constructed as to prevent any person from accidentally falling into the quarry, and

   (ii) by reason of its accessibility from a highway or place of public resort constitutes a danger to members of the public.

Highways include footpaths and bridle-ways as well as carriageways. Where a local authority or some person other than the owner incurs any expense in meeting these safety requirements, the Act allows the recovery of those costs from the owner.

The unauthorised removal of warning notices is a criminal offence.

1 The Quarries Regulations 1999 similarly requires operators of quarries to ensure that, where appropriate, a barrier suitable for the purpose of discouraging trespass is placed around the boundary of a quarry and is properly maintained.
2 But does not include mines (other than those for coal, stratified ironstone, shale or fireclay) that have not been worked since August 1872.
3 Includes mines that have not been worked since 1872.
4 Whether in the course of being worked or not.

RABBITS

See also Coursing; Cruelty to Animals; Game Licences; Game Rights; Hares; Killing Birds and Animals; Poaching; Traps and Snares

As with some other pest species, the Ministry of Agriculture, Fisheries and Food may under powers granted by the Agriculture Act 1947 require occupiers of land to control the rabbit populations by killing or capturing them, reducing their breeding sites or by taking whatever steps are necessary to prevent their spread to adjoining land. Rabbit Clearance Orders made under the Pests Act 1954 also empowers the Minister to designate areas from which wild rabbits are to be eliminated and these require that occupiers of land falling within any specified area take such steps as are necessary to kill the rabbits or, where that is not reasonably practicable, prevent them from causing any damage.

The need for crop protection and the responsibilities of occupiers is also reflected in the Ground Game Acts of 1880 and 1906. These Acts allow for occupiers to kill and take rabbits regardless of any other person's right to take game on the same land. Occupiers and authorised persons may, therefore, legally kill rabbits on their land even where the lease specifically reserves such rights for another. This concurrent right may be exercised through the use of any method of control although the use of a firearm is restricted to daylight hours unless the owner of the game rights has given their written permission.

Eradication methods may include traps and snares,[1] nets, poisoned seed or grain and authorised poisonous gas.[2] Myxomatosis is a particularly unpleasant, man-made and contagious disease that has had a dramatic effect on rabbit populations. So effective is this disease at rabbit clearance that restrictions were introduced in 1954[3] prohibiting the use of infected rabbits as a means of spreading the disease to unaffected parts of the country. Where spring traps are legally used they must be checked at least once during daylight hours to reduce the possibility of any cruelty being caused.

As wild animals, rabbits are also subject to the general protection offered by the Wildlife and Countryside Act 1981 and the Wildlife (Northern Ireland) Order 1985 that both restrict the means by which wild animals may be killed or captured. It is not permissible to use bows, crossbows, explosives[4] or live decoys, although exceptions may occur where the act is licensed for scientific purposes or for the protection of crops or growing timber.

In addition to their status as pests, rabbits are also considered to be a quarry species and fall under the provisions of the Night Poaching Acts 1828 and 1844, the Game Act 1831 and the Poaching Prevention Act 1862. Game licences are required to kill, take or pursue rabbits unless an exception applies.

The Wild Mammals (Protection) Act 1996, in the case of a wild rabbit, and the Protection of Animals Act 1911, in the case of any captive rabbit, offer protection from cruel treatment. The 1996 Act does not apply to anything done as an act of mercy or in the course of lawful shooting, hunting, coursing or pest control and the 1911 Act similarly excludes acts done in the coursing or hunting of any captive animal.

---

1   Spring traps may be used provided that they are placed within a rabbit hole (Pests Act 1954).

2   Poisoned seed or grain is permitted under the Protection of Animals Act 1911 for the destruction of insects and other invertebrates, rats, mice or small ground vermin where it is in the interests of public health or agriculture subject to all reasonable steps being taken to prevent injury to domestic animals and wild birds.

3   The Pests Act 1954.

4   Other than ammunition for firearms.

RABIES

Fear of the virulent disease of rabies spreading across Europe to these shores motivated the quarantine laws that currently impose severe restrictions on the importation of animals into this country. The validity of the original fear has been increasingly argued against in recent years and the open border approach of the European Union has brought the whole policy of quarantine into question. As a result, the Government has now announced a 'passports for pets' scheme involving an immunisation process combined with electronic tagging which it is hoped will ease the passage of animals into the UK. This is very new and the reality is that the current controls will remain in place for the majority of importees for some time to come.

If it is suspected that the infection has appeared in any area the Minister for Agriculture, Fisheries and Food has extensive powers under the Animal Health Act 1981 and the Rabies (Importation of Dogs, Cats and other Mammals) Order 1974 to act to prevent its spread. These powers may be as dramatic as requiring the mass destruction of every fox and other wild mammal within a specified area. While such a Destruction Order does not extend to include the killing of captive or domesticated animals it will require them to be kept under close control and domestic dogs may have to muzzled. Any failure to comply with an Order is an offence and may lead to any unmuzzled dog being destroyed.

The current legislation makes it an offence to land an animal into the UK from any other place with the exception of Northern Ireland, the Republic of Ireland, the Channel Islands or the Isle of Man, each of which have similar restrictions and procedures. An animal may only be brought into this country on a licence issued by the Ministry and is subject to the primary condition that the animal is immediately detained and isolated in suitable quarantine kennels for a minimum period of 6 months.[1] Any person found contravening this condition, or believed to have contravened it, is guilty of an offence[2] and liable to arrest by a police officer. The animal may be seized and destroyed.

1   At the owner's expense.
2   Punishable by a maximum fine of £5000.

RIFLES

See also Air Weapons; Deer; Firearms; Northern Ireland; Protests and Protestors; Shotguns

Rifles[1] are firearms for the purposes of the Firearms Acts 1968 to 1997.[2] Defined as 'lethal barrelled weapons', possession generally requires that a Section 1 Firearms Certificate has been issued by the local police in respect of that particular rifle. Certificates are only issued by the police where they are satisfied that the applicant can be permitted to own the firearm, and any ammunition, without danger to the public or to the peace. An interview and examination of security arrangements is likely to follow any application, to ensure that the details provided are accurate and that adequate measures have been taken to store the rifle in such a way as to minimise the risk of theft. Applicants are also required to provide photographs and sponsors to countersign[3] the application certifying that they know of no reason why the applicant should not be granted a certificate. The police may also access an applicant's medical records. Applicants must also provide a good reason for wanting the firearm and that reason must be applicable to the particular class or type of firearm applied for. The place where the weapon is to be used is also likely to be visited and inspected to ensure its suitability for that firearm's use.

If issued, a certificate will identify the rifle that may be possessed and the maximum amount of ammunition that may be kept at any one time. Other conditions may include specific security or territorial conditions[4] imposed by the police. Certificates are renewable every five years and similar procedures will apply on each renewal. Possession of a certificate is a necessary prerequisite for the purchase of a rifle and its details will be recorded on the certificate. Any other sales or transfers will also be recorded. Prior to the purchase or acquisition of any other rifles the certificate holder must obtain police approval. Exceptions to the general requirement that a certificate is needed for the possession of a rifle include any person:

(a) carrying a firearm or ammunition belonging to a certificate holder as a gun bearer. This requires the bearer to act under instruction from the certificate holder and for the rifle to be used only by the certificate holder for sporting purposes;

(b) of or over the age of 17 years, borrowing a rifle from the occupier of private premises. This exception requires that the gun is used only on those premises and in the presence of the occupier or their employee. Any conditions on the certificate must still be complied with, however, the borrower may purchase ammunition for use with the rife at that time. This is often referred to as an estate rifle;

(c) using a miniature rifle[5] at a miniature rifle range or gallery. This will include the type of shooting gallery that may be found at country fairs.

In addition to the requirement of certification, the law also limits possession by setting minimum ages at which rifles may be owned or possessed. No person under the age of 17 years may purchase or hire any firearm or ammunition although they may have one in their possession and may acquire one by way of a gift. Under the age of 14 years a person must not have in his possession any section 1 rifle or ammunition but this will not apply to any period when the young person is:

(a) acting as a bearer for sporting purposes;
(b) at a miniature rifle range;
(c) a member of an approved rifle club when engaged as a member and in connection with target shooting.

It is a criminal offence for any person of any age to have a loaded rifle in a public place[6] without some lawful authority or reasonable excuse.

Foreign visitors who wish to shoot in this country require the prior permission of the police to possess any firearm. A sponsor who is resident in this country must make an application on their behalf for a visitor's permit and sponsors may either act as individuals or as the representatives of shooting syndicates, estates or national shooting organisations. The grant of a visitor's permit is likely to be subject to the sort of conditions imposed on domestic certificates and will include, where appropriate, the possession of a valid European Firearms Pass.

When not in use rifles should be stored securely. If being transported reasonable measures must be taken to reduce the risk of theft, and if stored in a vehicle that is to be left unattended this should include concealment and perhaps the removal of important components such as the trigger mechanism. Generally the courts have accepted a lesser degree of security for firearms in vehicles than would be required at the place where it is normally kept.

Police officers are provided with sufficient powers under the legislation to enforce the law. This includes a power to seize and inspect any firearm found in a public place[6] in order to ascertain its type. Once the officer has ascertained that it is of a type requiring a certificate he may demand that the certificate is produced to him there and then. While the current laws do not specifically require that a rifle owner carry their certificate, if the document is not produced the police officer is empowered to seize it. Police officers also have extensive powers of arrest where they believe a firearm is possessed without a certificate or is being used illegally.

---

1 The legality of using different calibres for different species of deer is detailed on pp.50–3.
2 The Firearms Order (Northern Ireland) 1985 imposes slightly different licensing conditions within the area of the Royal Ulster Constabulary.
3 Currently two countersignatories are required for firearms of this category.
4 Territorial conditions relate to the land where the rifle is to be used and the police may wish to check that this land is suitable for a rifle of the type being applied for. Police forces in England and Wales require that the land is named and suitable, while in Northern Ireland the police require that the land is owned or leased to the applicant.
5 i.e. with a barrel diameter not exceeding .23 inch calibre.
6 Defined as a place where members of the public have access whether on payment or otherwise.
7 Or in a private place where the officer believes that the holder of the firearm is either a trespasser or is committing or about to commit an indictable offence or intends to resist or prevent the arrest of another.

RIVERS, STREAMS AND OTHER WATERCOURSES

See also Access – A Right to Roam; Bridle-ways; Fish and Fishing; Footpaths; Nuisances; Pollution; Trespass

Non-tidal rivers and streams are private property offering no general right of access, navigation or fishing unless specifically permitted by the landowner or in the few cases where a footpath or bridle-way runs alongside. Their maintenance, however, and of all watercourses including all rivers, streams, ditches, drains, cuts, culverts, dikes, sluices and passages through which water flows falls under the remit of the Environment Agency, which enforces the various Acts dealing with potential pollution and, together with internal drainage boards and local authorities, ensures that the flow of water is maintained.

Under the Public Health Act 1936 it is a statutory nuisance for any:

(a) pond, pool, ditch, gutter or watercourse to be so foul or in such a state as to be prejudicial to health, or to be a nuisance;

(b) part of a watercourse[1] to be so choked or silted up as to obstruct or impede the proper flow of water as to be a nuisance or to give rise to conditions prejudicial to health.

A healthy flow of water is also protected by the Water Resources Act 1991. This prohibits:

(a) any dredging operation from removing deposits from a river bed and then allowing those deposits to be carried away suspended in the waters;

(b) any person, without consent,[2] causing or permitting a substantial amount of vegetation to be cut or uprooted in any inland freshwater or to be cut or uprooted so near to one that it falls into it, without taking reasonable steps to remove the vegetation.

Other potential obstructions that also require prior consent include the erection of any mill dam, weir or other like obstruction.[3] Where any ordinary watercourse[4] is in such a condition that the proper flow of water is impeded[5] the drainage board[6] or local authority may, by a notice served on:

(a) any person having control;

(b) any owner or occupier of the adjoining land; or

(c) the person whose act or default has impeded the water flow;

require that person to remedy the problem. Where necessary the board or authority may carry out the work and recover their costs through the courts.

Pollution of watercourses through silage or slurry[7] created during farming operations is controlled by the Control of Pollution (Silage, Slurry and Agricultural Fuel Oil) Regulations 1991. These require that silage and slurry are kept properly stored in approved silos or slurry storage tanks which are sited at least 10m away from any inland water that the silage or slurry could enter if it were to escape.

The abstraction of water from any river or stream requires a licence and is subject to conditions imposed by the Water Resources Act 1991.

1 Not being a part ordinarily navigated by vessels employed in the carriage of goods by water.
2 Consent can only be provided by the Environment Agency.
3 The Land Drainage Act 1991.
4 Defined as a watercourse that does not form part of a main river.
5 Unless the condition is attributable to subsidence due to mining operations.
6 This may be the Environment Agency.
7 This is the excreta of livestock kept in any yard or building and may be combined with bedding, rainwater or washes from a building or yard.

SALMON AND TROUT

See also Fish and Fishing; Poaching; Theft

Coarse fishing, rights and licences are dealt with elsewhere but the separate status of salmon and trout as a valuable quarry species is recognised by specific provisions within the general fishing laws. The Salmon and Freshwater Fisheries Act 1975[1] restricts the methods by which salmon[2] and trout[3] may be caught by prohibiting the use of firearms, otter laths, jacks, wires, snares, crosslines, setlines, spears, gaffs,[4] stroke-hauls, snatches and lights.[5] The use of any of these is a criminal offence unless used for the purpose of developing or preserving a private fishery where the prior permission of the National Rivers Authority[6] has been granted. Other offences under this Act include:

(a) using any fish roe or buying, selling, exposing for sale or possessing any roe of salmon or trout for the purpose of fishing for salmon or trout;

(b) knowingly taking, killing, injuring or attempting to take, kill or injure any salmon or trout which is unclean[7] or immature;[8]

(c) buying, selling, exposing for sale or possessing any salmon or trout which is unclean or immature or any part of such a fish;[9]

(d) wilfully disturbing any spawn or spawning fish or any bed, bank or shallow on which any spawn or spawning fish may be, except in the exercise of a legal right to take materials from any waters;[10]

(e) shooting or working any seine or draft net for salmon or migratory trout across more than three-quarters of the width of the waters;

(f) taking or attempting to take salmon or migratory trout with any net[11] that has a mesh of less dimension than 2 inches (5cm) in extension from knot to knot,[12] or 8 inches (20cm) measured round each mesh when wet;[13]

(g) knowingly permitting to flow or putting or knowingly permitting to be put into any waters containing fish, any liquid or solid matter to such an extent as to cause the waters to be poisonous or injurious to fish or to the spawning grounds or food of fish;[14]

(h) using explosive, poisonous or noxious substances or electrical devices unless used for scientific purposes and with the written permission of the National Rivers Authority;

(i) placing or using an unauthorised fixed engine[15] in any inland or tidal waters which are within the area of any water authority;[16]

(j) the use of an unauthorised fishing weir[17] for the purpose of taking salmon or migratory trout. Where a fishing weir extends more than halfway across a river it may not be used to take salmon or migratory trout unless it has in it a free gap or opening situated in the deepest part of the river. Such openings must be between 3 and 40ft (1 and 12m) wide with the natural riverbed forming their bottom and must be parallel to the direction of the stream;

(k) the use of an unauthorised fishing mill dam[18] for the purpose of taking salmon or migratory trout unless it has attached to it an approved and maintained fish pass with a constant flow of water passing through it as will enable salmon and migratory trout to pass;

(l) wilfully altering or injuring a fish pass or doing any act whereby salmon or trout are obstructed in using a fish pass, or whereby a fish pass is rendered less efficient;

(m) the taking or killing,[19] scaring or disturbing of any salmon or trout at any place 50 yards (46m) above or 100 yards (91m) below any artificial or natural dam or obstruction or within such distance as may be prescribed by a bye-law, or in any artificial channel connected with a dam or obstruction;

(n) the taking or killing,[20] scaring or disturbing of any salmon or trout in any waters under or adjacent to any mill, or in the head or tail race of any mill, or in any waste race or pool communicating with any mill;[21]

(o) fishing for, taking, killing or attempting to fish, take or kill any salmon during the annual close season or weekly close time;

(p) fishing for, taking, killing or attempting to fish, take or kill any trout during the annual close season or weekly close time;

(q) fishing for, taking, killing or attempting to fish, take or kill any rainbow trout in any inland water during the annual close season;[22]

(r) fishing without a licence or in contravention of the conditions of a licence.

The taking of salmon or trout without any legal right or permission is specifically included as theft under the Schedules to the Theft Act 1968.

The 1975 Act also identifies the general seasons for salmon and trout in England and Wales, although these are subject to changes imposed by bye-laws aimed at protecting local stocks. As a result, slightly different close seasons will apply to different areas and anglers will need to note changes within their areas in order to avoid committing offences.[23] Minimum close seasons and weekly close times are set as below:

Close season	Minimum period
Salmon	153 days [24]
Salmon with rod and line	92 days
Trout close season	181 days
Trout with rod and line	153 days
Rainbow Trout [25]	93 days
Salmon/Trout with putts and putchers	242 days

Weekly close time	Minimum period
Salmon	42 hours
Trout	42 hours

Taking any salmon or trout within the close periods is a criminal offence. However, no offence will be committed if the actions are done for the purpose of the artificial propagation of fish or for some scientific purpose provided the written permission of the National Rivers Authority has first been obtained.

Scottish legislation includes many local Act and a history of piecemeal legislation that, while initially appearing to be a mish mash of rules and regulations, actually results in much the same control as that effected by the bye-laws under the 1975 Act. Once again some different controls will apply to different areas in order to meet local needs.[26] Many of the offences under the Salmon and Freshwater Fisheries Act 1975 are repeated under the Salmon and Freshwater Fisheries (Protection) (Scotland) Act 1951,[27] which, together with other Scottish legislation,[28] generally prohibits:

(a) fishing for or taking salmon or sea trout between midnight on a Saturday and midnight on a Sunday;

(b) fishing for or taking salmon or sea trout between 6 p.m. Friday and 6 a.m. the following Monday of any week other than by rod or line;

(c) fishing for salmon or sea trout in any inland waters other than by rod or line or, in some instances, coble and net;

(d) fishing for salmon or sea trout in any salmon fishery district other than inland waters other than by rod or line, coble and net, bag net, fly net or stake net;

(e) the taking of dead salmon or sea trout from rivers or waters;[29]

(f) the illegal possession of any salmon or sea trout;

(g) the illegal possession of any instrument, explosive, poison or noxious substance for the taking of any salmon or sea trout;

(h) the use of nets for salmon with a mesh of less than 3.5 inches (9cm);

(i) the use of nets at waterfalls and mill dams,

(j) fishing for salmon at any fish pass;

(k) the purchase or sale of trout less than 8 inches (20cm) in length.[30]

(l) fishing during the weekly or annual close seasons.[31]

In Scotland, unlike the remainder of the UK, theft is a common law crime that does not include the taking of fish. However, the Salmon and Freshwater Fisheries (Protection) (Scotland) Act 1951 specifically includes an offence whereby any person[32] who, without any legal right or the written authority of the person with the legal right, fishes for or takes any salmon[33] in any waters is liable. Fishing for salmon or sea trout by rod and line does not require a licence in Scotland. However, there is no public right to fish for salmon in tidal waters around the Scottish coastline.

The Salmon Act 1986 applies to the whole of the UK and provides powers for the licensing of salmon dealers. This Act also creates an offence of handling salmon in suspicious circumstances, which may be committed by any person who believes[34] that the salmon has been killed or taken in the course of the commission of an offence. It is also an offence to receive the salmon or undertake or assist in its retention, removal or disposal or to arrange to do so.[35]

---

1   The Salmon and Freshwater Fisheries (Protection) (Scotland) Act 1951 generally applies to Scotland although the 1975 Act will apply to the border stretches of the Esk and the Solway Firth.

2   Defined as all fish of the salmon species and includes any part of a salmon.

3   Defined as any fish of the salmon family commonly known as trout, including migratory trout and char, and includes any part of a trout.

4   This does not include a plain metal hook used as an auxiliary to angling with a rod and line.

5   For the definitions of these terms see pp.72–5.

6   Department of Agriculture and Fisheries for Scotland although this function will now be taken by a new department under the Scottish Executive.

7   This means that the fish is about to spawn or has recently spawned and has not yet recovered.

8   In relation to salmon, this means that the salmon is of a length of less than 12 inches (30cm) measured from the tip of the snout to the fork or cleft of the tail. A trout is immature if the fish is of a length less than that prescribed by the byelaws for the water in which it is taken.

9   (b) and (c) do not apply to any person who takes a fish accidentally and then returns it to the water with the least possible injury.

10 (a),(b), (c) and (d) are not offences where the acts take place for the purpose of the artificial propagation of salmon, trout or freshwater fish or for some scientific purpose or for the preservation and development of a private fishery and with the permission of the National Rivers Authority.

11 This does not include a landing net used as an auxiliary to fishing with rod and line.

12 The measurement to be made on each side of the square.

13 This offence is not committed where bye-laws permit the use of smaller nets but will include circumstances where two nets are used, one behind the other with the practical effect of diminishing the mesh of the nets so used.

14 No offence is committed where the act is done in the exercise of a legal right where the best practical means has been used, within a reasonable cost, to prevent such matter doing any injury.

15 Includes a stake net, bag net, putt or putcher, any fixed implement or engine for taking fish, any net secured by anchors (acting as more than a brake), any net or other implement fixed to the soil and any net placed or suspended in any inland or tidal waters unattended by the owner.

16 Does not include a fixed engine certified under the Salmon Fishery Act 1865 to be a privileged fixed engine or a fixed engine which was in use during the season of 1861 in pursuance of an ancient right, or a fixed engine authorised by bye-laws or in accordance with a general authorisation given by the Minister or Secretary of State.

17 A fishing weir is defined as any erection, structure or obstruction to the soil, either temporary or permanently, across or partly across a river or branch of a river, and used for the exclusive purpose of taking fish.

18 This means a dam used or intended to be used for the taking of fish and partly for the purpose of supplying water for milling or other purposes.

19 Other than with rod and line.

20 Other than with rod and line.

21 (m) and (n) do not apply to any legal fishing mill dam not having a crib, box or cruive or to any fishing box, coop, apparatus, net or mode of fishing in connection with and forming part of such a dam or obstruction for the purposes of fishing.

22 A general exception for (o), (p) and (q) occurs where the acts are done for the purpose of the artificial propagation of these fish, restocking or for some scientific purpose and with the permission of the National Rivers Authority or, in the case of rainbow trout, acts in connection with a several fishery (exclusive right) where salmon and trout are specially preserved.

23 The most recent bye-laws came into force on 15 April 1999 and can be obtained through the Environment Agency. The Fresh-Water Fisheries (Scotland) Act 1902 establishes the annual close season for brown trout in Scotland as being 7 October to 14 March inclusive. However, this does not apply to stocked waters and sea trout are regarded as salmon and fall under the salmon legislation.

24 A minimum of 168 days.

25 The annual close season for any rainbow trout for any waters is that fixed for those waters by bye-laws.

26 For example, Acts such as the Tweed Fisheries Act 1857 and the Solway Act 1804 apply rules to those rivers that may not apply elsewhere.

27 As amended by the Salmon Act 1996.

28 The Theft Act 1607, the Salmon Fisheries (Scotland) Act 1868, the Trout (Scotland) Act 1933, and the Freshwater and Salmon Fisheries (Scotland) Act 1976.

29 Includes the sea within 1 mile (1.6km) of the low tide mark. However, no offence is committed by water bailiffs, persons authorised by a fisheries board or any person with the right to fish.

30 The Trout (Scotland) Act 1933.

31 In Scotland the seasons are determined by the Salmon and Freshwater Fisheries (Protection) (Scotland) Act 1951. The weekly close time operates between midnight on a Saturday and midnight on a Sunday. The annual minimum is 168 days for salmon and generally operates between 1 November and 10 February inclusive. However, some rivers are controlled by local alternatives.

32 It is an aggravated offence liable to a higher penalty where two or more people act together to commit this offence.

33 This includes sea trout and the offence may be committed in any inland water on the sea up to one mile from the low water mark.

34 Or it would be reasonable for him to suspect that an offence has at any time been committed in relation to any salmon.

35 By or for the benefit of another.

SCOTLAND

See also Agencies; Badgers; birds and eggs; Bulls and Cattle; Crossbows and Archery; Cruelty to Animals; Damage; Dangerous and Destructive Animals; Deer; Diseases; Dogs; Firearms and Shooting; Fish and Fishing; Fly Tipping; Game Birds; Game Licences; Hares; Knives; Litter; Livestock; Noise; Plants and Flowers; Poaching; Pollution; Protected Animals; Protests and Protestors; Rabbits; Rabies; Salmon and Trout; Straying; Traps and Snares; Trespass

The law in Scotland is a mix of common and statute law and influenced by both Anglo-American and Franco-Germanic concepts of law. The common law dates back to early history and is founded on local traditions and accepted practices that need to be identified and clarified by the courts. Statute laws are those written by Parliament and interpreted by the courts.

While statute law has largely replaced the older rules and traditions accepted in countryside matters, police powers in Scotland still depend on the common law.[1] Statutes specify the powers that they grant. The common law power of arrest justifies a police officer arresting any person:

(a) seen to be committing a common law crime;

(b) seen to be running from the scene of such a crime and being pursued by others;

(c) accused by a credible witness of having committed a common law crime; or

(d) who is threatening danger to the public.

Crimes at common law relevant to the countryside include breach of the peace, mobbing and rioting, theft, damage,[2] and the culpable and reckless discharge of a firearm. Statute law appears in two forms: those particular to Scotland and those that apply generally within the UK. While Acts of general application are in the majority, this is unlikely to continue to be the case following the transfer of legislative powers to the new Scottish Assembly. Proposals already include radical changes to the land ownership system that has remained feudal in its approach, increased access to the countryside with a new Scottish Access Code, a revision of the law concerning SSSIs and the introduction of legislation to allow the creation of national parks.

Acts that are currently applicable to countryside issues include:

Scotland only

- The Game (Scotland) Act 1772 – offences relating to the killing or taking of game during the close seasons.
- The Game (Scotland) Act 1832 – reflects the Game Act 1831 in making out a variety of daytime poaching offences.
- The Hares (Scotland) Act 1848 – similar provisions to those in the corresponding Hares Act 1848 applicable in England, Wales and Northern Ireland.
- The Tweed Fishery Acts 1857 and 1859 – fishing controls specific to the River Tweed.
- The Trespass (Scotland) Act 1865 – offences of trespass.
- The Freshwater Fisheries (Scotland) Act 1902 – sets the close season for brown trout in waters other than stocked waters.
- The Protection of Animals (Scotland) Act 1912 – cruelty to animals legislation mirroring that of 1911 introduced into the rest of the UK.[3]
- The Trout (Scotland) Act 1933 – restricts the sale of small trout.
- The Agriculture (Scotland) Act 1948 – covers traps and snares.
- The Salmon and Freshwater Fisheries (Protection) (Scotland) Act 1951 – creates poaching offences and controls the methods of killing fish.
- The Deer (Scotland) Act 1959 – makes out an offence of poaching in relation to deer.
- The Civic Government (Scotland) Act 1982 – offence of possessing a firearm in a public place while drunk. This Act also provides the police with specific

powers of search where they suspect that stolen property that a person is in possession of stolen property.

- The Roads (Scotland) Act 1984 – deals with straying animals.
- The Deer (Close Seasons) (Scotland) Order 1984 – sets close seasons.
- The Deer (Firearms, etc.) (Scotland) Order 1985 – sets minimum firearm sizes for the killing of deer, controls use of light intensifying and heat sensitive sights.
- The Criminal Law (Consolidation) (Scotland) Act 1995 – deals with knives and other offensive weapons.
- The Deer (Scotland) Act 1996 – specifies close seasons and places controls on the poaching of deer, night shooting and illegal possession of venison.

UK

- The Night Poaching Act 1828 – concerned with poaching during the hours of darkness.
- The Game Licences Act 1860 – makes out the requirement for licences.
- The Poaching Prevention Act 1862 – grants police powers.
- The Ground Game Act 1880 – deals with an occupier's right to take hares and rabbits.
- The Dogs (Protection of Livestock) Act 1953 – details offences of sheep worrying.
- The Firearms Acts 1968 to 1997 – general firearms controls.
- The Control of Pollution Act 1974 – deals with pollution, including noise.
- The Dangerous Wild Animals Act 1976 – controls the keeping of certain animals.
- The Refuse Disposal (Amenity) Act 1978 – concerned with the abandonment of cars and litter.
- The Wildlife and Countryside Act 1981 – applies to Scotland, England and Wales.
- The Animal Health Act 1981 – deals with notifiable diseases.
- The Salmon Act 1986 – licensing and dealing controls applicable to Scotland.
- The Public Order Act 1986 – deals with trespass and other offences leading to disorder.
- The Crossbows Act 1987 – age limitations on crossbow possession.
- The Environmental Protection Act 1990 – includes sections regarding litter and the formation of Scottish Natural Heritage and the Scottish Environmental Protection Agency.
- The Protection of Badgers Act 1992 – restrictions on the killing and taking of badgers.

- The Control of Dogs Order 1992 – requires dogs to wear collars on any highway.
- The Criminal Justice and Public Order Act 1994 – trespass offences.

Wherever possible Scottish legislative controls have been identified where they differ from other nations within this book.

1   See pp.148–9 for powers available to police officers in other jurisdictions.
2   Offences may be committed at both common and statute law under the Criminal Law (Consolidation) (Scotland) Act 1995.
3   As amended by the Protection of Animals (Amendment) Act 1988.

SHOTGUNS

See also Clay Target Shooting; Deer; Firearms and Shooting; Killing Birds and Animals; Protests and Protestors; Rifles

With over one million shotguns[1] in the hands of 638 000 certificate holders in England and Wales alone, shotgun-based sports and pastimes remain popular despite the political pressures of recent years.[2] Once regarded very much as tools of the countryside, shotguns are defined by the Firearms Act 1968[3] as including any smooth bore gun other than an air weapon, which:

(a) has a barrel not less than 24 inches (61cm) in length or with a bore not exceeding 2 inches (5cm) in diameter;
(b) either has no magazine or has a non-detachable magazine incapable of holding more than two cartridges; and
(c) which is not a revolver gun.

Ownership under the Act requires the prior consent of the chief officer of police for an area and certificates should be issued on application, reflecting the different status accorded these weapons since the introduction of firearms control in the 1920s. Anyone who wishes to own a shotgun must first apply to the local police force by completing an application form and sending the appropriate fee and four recent photographs. The form requires the signature of one person of standing who has personally known the applicant for at least two years and, as with passports, one photograph must also be countersigned as being of a good likeness. Unlike the more onerous conditions to which rifle applications are now subjected, the police may only refuse to grant[4] a shotgun certificate if they are satisfied that the applicant:

(a) cannot be permitted to possess a shotgun without danger to the public safety or the peace, or is of unsound mind or intemperate habits;[5]

(b) is prohibited by the Firearms Act 1968 from owning or possessing a shotgun;[6]

(c) the applicant does not have a good reason for possessing, purchasing or acquiring one.

While an applicant for a rifle certificate is required to demonstrate a good reason for their application, shotgun certificate applicants have no such responsibility and the onus lies on the police to show that there exists no good reason or that the applicant is unfit. The legislation specifically provides that any sporting, competition or vermin control purpose is sufficient cause on which to base an application for a shotgun certificate. A desire for mere possession should be sufficient as the Act also states that an application shall not be refused merely because the applicant intends neither to use the gun himself nor lend it for anyone else to use. Once granted a shotgun certificate lasts for 5 years before renewal is necessary and the process for renewal should be similar to that for an initial grant.

Following the passing of the Firearms Act 1988 and the Firearms Rules 1989 there is now a general safekeeping requirement similar to that imposed on rifles. This demands that shotguns are stored securely so as to prevent, as far as reasonably practicable, any unauthorised access. Storage should ideally be in a locked gun cabinet or other secure cabinet, although the removal and secure storage of firing mechanisms may be an acceptable alternative.[7] A lesser degree of security is acceptable for guns in transit, although when in cars they should be concealed and the vehicle locked. There is no safekeeping requirement in respect of shotgun cartridges.

Whereas the acquisition of a rifle must be preceded by the placing of police authority on to the acquirer's certificate, the acquisition of a shotgun need only be recorded on to a shotgun certificate after the transaction has taken place and where possession is expected to exceed 72 hours. Purchases of shotguns together with details of any sales or transfer of a shotgun by way of hire, loan or gift must be notified to the police force that granted the licence by recorded delivery or registered post and within 7 days of the transaction.

There is no legal restriction on the number of shotguns or cartridges that may be possessed. While the legislation requires that purchasers of cartridges should produce their shotgun certificate at the point of sale, there is no legal requirement for any certification merely for the possession of shotgun cartridges acquired by other means.

The Firearms Acts make it an offence for any person to:

(a) possess of a shotgun without a certificate,
(b) fail to comply with any condition on the certificate,[8]
(c) sell or transfer a shotgun to a non-certificate holder;
(d) shorten a shotgun barrel to less than 24 inches (60cm); or
(e) fail to notify the sale or transfer of any shotgun within 7 days.

No one under the age of 17 years may purchase a shotgun and any person under 15 years may only have an assembled shotgun with him while supervised by someone aged 21 or where the gun is so covered that it cannot be fired.[9] Supervised possession will still require the young person to hold a certificate unless the weapon is being used at an approved clay target shooting ground. Certificates may currently be granted to an applicant of any age subject to the basic requirement that the countersignatory must have known them for at least 2 years.

Exceptions to a general requirement for possession to be authorised by a shotgun licence include auctioneers, carriers and people acting as a gun bearer for a certificate holder who is using the shotgun for sporting purposes. A shotgun may also be borrowed from the occupier of private premises and used on those premises in the occupier's presence without the need for a certificate.[10]

Visitor's permits may be granted to foreign visitors from within the European Union[11] and elsewhere. Certificates and permits only authorise possession and the use made of a shotgun should also comply with those laws relating to the killing or taking of wild animals, possession in public places, firing near highways and trespass dealt with in other sections. Police officers have powers to demand that a shotgun is handed to them for the purposes of inspection and, although carrying a certificate is not mandatory under the 1968 Act, officers are empowered to require its production. Any failure to produce the certificate may lead to the shotgun being confiscated until legal possession can be established.

1. 1 335 000 – Firearms Statistics for England and Wales 1996.
2. Restrictions followed the massacres at Hungerford and Dunblane, although neither of these involved the use of shotguns.
3. This Act applies in England, Wales and Scotland. Alternative licensing arrangements operate in Northern Ireland under the Firearms Order (Northern Ireland) 1985. This subordinate legislation provides for one certificate covering all types of firearms.
4. Or after 5 years renew.
5. This may include evidence of drug or alcohol abuse, anti-social behaviour as well as any other disturbing tendency.
6. i.e. following a conviction for an offence resulting in a term of imprisonment.
7. 'Firearms Law: Guidance to the Police.' HMSO Books, 1989.
8. Only a few statutory conditions may be imposed such as a requirement to notify the police on change of address and reporting the loss or theft of any shotgun.
9. It is an offence for a person to make a gift of a shotgun or ammunition for a shotgun to a person under the age of 15.
10. The lender must hold a certificate.
11. Provided that they hold a valid European Firearms Pass.

STRAYING

See also Common Land; Dogs; Highways and Roads

The Highways Act 1980 states that if any horses,[1] cattle, sheep, goats or pigs are at any time found straying or lying on or at the side of a highway, their keeper will be guilty of an offence.[2] For the purposes of this offence a highway will include a footpath or bridle-way but does not apply to any part of a highway passing over any common, waste or unenclosed land and no offence will be committed where there is a right of pasture at the side of any highway, footpath or bridle-way. If animals are found straying in contravention of this section they may be removed and any costs involved recovered from their owner. In Scotland the Roads (Scotland) Act 1984 provides for a similar offence if any animal[3] is left on or allowed to stray on any road, other than a road running through unenclosed countryside.[4]

Straying dogs are also a hazard near roads and any dog permitted to be in a highway needs to have a collar containing details of their owner.[5] This does not apply, however, to packs of hounds, dogs being used for sporting purposes, dogs driving cattle, police dogs and guide dogs for the blind. Any dog found without a collar may be treated as a stray and if a police officer has reason to believe that any dog found on a highway or in any public place is a stray dog then he may seize it and retain the animal until its owner has claimed it. As with other straying animals, any costs involved may be recovered from the animal's owner.[6]

1   The term includes any pony, ass or mule.
2   This offence is punishable by a fine of up to £2500.
3   This term is undefined under this enactment.
4   It is a defence to show that all reasonable steps were taken to prevent the animal from straying.
5   The Animal Health Act 1981.
6   The Dogs Act 1906. The Animals Act 1971 also imposes a civil liability on the owners of trespassing livestock for damage or loss caused.

THEFT

See also Damage; Fish and Fishing; Police; Salmon and Trout; Scotland

In Scotland theft is a common law crime involving the taking and appropriating of property without the consent of its rightful owner or other lawful authority. Across the remainder of the UK, theft is defined by the Theft Act 1968 as being the 'dishonest appropriation of property belonging to another with the intention to permanently deprive that other person of it'.

'Dishonest' is not defined by the Act, although it identifies actions that will not be considered to be dishonest as including:

(a) an appropriation of property where the person does so in the belief that he has a right in law to deprive the other of it;
(b) if he appropriates the property in the honest belief that he would have the owner's consent if that other had known of the circumstances;
(c) if he appropriates the property in the belief that the owner cannot be discovered by taking reasonable steps. This often applies where property is found which may have been lost or abandoned.

'Appropriation' is an assumption by any person of the rights of the owner of the property and this may include the taking away of any property or, in some cases, merely the use of someone else's property. 'Borrowing' may still amount to a theft if it is for a period or in such circumstances as to make it equivalent to an outright taking. 'Property' includes money and all other property but a person cannot steal land, or things forming part of land and severed from it except:

(a) when he is a trustee or personal representative, is authorised by power of attorney, is a liquidator of a company or otherwise to sell or dispose of land, and he appropriates the land or anything forming part of it by dealing with it in breach of the confidence placed in him; or
(b) when he is not in possession of the land, appropriates anything forming part of the land by severing it or causing it to be severed, or after it has been severed; or
(c) when, being in possession of the land under a tenancy, he appropriates the whole or part of any fixture or structure let to be used with the land.

Under the 1968 legislation, a person who picks[1] mushrooms[2] growing wild on any land, or who picks flowers, fruit or foliage from a plant[3] growing wild on any land does not steal what he picks unless he does it for reward or for sale or some other commercial purpose. Wild creatures, tamed or untamed, are regarded as property but a person cannot steal any wild creature not tamed or ordinarily kept in captivity[4] unless it has been reduced into captivity by another person[5] and possession of it has not since been lost or abandoned. For example a swarm of bees is not reduced into captivity until it is hived and can only be stolen after it has been hived. Tame, captive and domesticated animals will always be property and can be stolen or damaged.

From the offence of theft the legislation leads on to define other types of illegal appropriation. 'Burglary' is theft in circumstances where the thief has entered a building or part of a building as a trespasser. 'Robbery' involves theft accompanied by an assault while 'deception' involves theft achieved by some trick or lie. The Theft Act 1968 also deals with two instances where property may be illegally taken but the thief has no intention of keeping it. There have been cases where articles on display have been taken from places open to the public, but where the taker only intended to 'borrow' them for a temporary purpose. In such instances problems have arisen in subsequent proceedings as a charge of theft requires evidence of an intention to permanently deprive. To overcome such technical problems the Act creates an offence, where the public have access to a building in order to view the building or part of it,[6] or a collection[7] housed in it, for any person[8] to remove any article displayed or kept for display. This includes articles within the building or in its grounds.

Another circumstance where the lack of a permanent intention may create legal difficulty is that involving the taking of motor vehicles that is occasionally referred to as joy-riding. Under the Act, it is an offence for any person without having the consent of the owner or other lawful authority, to take any conveyance[9] for his own or another's use. This includes circumstances where, knowing that any conveyance has been so taken, a person drives it or allows himself to be carried in or on it. The penalties for offences under the Theft Act range between 14 years' imprisonment for an offence of burglary at a dwelling house to 6 months in the case of taking a conveyance and all are subject to arrest.

Fish stocks are also protected by the 1968 Act which makes it an offence[10] for any person to unlawfully take[11] or destroy, any fish in water which is private property or in which there is any private right of fishery.[12] There is also a power for any person to arrest someone they suspect, with reasonable cause, to be committing this offence. It is a slightly lesser matter[13] to fish by angling in the daytime and to unlawfully take, destroy or attempt to take or destroy any fish in water which is private property or in which there is any private right of fishery.

Courts have powers of forfeiture in respect of fishing equipment possessed at the time of the offence and for use in the taking or destroying of fish.

1 The term 'picking' does not include uprooting.
2 Includes any fungus.
3 Includes a shrub or tree.
4 Or the carcass of any such creature.
5 Or another person is in the course of reducing it into possession.
6 It is immaterial whether that access is limited to a particular period or occasion provided the taking occurs when the public had access.
7 Whether permanent or temporary.
8 Without some lawful authority.
9 i.e. any conveyance constructed or adapted for the carriage of a person or persons whether by land, water or air. It does not include a conveyance for use only under the control of someone not carried in or on it.
10 Punishable by imprisonment of up to 3 months and a fine of £1000.
11 Taking for the purposes of this offence does not require any intention to take any fish away. Keeping the fish in a keep net with the intention of returning it to the water is sufficient to complete the offence.
12 Rights are not easily obtained and long use of a stretch of water may still not be sufficient (*Hudson* v. *MacRae (1863)*). Similarly navigable, non-tidal rivers do not automatically provide a right to fish (*Smith* v. *Andrews (1891)*). Where land is leased, unless the right of fishing is expressly reserved, the right of fishery will pass to the tenant (*Jones* v. *Davies (1902)*).
13 Persons convicted of this offence are only liable to a fine of up to £200 and there is no accompanying power of arrest.

TOWN AND COUNTRY PLANNING

See also Clay Target Shooting; Conservation

The Town and Country Planning Act 1947 introduced a system of planning controls based on consultation with local planning authorities[1] that still offers extensive protection from inappropriate development and is now enshrined in the Town and Country Planning Act 1990.[2] The term 'development' is defined within this legislation as meaning the:

(a) carrying out of building,[3] engineering, mining[4] or other operations in, on, over or under land; or

(b) making of any material change in the use of any buildings or other land.

Unless falling into a category of exemption, all such development requires prior planning permission.[5]

The Act specifically excludes from its definition of 'development':

(a) maintenance, improvement or other alteration that affects only the interior of a building or does not materially affect its external appearance;

(b) work required for the maintenance or improvement of roads;

(c) the inspection, repairing or renewing of sewers, mains, pipes, cables or other apparatus;

(d) the use of any building or other land within the curtilage of a dwelling-house for any purpose incidental to the enjoyment of the dwelling-house;

(e) the use of any land for the purpose of agriculture or forestry and the use for either of these purposes of any building occupied with the land so used.

The deposit of refuse or waste materials on land is deemed to involve a material change of use.

Of the exclusions, (d) and (e) may be particularly controversial. The exception under (d) above generally removes the need for prior planning permission where some land use within the boundaries of a dwelling-house changes provided that the use is for any purpose incidental to the use of that dwelling. However this link must be a strong one and any reliance on this exception is likely to require some demonstration that its use is incidental to the use of the dwelling-house. For example, the simple storage of a caravan may not be sufficient.

Agricultural[6] and forestry purposes provide an exception that allows farmers and others to throw up almost any structure without having to seek planning permission, provided it is linked to their use of the land. Controversially this has seen the erection of dwellings that would otherwise have failed to gain planning permission.

Temporary changes of use that do not occur for more than 28 days[7] in each year do not require prior planning permission although this does not extend to the use of land as a caravan site or to motor sports or clay target shoots taking place within sites of special scientific interest.

Where required, planning permission is generally[8] granted by the local planning authority for an area following a formal application to develop some land. Permission may be granted unconditionally, or subject to such conditions as the planning authority thinks fit. Alternatively the authority may refuse the application in which case an appeals procedure lies to the Secretary of State. Once granted, planning permission may be revoked or modified by the authority concerned. Increasingly planning authorities are being required to consider the effects of development on the natural habitats that may be affected and it is often a condition of planning permission that steps are taken to reduce any environmental impact. With the adoption of European Directives concerned with habitat protection, it is increasingly likely that future developments will be restricted or refused purely on an environmental basis.

Earlier environment considerations saw the introduction of green belt policies that were initially adopted to reduce further encroachment by the London conurbation[9] and these were eventually adopted by the planning authorities of all the major towns and cities. Although the aim of such policies has been to provide a buffer zone there is no hard and fast rule on how local planning authorities should deal with such areas and their impact as been rather haphazard.

1   Unless the application fell into one of the many exceptions within the Act.
2   Town and Country Planning (Scotland) Act 1997.
3   This includes the demolition of buildings, rebuilding, structural alterations of or additions to buildings and other operations normally undertaken by a person carrying on business as a builder. A building is any structure or erection.
4   Includes the removal of material of any description from any mineral-working deposit, pulverised fuel ash deposit or other furnace ash or clinker or from a deposit of iron, steel or other metallic slags, and the extraction of minerals from a disused railway embankment.
5   In the case of buildings that are listed as being of some special historic or architectural interest other permissions may be required.
6   Agriculture includes horticulture, fruit growing, seed growing, dairy farming, the breeding and keeping of livestock (including any creature kept for the production of food, wool, skins or fur, or for the purpose of its use in

the farming of land), the use of land as grazing land, meadow land, osier land, market gardens and nursery grounds, and the use of lands for woodlands where that use is ancillary to the farming of land for other agricultural purposes.

7   This reduces to 14 days for markets and motor sports.
8   In some cases planning permission is deemed to have been granted, for example, where the authorisation of a government department is required by law.
9   The Metropolitan Green Belt Act 1938.

TRAPS AND SNARES

See also Agencies; Cruelty to Animals; Damage; Killing Birds and Animals; Northern Ireland; Pests; Protected Animals; Rabbits; Vermin

The Wildlife and Countryside Act 1981 and the Wildlife (Northern Ireland) Order 1985 restrict the use of traps and snares by setting controls on the types of trap that may be used against a particular species and also by regulating some of the circumstances in which traps may be used. Other than when done under the terms of a licence,[1] it will be an offence to:

(a) set in position any spring, trap, gin or snare which is of such a nature and so placed as to be calculated to cause bodily injury to any wild bird coming into contact with it;[2]

(b) use for the purpose of killing or taking any wild bird any of the articles in (a);

(c) set in position any self-locking snare which is of such a nature and so placed as to be calculated to cause bodily injury to any wild animal coming into contact with it;

(d) use for the purpose of killing or taking any wild animal any self-locking snare;[3]

(e) set in position any trap or snare which is of such a nature and so set as to be calculated to cause bodily injury to any wild animal included in Schedule 6;[4]

(f) use for the purpose of killing or taking any wild animal included in Schedule 6 any self-locking snare;[5]

(g) attempt to commit any of these offences;

(h) have in their possession anything capable of being used to commit one of the forgoing offences; or

(i) set in position any snare of such a nature and so placed as to be calculated to cause bodily injury to any wild animal coming into contact with it and then to fail, without reasonable excuse, to inspect it, or cause it to be inspected at least once every day.

Other legislation limiting or prohibiting the use of traps and snares include the Protection of Animals Act 1911[6] and, if a trap or snare is used to take or kill any domestic or captive animal, the Criminal Damage Act 1971. In Northern Ireland it is an offence to sell, offer or expose for sale, any self-locking snare with a view to its being used for the purposes that are unlawful under (a) and (b) above.

However, although restricted trapping remains an approved method of taking or killing some animals including many of the species generally regarded as pests or vermin and snares are popular as a method of rabbit control. All spring traps must be approved under the Pests Act 1954[7] by the Ministry of Agriculture, Fisheries and Food and the current Spring Traps (Approval) Order 1995[8] identifies those that are acceptable. Traps included under this Order may still be being used illegally if they are not operated in accordance with any limitation placed on the approval.[9] It is an offence under the 1954 Act for a person:

(a) for the purpose of killing or taking animals to use or knowingly permit the use of any spring trap other than an approved trap, or uses, or knowingly permits the use of an approved trap for animals or in circumstances for which it is not approved;

(b) to sell, or expose or offer for sale any spring trap other than an approved trap with a view to its being used for an unlawful purpose under (a);

(c) to have any spring trap in his possession for any of the purposes under a) or (b).

Unlawful circumstances include the use of a spring trap for the taking or killing of hares or rabbits other than in a rabbit hole.[10] There are no traps currently approved for the taking of hares. Some designs are immediately unacceptable and illegal, including the gin trap and pole trap and these 'leg-hold' traps are also banned under EC regulations. Approved traps are listed in the table overleaf:

Trap	Approval / Limitations
Aldridge spring activated snare	For large, non-indigenous mammalian carnivores
BMI Magnum 55	For rats, mice and small ground vermin in natural or artificial tunnels
BMI Magnum 110	As above and also for use against grey squirrels, stoats and weasels
BMI 116	As above and also for mink and rabbits
Fenn rabbit trap Mk1	For use against rabbits in natural or artificial tunnels
Fenn vermin trap Mk1, 2, 3, 4	For grey squirrels, mice, rats, stoats, weasels and other small ground vermin in natural or artificial tunnels
Fenn dual purpose trap Mk6	As above and for use against rabbits
Fuller trap	For grey squirrels in natural or artificial tunnels
Imbra Mk 1 & 2	Grey squirrels, mice, rabbits, rats, stoats, weasels and other small ground vermin in natural or artificial tunnels
Juby trap	As above
Kania trap 2000	Grey squirrels, mice, mink, rats, stoats, weasels and other small ground vermin in artificial tunnels
Sawyer and Lloyd traps	Grey squirrels, mice, rats, stoats, weasels and other small ground vermin in artificial tunnels

1   Unless licensed by the Ministry of Agriculture, Fisheries and Food, the Department of the Environment, English Nature or the Scottish, Welsh and Northern Ireland equivalents.
2   No animal traps are approved for the taking of wild birds although Larsen, Ladder and Cone traps which take birds alive may be used. Larsen traps employ live decoys which are not generally permitted under the 1981 or 1985 legislation. A general licence issued by the Department of the Environment permits their use, however, where the decoy is provided with food and water and has sufficient room to stretch its wings. Only crows, jackdaws, jays, magpies and rooks may currently be used as decoys. Cage traps and nets may be used to take game birds for the purpose of breeding.
3   Whether falling under (c) or not.
4   The Schedules correspond. It is a defence to show that the trap or snare was set in position in the interests of public health, agriculture, forestry fisheries or nature conservation or for the purpose of taking or killing any animal which could be lawfully taken by those means. This is provided the accused can show that he took all reasonable precautions to prevent injury to any animal included in Schedule 6 (see p.154 for details).
5   Whether falling under (c) or not.
6   The Protection of Animals (Scotland) Act 1912.
7   The Agriculture (Scotland) Act 1948.

8   The Spring Traps (Scotland) (Approval) Order 1996.

9   Defences include the use of traps under a licence issued by the Ministry of Agriculture, Fisheries and Food and the use of specified traps solely for the destruction of rats, mice and other small ground vermin.

10 Unless approved under either of the Spring Traps (Approval) Orders.

TREASURE TROVE

See also Metal Detectors

Historians contend that our countryside landscape has been in constant use for more than 2000 years with villages and settlements arising, changing and diminishing regularly over that time. Rather than a peaceful pastoral landscape, however, wars and disputes have seen artifacts, coins and other valuable items being hidden, lost or abandoned and the potential rewards of finding these attract hunters. Anyone finding an object which they believe to be 'treasure' is required by the Treasure Act 1996 to notify the coroner for that district within 14 days of the find or 14 days of first believing the object to be 'treasure'. Treasure, is deemed to be:

(a) any object at least 300 years old when found and —

  (i)   is not a coin[1] but has metallic content of which at least 10 per cent by weight is gold or silver,

  (ii) when found is one of at least two coins in the same find which are at least 300 years old at that time and have that percentage of gold or silver,

  (iii) when found is one of at least ten coins in the same find which are at least 300 years old at that time;

(b) any object at least 200 years old when found which has been designated to be of outstanding historical, archaeological or cultural importance.

Any object which is part of a find combining any of the above is also included but the term 'treasure' does not include objects which are unworked natural objects or minerals as extracted from a natural deposit. Any failure to report a find falling under the provisions of this enactment is a criminal offence.

1   'Coin' includes any metal token which was or can reasonably be assumed to have been used or intended for use as or instead of money.

TREES

See also Birds and Eggs; Hedges and Hedgerows; Highways and Roads; Nuisances; Protected Animals

Local planning authorities and county councils are empowered under the Town and Country Planning (Trees) Regulations 1999 to make Tree Preservation Orders. Once made an Order protects a tree or woodland from being cut, lopped or uprooted and from any wilful damage or destruction without the prior permission of the planning authority. All types of trees may be subject to an Order including those forming part of a hedge or hedgerow and details of preservation orders are kept in the local land charges register at local council offices. These Orders do not prohibit any necessary work, provided permission is sought and gained prior to the lopping, cutting or trimming taking place. However, permission is not necessary for work to a tree that is:

(a) dead or dying;

(b) dangerous;

(c) creating a statutory nuisance;

(d) a cultivated fruit tree for fruit production;

(e) in the way of development for which detailed planning permission has been granted;

(f) subject of an obligation imposed by another Act;

(g) subject of a request by a specified government department or organisation;

(h) subject of a Forestry Commission felling licence.[1]

In any of these instances local planning authorities should be given a minimum of 5 days' notice of the intended work and may require that any tree that is cut down and removed should be replaced at the owner's expense.[2] Where a protected tree is cut down, destroyed or damaged without authorisation, or without one of the exceptions applying, a criminal offence is committed.[3] If a Tree Preservation Order has the effect of causing any loss or damage compensation may be obtained from the local authority, although this will not apply to any loss of development value or other value of the land or to circumstances where the loss is valued at less than £500.

Local highways authorities have responsibility for the maintenance of highways and are empowered to cut and lop any trees that interfere or obstruct any highway or require the owner of any such tree to undertake the work.[4]

When work is required on any tree the various protective provisions of the wildlife and habitat protection legislation[5] as to the unnecessary disturbance of birds and habitats should be considered. The main nesting periods should be avoided and any cutting or lopping ought only to take place between the months of September and April.

1   Where an application for a felling licence includes a protected tree the Commission will consult the local planning authority before deciding whether to grant the licence.
2   See pp.81–2 for requirements as to tree felling licences.
3   Punishable by a fine of up to £20 000 on summary conviction or unlimited on indictment.
4   There is a presumption at common law that a tree situated on a highway belongs to the owner of the sub-soil, which may be the person whose lands front the highway and this presumption will operate unless any better title can be established.
5   The Wildlife and Countryside Act 1981, the Wildlife (Northern Ireland) Order 1985 and the Conservation (Natural Habitats, etc.) Regulations 1994.

TRESPASS

See also Bridle-ways; Common Land; Footpaths; Highways and Roads; Poaching; Protests and Protestors; Theft; Vagrancy

There is an assumption within English law that all land, including 'common land', is owned either by individuals, organisations or the State and as such any person who enters on to land that is not theirs may be doing so as a trespasser. It is immediately obvious that this is not the reality of the situation and that people have a number of ways in which they can find themselves on someone else's land without being a trespasser. The real issue, therefore, is not one of ownership so much as of rights; who has the right or authority to enter and be on another's land, and under what circumstances.

Footpaths, bridle-ways and other highways and roads provide a general right to pass and re-pass along a specified route without the traveller committing any trespass. These are not without legal boundaries however, and anyone who acts outside the limits of the right to pass immediately becomes a trespasser. As a result a horse rider on a footpath is a trespasser as is a protestor on a bridle-way or a person on common land who holds no right of common in relation to that land. Other means of access to land include:

(a) permission – this may be either an express permission where the landowner grants specific authority for someone to be on their land, or implied, where access is a necessary part of some agreement or contract such as those agreed when shooting rights are let;
(b) easements – these are legally enforceable rights of access onto or across another person's land in some cases as the only means by which a person may gain access to their own land; and
(c) powers of entry – a massive amount of legislation allows police officers, utility companies, customs and excise, and a variety of local authority and government inspectors to enter on to land within specific circumstances such as the inspection of livestock or when inquiring into possible criminal offences.

Once again these methods of access are restricted and any action that takes place outside the limits of the express permission, easement or conditional power granted by a statute will amount to a trespass. Simple trespass is not a criminal offence, however, and an owner's main course of action can only be to seek an injunction to curtail a person in circumstances where a trespass is regular or continual or to seek compensation if some trespass results in loss or damage. Isolated cases of trespass are difficult to deal with in this way and a landowner's only recourse may be to demand that the trespasser leave the land and, if necessary, use reasonable force[1] to eject the trespasser. As simple trespass is not a criminal matter the police may not be able to assist although they are under a duty to prevent breaches of the peace and where practicable they should be called.

Some forms of trespass have been specifically made criminal by

Parliament and in these instances the police are granted powers to act. These include:

(a) Theft Act 1968 – any trespass into a building or part of a building where the trespasser intends to steal, cause damage, rape, wound or cause grievous bodily harm is burglary;[2]
(b) Firearms Act 1968 – trespass on to land or into a building with a firearm is a serious offence;
(c) Night Poaching Act 1828, Game Act 1831, Deer Act 1991 and Theft Act 1968 – trespass in pursuit of game, deer or fish is deemed to be poaching;
(d) Criminal Law Act 1977, Vagrancy Act 1824 and Trespass (Scotland) Act 1865 – lodging in property to the detriment of intending occupiers, without the consent of the owner or occupier or for any unlawful purpose is an offence under these Acts.

The Criminal Justice and Public Order Act 1994 is concerned with instances of mass trespass, disorder and demonstrations. Where a senior police officer believes that two or more people are trespassing on land, that they are there with the common purpose of residing for any period and that reasonable steps have been taken by or on behalf of the occupier to ask them to leave then he may direct them to leave,[3] provided that:

(a) any of them has caused damage to the land or to property on the land or used threatening, abusive or insulting words or behaviour towards the occupier, member of his family, employee or agent; or
(b) those people have between them six or more vehicles on the land.

It is an offence[4] of aggravated trespass for a person to trespass on land in the open air and, in relation to any lawful activity which persons are engaging in or are about to engage in on that or any adjoining land in the open air, to do anything which is intended by him to have the effect of:

(a) intimidating those people so as to deter them from engaging in that activity;
(b) obstructing that activity; or
(c) disrupting that activity.

1 What force is reasonable in the circumstances is a matter for the courts should any allegations of assault follow.
2 Housebreaking is a common law crime in Scotland.
3 Similar powers exist in relation to 'raves' or other mass parties where 100 or more people gather to listen to music. Failure to obey a direction to leave is a criminal offence subject to a power of arrest by a constable in uniform.
4 In such a case the police are empowered to direct offenders to quit the land.

VAGRANTS

See also Damage; Fires and Smoke; Trespass; Vermin

Although less of a problem in the countryside than in the towns and cities, it is still possible to see tramps, vagrants and beggars walking the lanes or sleeping rough at the roadside. Vagrancy was a particular problem in the early nineteenth century and many of our current laws still date back to that time. The Vagrancy Act 1824 remains in force and deems any person who wanders around or who places themselves in any pubic place, street, highway, court or passage to beg to be an 'idle and disorderly' person. Courts are empowered to fine idle and disorderly persons and, in some cases, send them to prison. Under the 1824 Act it is an offence for any idle and disorderly person to lodge themselves in any barn or outhouse, or in any deserted or unoccupied building or in the open air, although no offence will be committed unless:

(a) the person had been directed to a reasonably accessible place of shelter and had failed to apply for or refused accommodation there;

(b) it is a person who persistently wanders and notwithstanding that a place of shelter is reasonably accessible lodges or attempts to lodge as above; or

(c) that by so lodging damage was caused to property or an infestation by vermin was caused, or other offensive consequence or such was likely.

The Act also makes it an offence for any such person to be found in or upon any dwelling-house, warehouse, coach-house, stable or outhouse, or in any enclosed yard, garden or area if they are there for any unlawful purpose. Anyone may arrest a vagrant found in these circumstances provided that they hand their prisoner over to a police officer or a court as soon as practicable. Fines or imprisonment[1] are available to magistrates as a means of punishing offenders.

In Scotland it is an offence under the Trespass (Scotland) Act 1865 for any person to lodge in any house, barn, stable, shed, loft, granary, outhouse, garden, stockyard, court, close or enclosed space or to occupy or encamp on any land, being private property, without the consent of the owner or legal occupier of such premises or land.

---

1 Up to a maximum of £1000 and 3 months' imprisonment.

VERMIN

See also Conservation; Insects and Other Invertebrates;
Killing Birds and Animals; Pesticides; Poison; Pests; Protected Animals

It is the duty of every local authority under the Prevention of Damage by Pests Act 1949 to take whatever steps are necessary to ensure that their districts are kept free from rats and mice and to this end they may:

(a) carry out such inspections as may be necessary;
(b) destroy rats and mice on land of which they are the occupier so as to keep, as far as practicable, that land free from rats and mice;
(c) enforce the duties of other owners and occupiers of land.

The Act also requires the owners and occupiers of land to notify their local authority if they find rats or mice living on or resorting to their land in substantial numbers[1] although this does not apply to agricultural land. If a local authority becomes aware of the existence of rats or mice on any land, whether by notification or otherwise, they may require the owner or occupier to take whatever reasonable steps are necessary to reduce those populations. The local authority may serve a notice on both the owner and occupier specifying the treatment to be applied, any structural repairs that they need to make together with any time limits within which the work must be carried out. If the occupier prevents the owner from carrying out the specified work a court may order the occupier to permit it. Where a notice has been served, if the required work is not carried out the local authority may themselves do whatever is necessary and recover their costs from the owner or occupier.

The Ministry of Agriculture, Fisheries and Food may make regulations controlling the acceptable methods of destroying rats, mice, insects or mites and may also license the killing or taking of any wild animal where such is necessary. Licences may be granted for scientific and educational purposes as well as for the prevention of serious damage to foodstuffs, crops, vegetables and fruit and for the prevention of the spread of disease. Poisons and traps are the usual methods employed.

Not all rodents are pests, however, and efforts must be made to identify the dormouse, which is a protected species under the Conservation (Natural Habitats, etc.) Regulations 1994. It is an offence under these Regulations to deliberately capture or kill dormice as well as deliberately disturbing them, damage or destroy any breeding site or resting place. It is also an offence[2] to keep, transport, sell or exchange or offer for sale or exchange them alive or dead and this includes any part of such an animal and anything derived from one. Under these Regulations there is a general defence regarding acts of mercy, incidental results of otherwise lawful operations and anything done in pursuance of a requirement by the Ministry of Agriculture, Fisheries and Food.[3]

1   Failure to notify the local authority is an offence.
2   It is a defence to show that the animal had been lawfully killed or taken or lawfully sold.
3   This exception is concerned with requirements under the Agriculture Act 1947 and the Agriculture (Scotland) Act 1948 for the prevention of damage by pests and Orders made under the Animal Health Act 1981, as amended.

VILLAGE GREENS

See also Access – A Right to Roam; Common Land

The Commons Registration Act 1965 was introduced with the aim of preserving common land and village greens for recreational use through a process of registration whereby local registers recorded these sites, the rights of common attached to them and the identity of the landowners, where known. Time limits were placed on this process of registration,[1] and where the ownership of such land was uncertain and the land remained unclaimed, then the Act allowed it to be vested in the local authority. The purpose of this legislation was to clear up any ambiguities surrounding waste and common land and to clearly identify rights of access, recreation and enjoyment. The reality, however, was that the task proved problematic for local authorities who were unable to resolve many of the outstanding issues within the time period allowed. Further legislation is now being proposed to redress this.

The 1965 Act classifies village greens as land which:

(A) has been allotted by or under any Act for the exercise or recreation of the inhabitants of any locality;

(B) on which the inhabitants of any locality have a customary right to indulge in lawful sports and pastimes;

(C) on which the inhabitants of any locality have indulged in such sports and pastimes as of right for not less than 20 years.

Referred to as classes: class (A) includes land specifically set aside for exercise and recreation either by an Act of Parliament or by the Commissioners who acted under the Inclosure Act 1845; class (B) concerns land where a right of use has arisen from immemorial custom;[2] class (C) requires that the inhabitants of a locality have, in fact, used the land as of right for lawful sports and pastimes for a period exceeding 20 years. The registration requirement of the 1965 enactment particularly affects classes (A) and (B), which should have been entered into the local registers of commons by 1970. Class (C), however, can continue to classify a piece of land as a town or village green provided the elements of the classification are fulfilled. These elements have recently been considered by the House of Lords in the case of R v. *Oxfordshire County Council and Others ex parte Sunningwell Parish Council (1999)*. Five law lords ruled that the term 'sports and pastimes' defined a composite class of activity that was not limited to historical sports: archery is no longer a requirement; dog walking and playing with children are sufficient informal recreation to be the main function of a village green. The lords also ruled that the term 'as of right' could be evidenced by the fact that residents had used the land for recreation for a period of at least 20 years without any secrecy, force or permission. Where these conditions are met, an area of land may be registered as a 'village green' to which local inhabitants will thenceforth have a right of access for exercise and recreation.

This is a restricted right for the benefit of the local populace however, and does not provide for open access by the general public. Members of the public have access as of right only to metropolitan commons[3] and commons falling wholly or partly within an area which was a borough or urban district prior to the local authority re-organisation of 1974. These are generally known as urban commons.

1   In the majority of instances the due date for registration was 1970.
2   In law this refers to a time that predates the accession of Richard I in 1189.
3   The Metropolitan Commons Act 1866.

WALES

See also Agencies

Until the devolution of powers that has so recently taken place, the English Parliament dictated the laws of Wales with little recognition of its national history or local needs. This universal application of English law is now set to change following the creation of the new Welsh Assembly under the Government of Wales Act 1998 with sufficient legislative powers to create its own laws. At the time of writing the Assembly was still taking its first steps towards creating a Welsh body of law and no new legislation affecting countryside issues has yet emerged from the parliamentary process. Countryside issues are obviously on their agenda, however, and one of the first acts of the Welsh Assembly was to confirm the status and consultative position of the Countryside Council for Wales.

WATER

See also Bridle-ways; Floods and Flooding; Footpaths; Highways and Roads; Pesticides; Pollution; Rivers, Streams and Other Watercourses

The water industry is subject to a multitude of laws controlling abstraction, quality, supply and the licensing of works in relation to these. Water abstraction and the prevention of pollution fall under the provisions of the Water Resources Act 1991 which makes out offences that occur:

(a) when any person abstracts water or constructs or extends any well, borehole or other work or installs or modifies machinery in order to abstract increased quantities of water, without a licence; or

(b) when any person causes or knowingly permits any poisonous, noxious or polluting matter or any solid waste matter to enter any controlled water.

The offence at (a) is not committed where only small quantities of water not exceeding 5 cubic metres[1] are abstracted or 20 cubic metres in 24 hours for domestic or agricultural purposes other than spray irrigation on contiguous land. Controlled waters for the purposes of (b) include inland freshwaters, the waters of any relevant lake, pond, river or watercourse as well as ground waters contained in underground strata. This Act also provides powers for the prohibition or limitation of abstraction during periods of drought, and where an ordinary or emergency Drought Order has been made it will be an offence for any person to contravene any of its provisions or to use water other than in accordance with the restrictions imposed by the Order.

Water supply is controlled by the Water Industry Act 1991 which:

(a) places a duty on water authorities to allow any person to take water for extinguishing fires;

(b) permits disconnection for maintenance and repair as well as for non-payment;[2]

(c) provides powers for the imposition of hosepipe bans; and

(d) creates offences of –

  (i) supplying water unfit for human consumption by means of pipes to any premises;

(ii) unnecessarily causing or allowing any underground water to run to waste from any well, borehole or other works;

(iii) abstracting from any well, borehole or other works water in excess of the person's reasonable requirement;[3]

(iv) polluting any water in any waterworks which is used or likely to be used for human consumption or domestic purposes or for the manufacturing of food or drink for human consumption.

Miscellaneous legislation concerned with water includes the Highways Act 1980, which contains extensive provisions for the maintenance of highways and roads and includes a prohibition on the flow of water onto any highway. The Act grants powers to local highways authorities enabling them to require the occupier of any premises adjoining a highway to maintain any channels, gutters or downpipes as may be necessary to prevent water falling onto anyone using a highway or flowing on to the footway of a highway. Any failure to comply is an offence that is punishable by a fine plus an additional amount for each day that the failure continues.

The Public Health Act 1936 provides similar powers allowing local authorities to deal with overflowing or leaking cesspools.

1   Or 20 cubic metres with the consent of the Environment Agency provided it is not part of a continuous operation or series of operation.
2   If disconnection is for longer than 24 hours the local authority must be informed.
3   It is a defence to (ii) and (iii) to show that the waste occurred as a result of testing the extent or quality of the water or when cleaning, sterilising, examining or repairing the well, borehole, etc. It is also a defence to show that the water interfered or threatened the carrying out of some underground works and there was no other reasonably practicable method of disposing of it.

WEEDS

See also Highways and Roads; Nuisances; Plants and Flowers; Poison

The Weeds Act 1959 states that the Minister of Agriculture, Fisheries and Food,[1] if satisfied that injurious weeds are growing upon any land, may serve a notice[2] requiring the occupier to take action in order to prevent the spread of those weeds. Any unreasonable failure to comply with a notice is an offence. The weeds that this legislation applies to are:

(a) spear thistle;
(b) creeping or field thistle;
(c) curled dock;
(d) broad-leaved dock;
(e) ragwort.[3]

The use of weed-killers or other poisons should be controlled in order to avoid the destruction of protected varieties of plants. Protected species are listed in the Schedules to the Wildlife and Countryside Act 1981 and the Wildlife (Northern Ireland) Order 1985. While it is an offence to kill any of these protected species the legislation recognises the problems in dealing with encroaching weeds situated among other plants and provides general defences. These include unintended acts occurring as part of an otherwise lawful operation and anything done under a licence from the Ministry.

In cases where injurious weeds affect adjoining land, and in the absence of a notice under the 1959 Act, civil action may be possible on the grounds that the spread of these weeds creates an unreasonable interference with the use or enjoyment of the neighbouring land. If such can be shown then the landowner is committing a private nuisance for which an injunction ordering the curtailment of the nuisance may be sought and, where damage or loss has occurred, compensation to redress that loss.

---

1   The Act also includes the Secretary of State for Wales, although this responsibility will now fall to the new national assembly.
2   In the case of a road this will be the local authority responsible for maintaining the highway.
3   The Ministry is empowered to add to this list where necessary.

WILD MAMMALS

See also Cruelty to Animals; Falconry; Killing Birds and Animals; Poison; Protected Species

The Protection of Animals Acts[1] prohibit cruel treatment to both domestic and captive animals but fail to include within their provisions any offences relating to the treatment of wild animals that are not captive. This loophole has now been dealt with by the Wild Mammals (Protection) Act 1996[2] which affords protection to wild animals from cruel acts in addition to the more general safeguards included in the Wildlife and Countryside Act 1981 and the Wildlife (Northern Ireland) Order 1985. The 1996 Act states that, save as permitted, any person who mutilates, kicks, beats, nails or otherwise impales, stabs, burns, stones, crushes, drowns, drags or asphyxiates any wild mammal with intent to inflict unnecessary suffering shall be guilty of an offence.[3] Exceptions include:

(a) the attempted killing of any such wild mammal as an act of mercy where the mammal had been so seriously disabled that there was no reasonable chance of it recovering;

(b) the killing in a reasonably swift and humane manner of any such wild mammal where the mammal is injured or taken in the course of lawful hunting, shooting, coursing or pest control;

(c) any authorised action under any Act;

(d) any act done by means of any snare, trap, dog or bird lawfully used for the purpose of taking or killing any wild mammal; and

(e) the lawful use of any poisonous or noxious substance on any wild mammal.

A wild mammal for the purposes of the Act is defined as any mammal which is not a domestic or captive animal within the meaning of the Protection of Animals Act 1911 or the Protection of Animals (Scotland) Act 1912. The expression 'captive animal' is defined by these Acts as meaning any animal of whatsoever kind or species and whether a quadruped or not, including any bird, fish or reptile, which is in captivity, or confinement, or which is maimed, pinioned, or subject to any appliance or contrivance for the purpose of hindering or preventing its escape. This does not include a temporary condition, however, and a wild animal temporarily unable to escape is not 'captive' for these purposes.[4] Between the Acts of 1911, 1912 and 1996 it would appear that all animals are now protected from cruel treatment.

Where a police officer has reasonable grounds for suspecting that an offence has been committed against the provisions of the Wild Mammals (Protection) Act 1996 and that evidence may be found on the suspect or in a vehicle, then he or she may stop and search that person and seize any evidence found. The courts have the power to order the confiscation of any vehicle or equipment used in the commission of the offence.[5]

---

1. These are the Protection of Animals Act 1911, the Protection of Animals (Scotland) Act 1912 and the Welfare of Animals Act (Northern Ireland) 1972.
2. This Act is not applicable in Northern Ireland.
3. Punishable by up to 6 months' imprisonment and/or a fine of £5000.
4. *Rowley* v. *Murphy (1964)*.
5. This element of the Act is not applicable to Scotland.

WILDFOWL

See also Birds and Eggs; Estuaries and Foreshore; Game Birds; Game Dealers; Killing Birds and Animals; Lead Shot; Northern Ireland

While not 'game' in the sense that they are not defined as such by any of the Game Acts wildfowl have long been an accepted quarry species, a status reflected by exceptions to the general protection offered by the Wildlife and Countryside Act 1981 and the Wildlife (Northern Ireland) Order 1985. These allow for the killing or taking of some species of wildfowl by authorised people outside 'close' season periods that generally reflect the breeding periods of these birds. Any killing or taking of wildfowl other than during their 'open' season by authorised people or under the terms of a licence,[1] is a criminal offence. Authorised persons are:

(a) owners or occupiers of any land or any person authorised by them;
(b) any person authorised by a local authority;
(c) any person acting with the written authority of one of the Nature Conservancy Councils, a district board for a fishery district[2] or a local fisheries committee;[3]
(d) any person authorised by the National Rivers Authority.

Wildfowl may not be shot in Scotland on a Sunday or on Christmas Day. In England and Wales there is no such general restriction, although some counties banned the taking of wildfowl on a Sunday under the Protection of Birds Act 1954. As a result shooting remains prohibited on Sundays in Anglesey, Brecknock, Caernarvon, Carmarthen, Cardigan, Cornwall, Denbigh, Devon, Doncaster, Glamorgan, Great Yarmouth, Isle of Ely, Leeds, Merioneth, Norfolk, Pembroke, Somerset and the North and West Ridings of Yorkshire. Where these counties no longer exist, the restriction remains over the areas that they used to cover. The Wildlife and Countryside Act 1981 provides powers for the Secretary of State to apply a Sunday ban to other areas and to prohibit the killing or taking of any wildfowl at any other time. This has occasionally resulted in a ban for a short period of up to 14 days during severe weather conditions where wildfowl are struggling to survive without the added attention of hunters.

Restrictions on the acceptable methods by which any wild bird may be killed or taken apply to wildfowl and the legislation prohibits the use of traps, snares, hooks and lines, electrical devices for killing, stunning or frightening together with poisonous, poisoned or stupefying substances. It is an offence for any person to use any bow or crossbow, explosive,[4] automatic or semi-automatic weapon, shotgun with a barrel diameter of more than $1^3/_4$ inches (4.5cm), any device for illuminating a target or any form of artificial light. The use of a sound recording to attract wildfowl is also prohibited. Provisions under the Environmental Protection (Restriction on Use of Lead Shot) (England) Regulations 1999 prohibit the use of lead shot against certain wildfowl, although this is as a result of environmental concerns rather than worries over the suitability of the method. The wildfowl against which lead shot cannot now be used are coots, ducks, geese, swans, moorhens and golden plovers.[5]

The 1981 and 1985 Acts identify[6] which species of wildfowl may be killed, the periods during which this may take place and the dead wildfowl that may be sold. None of the quarry species of geese are included under Schedule 3, resulting in an effective ban on the sale of dead geese.

Schedule 2[7] Birds which may be killed or taken

Part 1 Outside the close season

Common name	Scientific name	Common name	Scientific name
Coot[8]	*Fulica atra*	Moorhen[11]	*Gallinula chloropus*
Duck, Tufted	*Aytha fuligula*	Pintail	*Anas acuta*
Gadwall	*Anas strepera*	Plover, Golden	*Pluvialis apricaria*
Goldeneye	*Bucephala clangula*	Pochard	*Aythya ferina*
Goose, Canada [9]	*Branta canadensis*	Shoveler	*Anas clypeata*
Goose, Greylag	*Anser anser*	Teal	*Anas crecca*
Goose, Pink-footed[10]	*Anser platyrhynchos*	Wigeon	*Anas penelope*
Mallard	*Anas platyrhynchos*		

Schedule 3 Birds which may be sold

Part 3[12] Dead from 1 September to 28 February

Common name	Scientific name	Common name	Scientific name
Coot	*Fulica atra*	Pochard	*Aythya ferina*
Duck, Tufted	*Aytha fuligula*	Shoveler	*Anas clypeata*
Mallard	*Anas platyrhynchos*	Teal	*Anas crecca*
Pintail	*Anas acuta*	Wigeon	*Anas penelope*
Plover, Golden	*Pluvialis apricaria*		

The open seasons for wildfowl are:

	Inland	Foreshore
Geese		
Canada	1 September – 31 January	1 September – 20 February
Greylag	1 September – 31 January	1 September – 20 February
Pink-footed	1 September – 31 January	1 September – 20 February
White-fronted	1 September – 31 January	1 September – 20 February

	Inland	Foreshore
Ducks		
Common Pochard	1 September – 31 January	1 September – 20 February
Gadwall	1 September – 31 January	1 September – 20 February
Goldeneye	1 September – 31 January	1 September – 20 February
Mallard	1 September – 31 January	1 September – 20 February
Pintail	1 September – 31 January	1 September – 20 February
Shoveler	1 September – 31 January	1 September – 20 February
Teal	1 September – 31 January	1 September – 20 February
Tufted	1 September – 31 January	1 September – 20 February
Wigeon	1 September – 31 January	1 September – 20 February
Waders (above or below the mean high water mark)		
Golden Plover	1 September – 31 January	
Miscellaneous		
Coot	1 September – 31 January	
Moorhen	1 September – 31 January	

1. No offence is committed by any action authorised by a licence issued by the Ministry of Agriculture, Fisheries and Food for the protection of crops etc.
2. Under the terms of the Salmon Fisheries (Scotland) Act 1862.
3. The Sea Fisheries Regulation Act 1966.
4. Other than ammunition for a firearm.
5. These Regulations currently apply only to England.
6. The lists have been adapted for the purposes of this section.
7. The Schedule numbers correspond.
8. Not included in the Schedule to the Wildlife (Northern Ireland) Order 1985, which does include the curlew and scaup.
9. Not included in the Schedule to the Wildlife (Northern Ireland) Order 1985.
10. In England and Wales only.
11. Not included in the Schedule to the Wildlife (Northern Ireland) Order 1985.
12. This Part is not included under the 1985 Order.

ZOOS AND ANIMAL PARKS

See also Cruelty to Animals; Dangerous and Destructive Animals

Increasing recreational use of the countryside has seen the creation of a number of animal parks as a modern alternative to the traditional zoo. The keeping of dangerous wild animals in any circumstances is subject to a licensing requirement[1] and the Zoo Licensing Act 1981 applies a similar precondition to the establishment of zoos and animal parks.[2] This Act applies to any place[3] where wild animals[4] are kept for exhibition to the public provided that the public has access, with or without payment, on more than 7 days in any period of 12 months and it is unlawful to operate such a premises or place except under the authority of a licence.

While the Department of the Environment, Transport and the Regions has responsibility for setting standards of care to be followed, licences are issued by the local authority for the area in which the zoo or park is mainly situated. Conditions will be applied to any licence issued and these will provide for the keeping of animal specimens in suitable conditions with adequate space and care and for regular inspection by a veterinary practitioner or other competent person. It is an offence[5] under the Act to:

(a) operate a zoo or animal park without a licence, or
(b) fail to comply with any of the conditions of a licence.

---

1. Zoos are exempt from the Dangerous Wild Animals Act 1976.
2. Similar provisions for Northern Ireland are contained in the Welfare of Animals Act (Northern Ireland) 1972.
3. Circuses and pet shops are not included under this legislation.
4. A wild animal is defined by the Act as any animal not normally domesticated in Great Britain. As captive animals the provisions of the Protection of Animals Act 1911 and the Protection of Animals (Scotland) Act 1912 will apply to cases of cruel treatment.
5. Punishable by fines of up to £2500.

INDEX

Access ... 1, 2, 33, 34, 82, 83
Agencies ... 3, 4, 5, 6, 31, 33, 34, 35, 46
Agriculture ... 62, 98, 184
Agricultural vehicles ... 26
Air weapons ... 7, 8, 25, 33
Amphibians ... 8
Ammunition
    deer ... 50, 51, 52, 54
    firearms, for ... 69
Ancient monuments ... 4, 76, 123, 124, 125
Angling
    lead weights ... 73
    rods ... 5, 72, 182
    salmon ... 170
    trout ... 170
Animal parks ... 207
Animals
    abandonment ... 43
    badgers ... 10
    captive ... 38, 41
    cruelty ... 41
    dangerous ... 47
    destructive ... 48
    disease ... 55
    fighting ... 29, 42
    Northern Ireland ... 130
    nuisances ... 135
    poaching ... 143
    protected ... 152
    theft ... 181
    transporting ... 87, 103
    traps ... 186
    wild mammals ... 202
    zoos ... 207
Arable Areas Payment Scheme ... 63
Archaeological sites ... 4, 98, 124, 125
    flooding ... 76
    metal detectors ... 123
    treasure trove ... 189
Archery ... 40, 41, 84, 111
    crossbows ... 40, 84
    deer ... 53
Areas of Outstanding Natural Beauty ... 4, 32

Arrest
    civil ... 144, 158
    gamekeepers, by ... 93, 144
    police, by ... 149
    protestors ... 157, 158
Arson ... 47, 71
Artificial insemination ... 122

Badgers ... 10, 154
Barbed wire ... 66
Bats ... 12, 153
Bees ... 13
Bicycles ... 19, 45, 94
Birds ... 14, 35, 36
    game ... 14
    Northern Ireland ... 131
    pests ... 138
    poaching ... 143
    poisons ... 147
    protected by special penalties ... 16
    rare, migratory and ... 36
    traps ... 186
    which may be killed ... 17
    which may be sold ... 18
    wildfowl ... 203
Boats ... 22, 23
Bridle-ways ... 2, 19, 83, 95
    bulls on ... 21
    crops on ... 39
    cycles on ... 19, 45
    dogs on ... 57
    driving on ... 59
    gates and stiles ... 20, 66
    highways, as ... 99, 100
    horses on ... 100, 103, 179
    trespass ... 192
    width ... 20
British Waterways Board ... 3, 22, 23
Buildings
    animals in ... 12, 152
    bats in ... 12
    historic ... 4
    listed ... 4, 47
    listed, damage to ... 47
    planning ... 183
Bulls ... 20, 21

Byways open to all traffic (BOAT)
  cycles on ... 45
  green lanes ... 94
  horses ... 103

Camping ... 24, 25, 79
Canals ... 22, 23, 24
Caravans ... 24, 25, 26, 183
Cattle
  bulls and ... 21
  carcasses, unburied ... 58
  driving ... 19, 21
  dogs ... 56, 57
  highways, on ... 79, 100
  movement ... 22
  straying ... 10, 85
  transport ... 122
Certificates
  firearms, for ... 67
  shotguns, for ... 176
Children ... 26, 27
  air weapons ... 7
  crossbows ... 40
  firearms ... 67
  horses ... 104
  rifles ... 167
  shotguns ... 178
Clay target shooting ... 27, 28, 67, 117
  planning permission ... 184
Cockfighting ... 29
Common land ... 1, 30, 31
  animals straying onto ... 179
  cycles on ... 45
  driving onto ... 59
  village greens ... 196
Community forests ... 4, 32
Conservation ... 31, 32, 33, 34, 35, 36
  farming ... 62, 63, 64, 65
  special areas of ... 5
  wild birds, of ... 34, 36
Country parks ... 33, 45
Countryside
  Agency ... 3, 32
  Commission ... 3, 4, 6, 32
  Council for Wales ... 4, 6, 31
  Stewardship Scheme ... 63
Coursing ... 37, 38, 43, 56, 106, 161

Crops ... 38, 39, 40
  burning ... 70
  damage ... 15, 84, 96, 138
  damage by deer ... 50, 53, 138
  footpaths, on ... 80
  hares ... 96
  highways, on ... 20, 101
  pesticides ... 137
  pests ... 15, 138, 160
  rabbits ... 160
Crossbows ... 40, 41, 84, 111, 204
  deer ... 53
  poaching ... 93, 144
  rabbits ... 161
Crown Estates
  conservation ... 35
  foreshore ... 60
Cruelty ... 41, 42, 43
  coursing ... 37
  dogs ... 58, 106
  falconry ... 61
  fox hunting ... 84, 106
  game birds ... 87
  horses ... 103
  livestock ... 22, 123
  poisons ... 146
  rabbits ... 161
  wild mammals ... 202
Cycles ... 44, 79, 95

Damage ... 7, 23, 39, 45, 46, 47, 76, 83
  fire, by ... 47, 71
  metal detectors, by ... 123
  protestors, by ... 157
Dangerous animals ... 47, 48, 49, 207
Decoys ... 111, 112
Deer ... 49, 50, 51, 52, 53, 54
  Forestry Commission ... 82
  licences ... 88, 90, 91
  livestock, as ... 121
  Northern Ireland ... 49
  pests, as ... 138
  poaching ... 144
  seasons ... 53
  Scotland ... 51
  transport ... 121, 122
  venison ... 51, 52, 88
Demonstrations ... 85, 156, 157, 158
Disease ... 14, 15, 22, 38, 55, 82, 121

210 INDEX

Dogs ... 56, 57, 58
    badger setts, in ... 10
    cattle carcasses, unburied ... 58
    coursing ... 37
    cruelty ... 43, 58
    dangerous ... 57
    footpaths ... 79
    guard ... 57
    hunting with ... 106
    poisons ... 147
    rabies ... 162
    sheep, and ... 56, 57
    straying ... 57, 180
    woodland, in ... 82

Dormice ... 196

Driftways ... 19

Driving
    off road ... 20, 59
    prohibition of ... 2

Eagles ... 61

Eggs ... 15

English Heritage ... 4, 123

English Nature ... 6, 31, 83, 119

Environment and Heritage Service ... 5, 31, 33

Environment
    Agency ... 5, 6, 75, 150, 166
    Department of ... 1, 3, 31, 34, 46, 95, 207

Environmentally Sensitive Areas ... 5, 33
    Scheme ... 64

Estuaries ... 60

Falconry ... 61, 62, 106

Farming ... 33, 38, 62, 63, 64, 65

Farming and Rural Conservation Agency ... 5

Farm Woodland Premium Scheme ... 64

Fences ... 1, 23, 47, 66, 67, 159

Ferreting ... 106

Fighting animals ... 29, 42

Firearms ... 67, 68, 69, 70, 93, 111, 130
    air weapons ... 7
    certificates ... 68, 163
    deer ... 49, 50, 51, 52
    ground game ... 96, 160
    highways, on or near ... 69, 101
    poaching ... 93
    rifles ... 163
    shotguns ... 176

Fires ... 47, 70, 71, 101

Fish ... 71, 72, 73, 74, 75
    salmon and trout ... 167, 168, 169, 170, 171, 172
    theft of ... 145, 182

Fisheries ... 3, 5, 15, 71, 84, 169, 170, 171, 172, 182

Fishing ... 71, 72, 73, 74, 75, 106
    common law rights ... 30
    foreshore ... 60
    lead weights ... 73, 117
    licences ... 5, 73
    tidal waters ... 60, 71

Flooding ... 75, 76, 125

Floods ... 6, 75, 76

Flowers ... 39, 139, 140, 141, 142, 181

Fly tipping ... 77, 184

Footpaths ... 23, 60, 79, 80, 81, 83, 95, 159
    bulls on ... 21
    creation ... 2, 79
    crops on ... 39, 80
    closure of ... 80
    diversions ... 80
    dogs on ... 57, 80
    driving on ... 59
    fishing from ... 72
    football on ... 80
    gates across ... 66
    highways, as ... 99, 100
    horses on ... 103
    litter ... 120
    metal detectors, on ... 124
    obstruction of ... 79
    protests from ... 79
    signs ... 81
    stiles ... 66
    trespass ... 192

Footways ... 99

Foreshore ... 60, 71

Forestry ... 81, 98, 184
    Commission ... 2, 4, 5, 35, 81, 82, 127
    community forests ... 4, 32

Forest Enterprise ... 5

Forest Research ... 5

Forests
    community... 4, 32
    damage to timber... 15
    trees... 190
Fossils... 83
Foxes... 83, 84, 85
    badger setts... 10, 11
    hunting... 83, 106
    pests, as... 138
    rabies... 162
Frogs... 8, 153
Fruit... 15, 38, 50, 53, 84
Fungi... 126

Game
    birds... 14, 85
    definition... 90, 94
    licences... 87, 88, 89, 90, 96
    poaching... 144
    poisons... 146
    rights... 91, 144
    selling, dead... 87, 88, 89, 170
    wildfowl... 203, 204, 205
Game dealers... 86, 87, 88, 89
    salmon... 170
    venison... 52
    wildfowl... 205
Game licences... 87, 88, 89, 90, 93, 144
Game rights... 91, 92
Gamekeepers... 90, 93, 94, 144
Gardens... 1
Gates... 1, 66, 67, 80
Grain... 38, 39, 40
Green belt... 185
Green lanes... 94, 95
Ground game
    hares... 95, 96, 97
    rabbits... 160, 161
Grouse... 86, 88, 90, 144, 148
Habitat Scheme... 64
Habitats
    animals, protected... 152, 153, 154, 155
    bats... 12
    Directive... 2, 6, 35
    flooding... 76
    hedges... 98
    limestone... 119

plants... 139
    rodents... 195
    special areas of conservation... 35
    trees... 191
    wetlands... 34
Handguns... 67
Harassment... 85, 107
Hares... 95, 96, 97, 148
    coursing... 37
    licences... 90, 91
    pests, as... 144
    poaching... 144, 145
    traps... 187
Hawks... 61, 62
Hedgerows... 98, 99, 190
Hedges... 1, 23, 98, 190
Heritage coastline... 4, 32
Highways... 59, 60, 99, 100, 101, 102, 192
    animals straying on... 179
    articles, abandoned... 77
    bridle-ways... 19
    crops... 39
    cycles... 44
    diversions... 2, 102
    dogs, straying... 57
    fencing in... 66
    firearms... 69
    fires... 70
    footpaths... 79, 80
    green lanes... 98
    hedges... 99
    horses, on... 102
    obstruction of... 101
    rubbish on... 77, 120
    smoke on... 70
    trees... 191
    water on... 200
Historic sites... 123, 124
Horses... 95, 102, 103, 104, 105
    children... 26
    cruelty... 42, 103
    highways, on... 100
    straying... 179
    transport... 103
Hunting... 92, 105, 106, 107, 161
    coursing... 37
    cruelty... 43, 106
    deer... 49
    dogs... 56
    foxes... 84
    game birds... 85

shooting ... 67
Insects ... 107, 138, 147
Invertebrates ... 107

Joint Nature Conservation Committee ... 6

Killing ... 38, 110, 111, 112, 113, 147
    animals ... 110, 152, 153, 154, 155
    birds ... 15, 85, 110
    bows ... 40, 41
    coursing ... 37
    crossbows ... 40
    cruelty ... 42
    deer ... 49, 52, 53
    firearms ... 69
    fish ... 72, 73
    foxes ... 83, 84
    hares ... 96
    licences ... 90
    Northern Ireland ... 130
    pests ... 138
    protected species ... 152, 153, 154, 155
    rights ... 91
    traps ... 186, 187
    wildfowl ... 203
Knives ... 113, 114

Land ... 114, 115, 116, 117
    adverse possession ... 115
    aggravated trespass ... 107
    change of use ... 184
    common ... 30, 59
    moorland ... 59
    nuisances ... 134, 135, 136
    occupiers ... 26, 27, 93, 114, 144
    theft of ... 181
    trespass ... 191
Lead shot ... 28, 117, 118
Lead weights ... 73
Licences ... 116
    air weapons ... 7
    birds ... 15
    caravan sites ... 24
    dangerous animals ... 48
    falconry ... 16
    fishing ... 72, 73
    foxes ... 84
    game ... 87, 88, 89, 90, 96
    game dealers ... 86

    net ... 5
    photography ... 16
    rifles ... 163
    rod angling ... 5, 72
    shotguns ... 176
    taxidermy ... 16
    vermin ... 196
    zoos ... 207
Limestone pavements ... 119
Litter ... 24, 77, 79, 120, 121, 151
Livestock ... 121, 122, 123
    bulls ... 21, 22
    cruelty ... 123
    damage to ... 15, 84
    disease ... 55, 121
    dogs ... 56, 57
    markets ... 122
    movement orders ... 55
    poaching ... 145
    straying ... 179
    transport ... 42
Local authorities ... 2, 4, 21, 59, 90, 119
    animal licences ... 48
    bridle-ways ... 19, 20
    common land ... 30
    footpaths ... 2, 79, 95
    game dealers ... 87
    highways ... 100, 101
    motor vehicle trials ... 20
    nature reserves ... 33
    pest control ... 138
    trees ... 190
    vermin ... 195
    zoo licences ... 207
Local nature reserves ... 33
Local planning authorities ... 3, 5, 80, 183

Marine Nature Reserves ... 33
Metal detectors ... 123, 124, 189
Mines ... 159
Ministry of Agriculture, Fisheries and Food ... 3, 5, 31, 38, 62, 83, 86, 98, 152, 162
    deer, licences ... 53
    disease ... 22, 55
    pesticides ... 137
    rabbit clearance ... 160
    rabies ... 162
    schemes ... 62, 63, 64, 65
    sensitive areas ... 33

vermin ... 196
weeds ... 200, 201
Ministry of Defence ... 35
Monuments ... 4, 76, 123, 124, 125
Moorland Scheme ... 64
Moors ... 1, 59
Motor sports ... 20, 186
Motor vehices
   abandoned ... 77, 78, 120
   bridle-ways, on ... 20
   deer ... 50, 51, 53
   driving, off-road ... 59, 94
   green lanes ... 94, 95
   noise ... 129
   trials ... 20
Mushrooms ... 39, 46, 125, 126, 181
Muskrats ... 48
Myxomatosis ... 161

National Assemblies ... 3, 130, 173, 198
National Nature Reserves ... 4, 6, 34
National Parks ... 2, 4, 32, 45, 126, 127, 128
   Commission ... 4
   Parks Authority ... 127
National Rivers Authority ... 5, 6, 73, 150, 169
National Scenic Areas ... 6, 34
National Surveying Authority ... 1
National Trails ... 4
National Trust ... 2, 127
Natura 2000 ... 36
Nature Conservancy Council ... 4, 6
Nature Conservation Orders ... 34
Navigations ... 22, 23
Newts ... 8
Noise ... 128, 129, 135
        clay shooting ... 28
Northern Ireland ... 5, 32, 129, 130, 131, 132, 133, 134
   deer ... 49
   Environment and Heritage Service ... 5
   firearms ... 68
   game birds ... 86
   game dealers ... 88
   Rivers Agency ... 6
   seasons ... 86

traps ... 186
Nuisances ... 20, 134, 135, 136
   fires ... 71
   noise ... 128
   trees ... 190
   watercourses ... 166
   weeds ... 201

Obstructions ... 1, 79, 101

Parks ... 1, 4, 32, 126, 127, 128 ...
Partridge ... 86, 88, 91, 94, 105, 144, 148
Pesticides ... 137, 138, 146
Pests ... 14, 43, 83, 95, 138, 139, 161, 195
   traps for ... 188
Pheasants ... 86, 88, 90, 94, 144, 148
Pistols ... 8, 67
Planning ... 3, 5, 183
Plants ... 82, 137, 139, 140, 141, 142, 143, 181
   Northern Ireland ... 133
Ploughing ... 20, 38, 39, 80, 101
Poaching ... 50, 57, 86, 90, 92, 93, 96, 143, 144, 145, 146
Poisons ... 42, 73, 97, 110, 146, 147, 148, 160, 200
Police, powers ... 148, 149
   aggravated trespass ... 107, 193
   air weapons ... 7
   badgers ... 10
   birds ... 16
   caravans ... 25
   crossbows ... 40
   deer ... 53
   demonstrations ... 157
   firearms ... 69, 165, 179
   fires ... 71
   harassment ... 107
   poaching ... 145
   protestors ... 107, 157
   rabies ... 162
   rifles ... 165
   Scotland ... 173
   shotguns ... 179
   trespass ... 193
   wild mammals ... 203
Pollution ... 5, 6, 46, 73, 117, 128, 150, 151, 166, 167
Poultry ... 14, 29, 56, 123

Protection areas ... 5
Protestors ... 85, 107, 156, 157, 158, 193

Quarries ... 1, 159
    fencing ... 66, 159
Quarry Species
    birds ... 15, 85, 86, 87
    deer ... 49, 50, 51, 52, 53
    foxes ... 83, 84
    game ... 85
    hares ... 95, 96
    rabbits ... 160
    salmon and trout ... 167
Rabbits ... 37, 88, 90, 94, 138, 143, 144, 145, 147, 160,161, 187, 188
Rabies ... 55, 162
RAMSAR sites ... 34
Rats ... 147, 188, 195
Riding ... 59, 60, 104, 105
Rifles ... 68, 163, 164, 165
    deer, for ... 50, 51, 52, 53
Rights
    access, of ... 59, 81
    cattle, to drive ... 19
    common land ... 30, 97
    fishery, of ... 60, 72
    footpaths ... 79
    game, to ... 91, 96
    green lanes ... 94
    ground game, to ... 96, 160, 161
    kill, to ... 91
    navigation, of ... 60, 72
    passage, of ... 19, 20, 79, 80, 99, 100, 101
    roam, to ... 1
    squatters ... 115
    towpaths ... 23
    village greens ... 196, 197
    Way, of ... 2, 99, 100
Rivers Agency ... 6, 75
Rivers ... 3, 22, 166, 167
Roads ... 21, 25, 44, 99, 100, 101
    Used as Public Paths (RUPP) ... 2, 45, 94, 101
Rural Development Commission ... 3, 32

Saboteurs ... 107
Salmon ... 5, 72, 89, 145, 147, 167, 168, 169, 170, 171,172
Schedules
    animals ... 153, 154, 155
    birds ... 16, 17, 18, 61, 62, 89, 139, 205
    fish ... 74
    fungi ... 126
    insects ... 108, 109
    Northern Ireland ... 131, 132, 133, 134
    plants ... 140, 141, 142
Scotland ... 25, 34, 47, 51, 60, 72, 73, 74, 79, 90, 102, 114, 117, 144, 156, 169, 170, 173, 179, 180, 195, 204
Scottish Environment Protection Agency ... 6
Scottish Natural Heritage ... 6, 31
Seasons
    birds ... 15, 85, 86, 87
    coursing ... 37
    deer ... 53
    fish ... 73, 169
    game birds ... 86
    hares ... 96
    salmon and trout ... 169
    wildfowl ... 205
Set-aside ... 63
Sheep ... 56, 57
Shooting ... 20, 27, 43, 67, 68, 69, 70, 85, 93, 105, 117, 118, 161
Shotguns ... 27, 50, 52, 53, 68, 117, 176, 177, 178, 179, 204
Signs ... 1, 80
Silage ... 167
Sites of Special Scientific Interest ... 4, 6, 28, 33, 34, 35
Smoke ... 135, 151
Snares ... 43, 84, 97, 110, 111, 160, 167, 186, 187, 188, 204
Special Areas of Conservation ... 5, 35
Special Protection Areas ... 36
Squatters ... 115
Squirrels ... 188
Stables ... 104

Stiles ... 66, 67, 80
Straying ... 21, 57, 105, 179, 180
Streams ... 166

Taxidermy ... 16
Theft ... 14, 39, 72, 86, 92, 126, 143, 169, 180, 181, 182, 183
Timber ... 15, 38, 50, 53, 81, 82, 138, 160, 161
Tipping ... 77, 78, 120, 125, 151
Toads ... 8, 154
Towing paths ... 23, 45
Town and Country Planning ... 183, 184, 185, 190
Traps ... 42, 43, 97, 110, 111, 160, 161, 186, 187, 188, 204
Treasure trove ... 189
Trees ... 15, 50, 81, 82, 101, 135, 138, 181, 190, 191
   felling licences ... 82
Trespass ... 19, 25, 26, 47, 59, 60, 70, 83, 84, 85, 107, 115, 126, 148, 191, 192, 193, 194
   adverse possession ... 115
   aggravated ... 107, 144, 157
   air weapons, with ... 7
   poaching ... 90, 93, 143
   protestors ... 85, 157
   Scotland ... 70, 174
Trout ... 72, 167, 168, 169, 170, 171, 172

Vagrants ... 194
Vegetables ... 15, 38, 50, 53
Venison ... 51, 52, 88
Vermin ... 57, 188, 195, 196
Vessels ... 23
Village greens ... 196, 197, 198

Wales ... 198
   Countryside Council for ... 4, 31, 198
Waste ... 5, 77, 78, 120, 150, 184
Water ... 34, 136, 150, 199, 200
   abstraction ... 166, 167, 199
Water bailiffs ... 74, 145
Watercourses ... 166

Waterways
   cruising ... 22
   fishing ... 72
   inland ... 5
   tidal ... 60
Weeds ... 39, 200, 201
   pesticides ... 138
Wetlands
   Convention ... 34
   lead shot ... 117
Wild
   birds ... 14
   Birds Directive ... 36
   mammals ... 202
Wildfowl ... 203
   hunting ... 106
Wildlife
   damage ... 46
   disturbance ... 2
   English Nature ... 4
   management ... 3
Woodland
   recreation ... 82
   trees ... 190

Zoos ... 207